○ YITZHAK RABIN   □ ASSASSIN THAT WILL ASSASSINATE

'On 1 September 1994, I flew to Israel and met in Jerusalem
with a close friend of Prime Minister Yitzhak Rabin, the poet Chaim Guri.
I gave him a letter which he immediately gave to the Prime Minister.

**"An Israeli mathematician has discovered a hidden code in the Bible
that appears to reveal the details of events that took place thousands
of years after the Bible was written,"** my letter to Rabin stated.
**"The reason I'm telling you about this is that the only time your full
name – Yitzhak Rabin – is encoded in the Bible, the words
'assassin that will assassinate' cross your name."**

On 4 November 1995, came the awful confirmation, a shot in the back
from a man who believed he was on a mission from God, the murder
that was encoded in the Bible three thousand years ago.'

Michael Drosnin is a reporter, formerly at the *Washington Post* and the *Wall Street Journal*. He is the author of the *New York Times* bestseller *Citizen Hughes*. He lives and works in New York City.

THE
BIBLE
CODE

MICHAEL
DROSNIN

ORION

An Orion Paperback
First published in Great Britain by
Weidenfeld & Nicolson in 1997
This paperback edition published in 1997 by
Orion Books Ltd,
Orion House, 5 Upper St Martin's Lane,
London WC2H 9EA

This edition published by arrangement
with Simon & Schuster Inc.

A CIP catalogue record for this book
is available from the British Library.

ISBN: 0 75280 932 6

Typeset by Selwood Systems, Midsomer Norton
Printed and bound in Great Britain by
Clays Ltd, St. Ives plc

For my family,
for my friends,
for all who kept the faith,
again

'But thou, O Daniel, shut up the words and seal the book until the time of the End.'

— Book of Daniel 12:4

'The distinction between past, present, and future is only an illusion, however persistent.'

— Albert Einstein, 1955

CONTENTS

Introduction   1

1 The Bible Code   3
2 Atomic Holocaust   35
3 All His People to War   49
4 The Sealed Book   61
5 The Recent Past   77
6 Armageddon   91
7 Apocalypse   105
8 The Final Days   121
  Coda   141

  Notes   143
    Chapter Notes   145
    Notes on Illustrations   179
  Appendix   195
  Acknowledgements   219
  Index   221

INTRODUCTION

Reporting is the first rough take on history. This book is the first full account of a code in the Bible that reveals events that took place thousands of years after the Bible was written.

So, perhaps, it is the first rough take on the future.

We have just begun to understand the Bible code. It is like a jigsaw puzzle with an infinite number of pieces, and we only have a few hundred, or a few thousand. We can only guess at the complete picture.

The only thing I can state with certainty is that there is a code in the Bible, and in a few dramatic cases it has foretold events that then happened exactly as predicted.

There is no way to know if the code is also right about the more distant future.

I have tried to deal with this story the way I've dealt with every other story: as an investigative reporter. I've spent five years checking out the facts.

Nothing is taken on faith.

I have confirmed every discovery in the Bible code on my own computer, using two different programs – the same one used by the Israeli mathematician who first found the code, and a second program written independently of him.

I also interviewed the scientists in the United States and Israel who investigated the code.

Many of the events described in the book were witnessed by me. Accounts of other events are based on interviews with persons directly involved, or were confirmed by published news reports.

Detailed notes on each chapter, notes on all the illustrations, and a reprint of the original experiment that proved the reality of the Bible code, appear at the end of the book.

My goal has been to report what is encoded in the Bible exactly as I would have reported a story from the police blotter when I was at the Washington Post, exactly as I would have reported a story from a corporate boardroom when I was at the Wall Street Journal.

I am not a rabbi or a priest, not a Bible scholar. I have no pre-conceived beliefs, and only one test – the truth.

This book is not the last word. It is the first report.

CHAPTER ONE

THE BIBLE CODE

On 1 September 1994, I flew to Israel and met in Jerusalem with a close friend of Prime Minister Yitzhak Rabin, the poet Chaim Guri. I gave him a letter which he immediately gave to the Prime Minister.

'An Israeli mathematician has discovered a hidden code in the Bible that appears to reveal the details of events that took place thousands of years after the Bible was written,' my letter to Rabin stated.

'The reason I'm telling you about this is that the only time your full name – Yitzhak Rabin – is encoded in the Bible, the words "assassin that will assassinate" cross your name.

'That should not be ignored, because the assassinations of Anwar Sadat and both John and Robert Kennedy are also encoded in the Bible – in the case of Sadat with the first and last names of his killer, and the date of the murder, and the place, and how it was done.

'I think you are in real danger, but that the danger can be averted.'

On 4 November 1995 came the awful confirmation, a shot in the back from a man who believed he was on a mission from God, the murder that was encoded in the Bible three thousand years ago.

The assassination of Rabin is dramatic confirmation of the reality of the Bible code, the hidden text in the Old Testament that reveals the future.

The code was discovered by Dr Eliyahu Rips, one of the world's leading experts in group theory, a field of mathematics that underlies quantum physics. It has been confirmed by famous mathematicians at Harvard, Yale, and Hebrew University. It has been replicated by a senior code-breaker at the US Department of Defense. It has passed three levels of secular peer review at a leading US math journal.

Rabin's assassination was not the only modern event found. In addition to the Sadat and Kennedy assassinations, hundreds of other world-shaking events are also encoded in the Bible – everything from World War II to Watergate, from the Holocaust to Hiroshima, from the Moon landing to the collision of a comet with Jupiter.

And the Rabin assassination was not the only event found in advance. The Jupiter collision was found, with the exact date of impact, before it happened, and the dates of the Gulf War were found in the Bible before the war started.

It doesn't make ordinary sense in our secular world, and since I am not religious, I would normally be among the first to dismiss it as millennium fever.

But I have known about this for five years. I have spent many weeks with the Israeli mathematician, Dr Rips. I learned Hebrew, and checked the code on my own computer every day. I talked to the man at the Defense Department, who independently confirmed that the Bible code does exist. And I went to Harvard and Yale and Hebrew University to meet with three of the world's most famous mathematicians. They all confirmed that there is a code in the Bible that reveals the future.

I did not fully believe it until Rabin was killed.

I found the Bible code's prediction of his assassination myself, a clear warning that he would be killed in the Hebrew year that began in late 1995, but never really believed it would happen. When he was killed, as predicted, when predicted, my first thought was, 'Oh my God, it's real.'

○ YITZHAK RABIN   □ ASSASSIN THAT WILL ASSASSINATE

It could not be a coincidence. The words 'assassin that will assassinate' cross the name 'Yitzhak Rabin' the only time his full name appears in the Old Testament. The Bible code stated he would be killed in the Hebrew year that started in September 1995. Now, on 4 November, he was dead.

Rabin's friend, Chaim Guri, told me it was also the first thing he thought of when the Prime Minister was shot.

'It was like a knife in my heart,' said Guri. 'I called the chief of staff, General Barak, and said, "The American reporter, he knew it a year ago, I told the Prime Minister. It was in the Bible."'

When I first found the Rabin murder encoded, I remembered the first question my book editor had asked me: 'What if you had known about the Sadat assassination before it happened? Could you have warned him, and kept it from happening?'

With Rabin, I tried and failed. Before the assassination no one was able to find the name of the gunman, or the exact date. A few days after I first contacted the Prime Minister, Dr Rips and I met with the chief scientist at the Ministry of Defense, Gen. Isaac Ben-Israel. We searched for details. But only the year of the predicted murder was apparent.

After Rabin was killed, the name of his assassin, 'Amir,' was immediately found in the Bible code. It was always there, right above Rabin's name, but hidden in plain sight.

'Amir' was encoded in the same place as 'Yitzhak Rabin' and 'assassin who will assassinate.' Moreover, the words 'name of the assassin' appeared in the plain text of the Bible in the same verse that the name 'Amir' appeared in the hidden text. And also, in that same verse, the hidden text stated, 'He struck, he killed the Prime Minister.'

He was even identified as an Israeli who shot at close range: 'His killer, one of his people, the one who got close.'

The code revealed when and where it would happen. 'In 5756,' the Hebrew year that began in September 1995, crossed both 'Tel Aviv' and 'Rabin assassination.' 'Amir' appeared again in the same place.

But before Rabin was killed we knew only that the Bible code predicted his murder 'in 5756.' And Rabin ignored the warning.

'He won't believe you,' his friend Guri had told me when I first

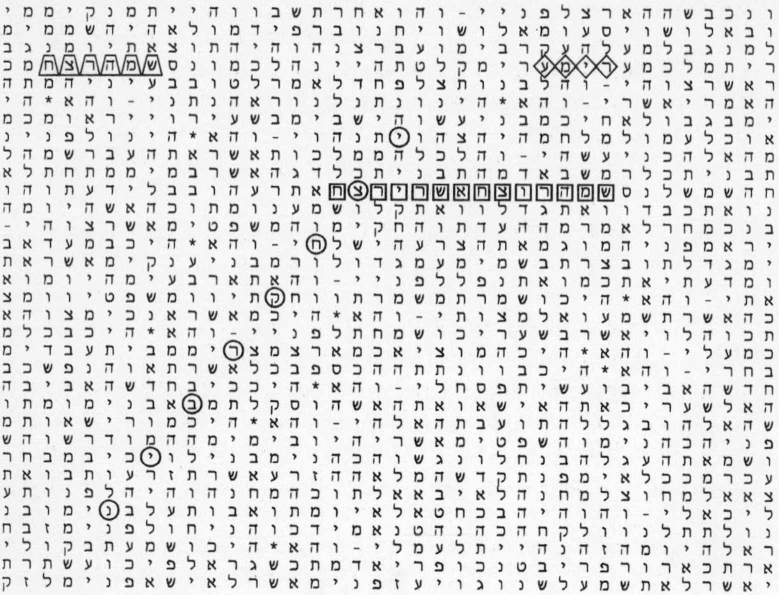

○ YITZHAK RABIN   ☐ NAME OF ASSASSIN WHO WILL ASSASSINATE

◇ AMIR   △ NAME OF ASSASSIN

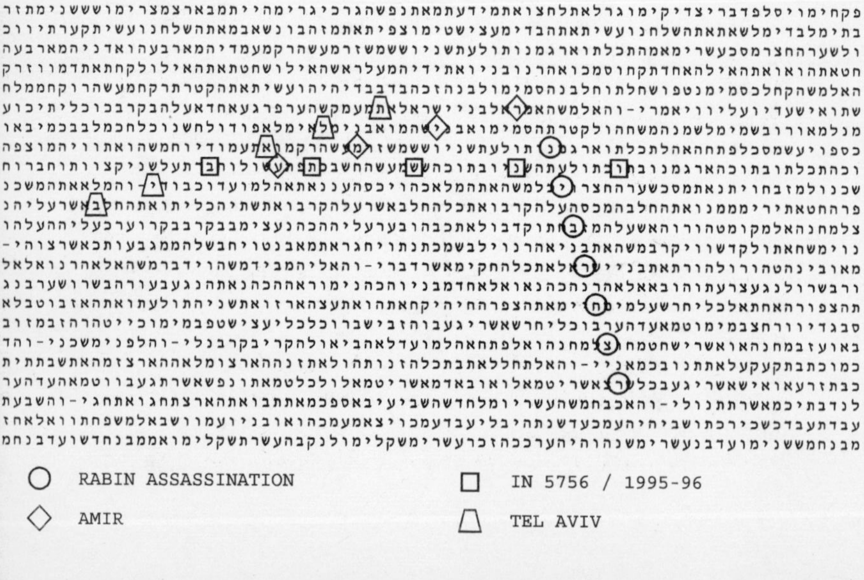

○ RABIN ASSASSINATION   ☐ IN 5756 / 1995-96

◇ AMIR   △ TEL AVIV

gave him the letter. 'He's not at all a mystic. And he is a fatalist.'

So, I still don't know if the assassination could have been prevented. I only know what I told the Prime Minister in my letter: 'No one can tell you whether an event that is encoded is predetermined, or is only a possibility. My own guess is that it is only a possibility – that the Bible encodes all the probabilities, and what we do determines the actual outcome.'

We had not been able to save Rabin's life. But suddenly, brutally, I had absolute proof that the Bible code was real.

Five years ago, when I first flew to Israel, the Bible code and the Bible itself were the furthest things from my mind. I was there to meet with the chief of Israeli intelligence about the future of warfare.

But while I was there I learned of another mystery, one that suddenly pulled me back several millennia – 3200 years, to be exact, to the time when according to the Bible God spoke to Moses on Mount Sinai.

As I was leaving intelligence headquarters, a young officer I'd met stopped me. 'There's a mathematician in Jerusalem you should see,' he said. 'He found the exact date the Gulf War would begin. In the Bible.'

'I'm not religious,' I said, getting into my car.

'Neither am I,' said the officer. 'But he found a code in the Bible with the exact date, three weeks before the war started.'

It all seemed beyond belief. But the man at Israeli intelligence was as secular as I was, and the man who had discovered the code was considered a near genius in the world of mathematics. I went to see him.

Eli Rips is a modest man. He is so self-effacing that he tends to give other people credit for his own work, and one would never guess he is a world famous mathematician. When I first met with him in June of 1992, at his home outside Jerusalem, I assumed that by the end of the evening I would know there was nothing to his claim.

Rips pulled down a volume from his bookshelf, and read to me quoting an eighteenth century sage, a man called the Genius of Vilna: 'The rule is that all that was, is, and will be unto the end of time is included in the Torah, from the first word to the last word.

And not merely in a general sense, but as to the details of every species and each one individually, and details of details of everything that happened to him from the day of his birth until his end.'

I picked up a Bible from the desk in his study, and asked Rips to show me the Gulf War. Instead of opening the Bible, he turned on his computer.

'The Bible code is a computer program,' he explained.

On the computer screen appeared Hebrew letters highlighted in five different colors creating a crossword puzzle pattern.

הכנעניוהפרזיאזישבבארצואימראברברמאללוטאלאתחימריבהביניירבינכוביינרעייובינרעיכביאנש
לאכלתהארצלפניכתבפרדנאמעליאמתהשמאלואימנחוואמחימינאשמאילתחוישאלוטאתעיניוויראאתכלכב
שקתהלפניישחתיוהאתשדמדואתמעמרהכגניוהכארצמצריםבאכצאריויכחרלולוטאתכלכבהחרדנויוסעל
אישמעלאחאיואברמישבבארצכנעעלוטוישבבעריהכברויאהלעדסדמואנשיסדמרעימוₒₒₓⓢ - והמאד
רמאחריהפרדלוטמעמואשאנעייניכוראהמנהמקומאשארואתהשמצפנהונחונגבהוקדמהיימהכיאתכלהארצאשר
הולוראעכעלעונלמדישמתיאתזרעכעפרהארצאאשארימיובלאישלמנהיזאתאפרהארצגמזרעכזימרהלהלג
חבהכילכאתהכנהויאהלאבממדיבאוישבבאלניממראאשרבחברניויבנשמימזבחליוהויחיביאמיזאמרפלמ
לכאלסרכדרלעמרכמלכעיילמותדעלמלכלכגיימעשומלחמחהאתברעמלכסדמואתברשעמלכעמרהשוₐⓝₗₐₐₐ מה
[further Hebrew grid lines] ⓦ ⓢ ⓦ
 יומולכבכלעלהₐₐצרכלאלהחברראולעמקהשדימרואהממלחמחשמעמלכשרסוהנעהעבדואתאכדרלעמרשולשₐₑₐ שה
עשרהתשנהבאכדרלעמרזהמלכימאשארו, ₐₐₐₐₐₐ ₐₐₐₐₐ אⓑ וה
יברהרמשעירעדאילפארןאשרעלהמדברישבוייבאולעלייבאולעלעטהⓜⓛⓒⓗⓜⓗ מⓗₐ ⓖ את
צנתמרויצאמלכסדמומלכעמרהומלכאדמהומלכצביימ ⓜⓗⓜⓗⓗₐ ₑₘₐⓠ ⓗ ימ
עיללמותדעלמלכלכגיימואמרפלמלכלשנערארימלכואלסⓐⓧ בעהמלכימאדⓗ ⓗחמשהועמקהשדימבאⓐ ⓑאⓡⓣ
דמעמרהתיפלושמהותנשאר ... מלכיסדמ ... ⓡₐ ... ⓢ ... ⓜ ... ⓥₐ ... עמרהאתאכלכמⓥ ... כלכמויילכוויקחמואתל ... ⓣ את
מויילכווי ... הⓟ ... באתפ ... ⓟ ... ₐₐⓥ ... ₓₐ ... ⓥ ... דלאברמהעבריויהואשבכנבאלניממראאמריאחימראשכלואחיענרו

○ FIRE ON 3rd SHEVAT (JANUARY 18, 1991)   ◇ MISSILE   □ WAR
△ HUSSEIN (PICKED A DAY)   ▭ SADDAM   □ ENEMY

Rips handed me a print-out. 'Hussein,' 'Scuds,' and 'Russian missile' were all encoded together in Genesis. The full code sequence stated 'Hussein picked a day.'

'Here, in Genesis, Chapter 14, where we have the story of Abraham's wars with the surrounding kingdoms, we found the date – "fire on 3rd Shevat."'

Rips looked up from his computer. 'That's the date in the Hebrew calendar equivalent to January 18, 1991,' he explained. 'It's the day Iraq launched the first Scud missile against Israel.'

'How many dates did you find?' I asked.

'Just this one, three weeks before the war began,' he replied.

'But who knew 3000 years ago that there would be a Gulf War, let alone that a missile would be fired on January 18th?'

'God.'

The Bible code was discovered in the original Hebrew version of the Old Testament, the Bible as it was first written. That book, now translated into every language, is the foundation of all Western religion.

The Bible code is ecumenical, the information is for everyone. But the code only exists in Hebrew, because that is the original language of the Bible.

Rips told me that the first hint of the encoding had been found more than 50 years ago by a rabbi in Prague, Czechoslovakia. The rabbi, H.M.D. Weissmandel, noticed that if he skipped fifty letters, and then another fifty, and then another fifty, the word 'Torah' was spelled out at the beginning of the Book of Genesis. And that the same skip sequence again spelled out the word 'Torah' in the Book of Exodus. And in the Book of Numbers. And in the Book of Deuteronomy.

'I heard about it totally by chance, talking to a rabbi in Jerusalem,' said Rips. 'I tried to find the original book, and finally found the only copy that apparently exists, at the National Library in Israel. There were only a few pages about the code, but it seemed interesting.'

That was twelve years ago. 'At first I tried just counting letters like Weissmandel,' said Rips. 'You know, Isaac Newton also tried to find the code in the Bible, and he considered it more important than his Theory of the Universe.'

The first modern scientist, the man who figured out the mechanics of our solar system and discovered the force of gravity, Sir Isaac Newton, was certain that there was a hidden code in the Bible that would reveal the future. He learned Hebrew, and spent half his life trying to find it.

In fact, it was for Newton, according to his biographer John Maynard Keynes, an obsession. When Keynes became provost at Cambridge University, he discovered there the papers that Newton had packed up in 1696 when he retired as provost. Keynes was shocked.

Most of the million words in Newton's own handwriting were not about mathematics or astronomy, but esoteric theology. They revealed that the great physicist believed there was hidden in the Bible a prophecy of human history.

Newton, said Keynes, was certain the Bible, indeed the whole universe, was a 'cryptogram set by the Almighty,' and wanted to 'read the riddle of the Godhead, the riddle of past and future events divinely fore-ordained.'

Newton was still searching for the Bible code when he died. But his lifetime quest failed no matter what mathematical model he applied.

Rips succeeded. The discovery that had eluded Sir Isaac Newton was made by Eliyahu Rips because he had the one essential tool that Newton lacked – a computer. The hidden text of the Bible was encoded with a kind of time-lock. It could not be opened until the computer had been invented.

'When I applied a computer, I made the breakthrough,' Rips explained. 'I found words encoded far more than statistics allowed for by random chance, and I knew I was on to something of real importance.'

'It was the happiest time in my life,' said Rips, who came to Israel from Russia more than twenty years ago, and still speaks with an accent that is both Hebrew and Russian.

Although he is religious, and in the top right corner of every page of his calculations writes two Hebrew letters thanking God, for him, like for Newton, the math is also sacred.

Rips told me he had developed a sophisticated mathematical model that, when implemented by a computer program, confirmed that the Old Testament is in fact encoded.

He was stalled however in making the final breakthrough, a way to prove the reality in a simple and elegant way. Then he met another Israeli, Doron Witztum.

Witztum is a physicist but not connected to any university and, compared to Rips, is unknown to the world of science. But it was Witztum who completed the mathematical model, and Rips considers him 'a genius like Rutherford.'

He handed me a copy of their original experiment, 'Equidistant

Letter Sequences in the Book of Genesis.' The abstract on the cover page read, 'Randomization analysis indicates that hidden information is woven into the text of Genesis in the form of equidistant letter sequences. The effect is significant at the level of 99.998%.'

I read through the paper as we sat in his living room. What Rips and his colleagues had done was to search for the names of thirty-two great sages, wise men from Biblical to modern times, to determine whether their names, and the dates of their birth and death, were encoded in the first book of the Bible. They looked for the same names and the same dates in the Hebrew translation of *War and Peace* and in two original Hebrew texts. In the Bible the names and the dates were encoded together. In *War and Peace* and the two other books, they were not.

And the odds of finding the encoded information by random chance were ultimately found to be 1 in 10 million.

In his final experiment, Rips took the thirty-two names and sixty-four dates and jumbled them in 10 million different combinations, so that 9,999,999 were a mismatch, and only one was a correct pairing. He then did a computer run to see which of the ten million examples got a better result – and only the correct names and dates came together in the Bible.

'None of the random pairings matched,' said Rips. 'The results were 0 vs. 9,999,999, or one in 10 million.'

A senior code-breaker at the top secret National Security Agency, the clandestine US government listening post near Washington, heard about the startling discovery in Israel, and decided to investigate.

Harold Gans had spent his life making and breaking codes for American intelligence. He was trained as a statistician. He spoke Hebrew. And he was sure that the Bible code was 'off-the-wall, ridiculous.'

Gans was certain he could prove that the code did not exist. He wrote his own computer program, and he looked for the same information the Israelis had found. He was surprised. It was there. The dates that the sages were born and died were encoded with their names.

Gans could not believe it. He decided to look for entirely new information in the Bible code, and thereby expose the flaw in Rips' experiment, possibly even reveal a hoax.

'If this was real,' said Gans, 'then I figured that the cities where these men were born and died ought to be encoded as well.'

In his 440-hour experiment Gans checked not only the names of the thirty-two sages Rips finally used, but also thirty-four others from an earlier list, checking all sixty-six against the names of the cities, and the results made him a believer.

'It sent a chill up my spine,' recalled Gans. The cities also matched the names of the sages in the Bible code.

The Pentagon code-breaker, using his own computer program, had independently replicated the Israelis' results. Men who lived hundreds and thousands of years after the Bible was written were encoded in detail. Rips had found the dates. Gans had found the cities. The Bible code was real.

'We conclude that these results provide corroboration of the results reported by Witztum, Rips, and Rosenberg,' wrote Gans in a final report of his investigation.

'In evaluating the Bible code,' he later said, 'I was doing the same kind of work I did at the Department of Defense.'

'At first, I was 100% skeptical,' said the Pentagon code-breaker. 'I thought this was all just silly. I set out to disprove the code, and ended up proving it.'

The Bible was encoded with information about the past and about the future in a way that was mathematically beyond random chance, and found in no other text.

Rips and Witztum submitted their paper to a leading American math journal, Statistical Science. The editor, Robert Kass, a professor at Carnegie-Mellon, was skeptical. But he decided to have it checked out by other experts, the peer review process standard in all serious scientific journals.

To Kass' surprise, the Rips-Witztum paper passed. The first referee said the math was solid. Kass called in a second expert. He, too, said the numbers held up. Kass did something unprecedented – he called in a third expert.

'Our referees were baffled,' said Kass. 'Their prior beliefs made them think the Book of Genesis could not possibly contain meaningful references to modern-day individuals. Yet, when the authors carried out additional checks, the effect persisted.'

Kass sent an E-mail message to the Israelis: 'Your paper has passed the third peer review. We will publish it.'

Despite the automatic skepticism of secular mathematicians, no one could find fault with the math. No one could raise an unanswered question about the experiment. No one could explain away the startling fact that the Bible was encoded – that it revealed events that took place after the Bible was written.

The Bible is constructed like a giant crossword puzzle. It is encoded from beginning to end with words that connect to tell a hidden story.

Rips explained that each code is a case of adding every fourth or twelfth or fiftieth letter to form a word. Skip X spaces, and another X spaces, and another X spaces, and the hidden message is spelled out. As in this paragraph.*

But it is more than a simple skip code. Criss-crossing the entire known text of the Bible, hidden under the original Hebrew of the Old Testament, is a complex network of words and phrases, a new revelation.

There is a Bible beneath the Bible.

The Bible is not only a book – it is also a computer program. It was first chiseled in stone and handwritten on a parchment scroll, finally printed as a book, waiting for us to catch up with it by inventing a computer. Now it can be read as it was always intended to be read.

To find the code, Rips eliminated all the spaces between the words, and turned the entire original Bible into one continuous letter strand, 304,805 letters long.

In doing that, he was actually restoring the Torah to what great sages say was its original form. According to legend, it was the way Moses received the Bible from God – 'contiguous, without break of words.'

---

* Start at the first letter of the above paragraph, skip every three letters, and the code is revealed: 'Rips ExplAineD thaT eacH codE is a Case Of adDing Every fourth or twelfth or fiftieth letter to form a word.' The hidden message – **'READ THE CODE.'**

The computer searches that strand of letters for names, words, and phrases hidden by the skip code. It starts at the first letter of the Bible, and looks for every possible skip sequence – words spelled out with skips of 1, 2, 3, all the way up to several thousand. It then repeats the search starting from the second letter, and does it over and over again until it reaches the last letter of the Bible.

After it finds the key word, the computer can then look for related information. Time after time it finds connected names, dates, and places encoded together – Rabin, Amir, Tel Aviv, the year of his assassination, all in the same place in the Bible.

The computer scores the matches between words, using two tests – how closely they appear together, and whether the skips that spell out the search words are the shortest in the Bible.

Rips explained how it works, using the Gulf War as an example. 'We asked the computer to search for Saddam Hussein,' he said. 'Then we looked for related words to see if they came together in a way that was mathematically significant. With the Gulf War, we found Scuds with Russian missiles, and the date the war would begin encoded with the name Hussein.'

The words formed a crossword puzzle. Consistently, the Bible code brings together interlocking words that reveal related information. With Bill Clinton, President. With the Moon landing, spaceship and Apollo 11. With Hitler, Nazi. With Kennedy, Dallas.

In experiment after experiment, the crossword puzzles were found only in the Bible. Not in *War and Peace*, not in any other book, and not in ten million computer-generated test cases.

According to Rips, there is an infinite amount of information encoded in the Bible. Each time a new name or word or phrase is discovered in the code, a new crossword puzzle is formed. Related words cross vertically, horizontally and diagonally.

We can use the Rabin assassination as a case study.

First we asked the computer to search the Bible for the name 'Yitzhak Rabin.' It appeared only once, with a skip sequence of 4772.

The computer divided the entire Bible – the whole strand of 304,805 letters – into 64 rows of 4772 letters. The Bible code print-out is a snapshot of the center of that matrix. In the middle of the snapshot is the name 'Yitzhak Rabin,' with each letter circled.

○ YITZHAK RABIN

If 'Yitzhak Rabin' was spelled out with a skip code of 10, then each row would instead be 10 letters long. If the skip was 100, then the rows would be 100 letters long. And each time the rows are re-arranged a new set of interlocking words and phrases is created.

Each code word determines how the computer presents the text of the Bible, what crossword puzzle is formed. Three thousand years ago, the Bible was encoded so that the discovery of Rabin's name would automatically reveal related information.

Crossing the name 'Yitzhak Rabin' we found the words 'assassin will assassinate.' It appears on the table below with each letter in a square:

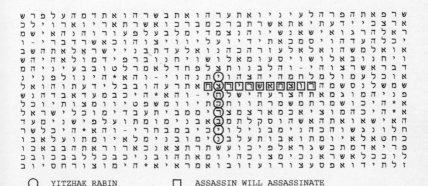

○ YITZHAK RABIN   ☐ ASSASSIN WILL ASSASSINATE

The odds against Rabin's full name appearing with the prediction of his assassination were at least 3000 to 1. Mathematicians say a hundred to one is beyond chance. The most rigorous test ever used is 1000 to 1.

I flew to Israel to warn Rabin on 1 September 1994. But it was only after he was killed a year later, that we found the name of his assassin. 'Amir' was encoded in the same place as 'Yitzhak Rabin' and 'assassin who will assassinate.'

○ YITZHAK RABIN   □ (ASSASSIN) WILL ASSASSINATE   ◇ AMIR

Amir's name had been there for 3000 years, waiting for us to find it. But the Bible code is not a crystal ball – you can't find anything without knowing what to look for.

Clearly, this was not Nostradamus, not 'A Star Will Rise in the East and a Great King Will Fall,' words that can later be read to mean anything that actually does happen.

Instead, there were details as precise as the story reported on CNN – the full name of Rabin, the name of his assassin, the year he was killed – all but Amir found before it happened.

Still, it was hard to believe. I asked Rips if it were not possible to find similar information in any text, random letter combinations that had no actual meaning. Perhaps finding the date of the Gulf War, even the assassination of Rabin, was just a coincidence.

Rips took a coin out of his pocket and flipped it in the air. 'If this is a fair coin,' he said, 'then half of the time it should come up heads, and half of the time it should come up tails. If I flip the coin twenty times and each time it comes up heads, then everyone would assume the coin is weighted. The probability that the same side would come up twenty times in a row is less than one in a million.'

'The Bible is like the weighted coin,' said Rips. 'It is coded.'

He cited his original experiment, the sages encoded in Genesis. 'The only other possibility is that a random event happened – that we, by chance, found the best match of thirty-two names and sixty-four dates – and that would only happen one time in 10 million.'

But if Rips is right, if there is a Bible code, if it foretells the future, then conventional science can't yet explain it.

Not surprisingly, some conventional scientists can't accept that. One, an Australian statistician, Avraham Hasofer, attacked the Bible code before Rips published his experiment, before the mathematical evidence was known. 'Certain types of patterns must inevitably occur in large data sets,' he said. 'You can no more find a patternless arrangement of digits or letters than you can find a cloud without a shape.'

'In any event,' said Hasofer, 'the use of a statistical test in matters of faith raises grave problems.'

Rips says his critic is wrong on the science, and wrong on the religion. Hasofer, he notes, never did a statistical test, never checked the math, and he never looked at the Bible code itself.

'Of course you can find random letter combinations in any text,' says Rips. 'Of course, you will find "Saddam Hussein" in any large enough data base, but you won't find "Scuds," "Russian missiles," and the day the war began, all in the same place, in advance. It doesn't matter if we're looking in a text of 100,000 or 100,000,000 letters, you will not find coherent information – except in the Bible.

'A great part of mankind now assumes that the Bible is just old folklore, myth, that science is the only reliable picture of reality. Others say that the Bible, as the word of God, must be true, and therefore science must be in error. I think that, finally, when we understand both well enough, religion and science will come together – we will have a Unified Field Theory.'

In the nearly three years since the Rips-Witztum paper was published, no one has submitted a rebuttal to the math journal.

The major scientists who actually examined the Bible code

confirm it. The Pentagon code-breaker, the three referees at the math journal, the professors at Harvard, Yale, and Hebrew University all started out skeptics, and ended up believers.

Einstein once said, 'The distinction between past, present, and future is only an illusion, however persistent.' Time, said Einstein, is not at all what it seems. It does not flow in only one direction, and the future exists simultaneously with the past.

The other great physicist who defined our universe, Newton, not only said that the future already exists, but believed that it could be known in advance, and in fact himself searched for the hidden code in the Bible that would reveal it.

Now some scientists, including the leading physicist in the world today, Stephen Hawking, believe that people might one day actually be able to travel in time. 'Time travel,' says Hawking, 'might be within our capabilities in the future.'

Maybe the poet T. S. Eliot was right: 'Time present and time past/Are both perhaps present in time future,/And time future contained in time past.'

But I was not prepared to believe that the future was encoded in the Bible without the kind of evidence a reporter trusts, information that can be checked out in the real world.

I spent an entire week with Eli Rips, working with him at his computer. I asked him to find things related to current world events, to a comet that had just been sighted, to modern science, and time after time he found the information I asked for encoded in the Old Testament. When we checked the control text, *War and Peace*, the information was not there. When we checked the Bible, it was.

In that week, and in six subsequent trips to Israel, and in my own investigation over the next five years, we found ten and then one hundred and then one thousand world events encoded in the Bible. It was possible on any given day to pick up the New York Times or the Jerusalem Post, and if the story on the front page was important enough, find it encoded in a document that had been written 3000 years ago.

The information, time after time, proved as accurate as the current newspaper accounts, the names, the places, the dates all encoded in Genesis through Deuteronomy. And sometimes it was found in advance.

Six months before the 1992 election, the code revealed Bill Clinton's victory. Connected to 'Clinton' was his future title, 'President.'

אבהההששההלהכתכחרכחריככנתממשעתיתקאתתנבתאקזיא
ישאחנדנחנדנחמאיככנוחנזיתאידבעועהיאמיכרמפכ
לאתהדכלזהחרוברבנ דעני נולמלכ יהתרתוהתיילעומאם
רכבאשרירכבעלקרקךחהזוירה יעמ יהתהשממבמיותההפ
מחחמאומקדשאדתדסקרבזהורי יבכ לכאלרשש יולעכרתהיה
ששבשלישבאמנדקרי י'כרק מהחפש רוט יב'יתאבקדר
אששרהקפצתאתהיוה-יחאא★ר מדמדבכ'ירהמשחפשמ ייצראת
הלאההיומהההוראמרתורצתורברתוערוארצאמלכאהל

○ CLINTON   □ PRESIDENT

The greatest recent upheaval in America, the fall of Richard Nixon in the Watergate crisis, is also encoded in the Bible. 'Watergate' appears with 'Nixon' and the year he was forced to resign, 1974.

Where 'Watergate' is encoded, the hidden text of the Bible asks a question: 'Who is he? President, but he was kicked out.'

אצייברעתאחהלשיי.ושעשרשאבתההנולחתאחנ נחתפי ו
אללי חיו הי יביתו מאלבשלי שבתבשיושבלדגבוא
לי יבלתהזיזבעתלאמההאלתערגזיתיונ ולככיבאלחלש
ולעככרדסבתי יחנצראומעלבכנ יכתנ ימי תיתפשהעמעת
ומבאירבדויוניפרונעילקרקנלועמהדי עי ירבחפכתכדר
רשתבאשאמטממשפעלגחנוהלענ ועההמהחמתאהפמ אלחרג
אי יוחתטשחהאאכלעתורהזההרורהלעאממ בל רה אזחקל
ההרודהדלההאמהישנ באיאאלשי ישנוערוט הי יופצק יו
שאלכחהובהבהותטפומוהנ יהקרברח יפלחרוכזורלכתאת

○ WATERGATE   □ WHO IS HE? PRESIDENT, BUT HE WAS KICKED OUT

The Great Depression is encoded with the crash of the stock market. 'Economic collapse' and 'Depression' appear together in the Bible, with the word 'Stocks.' The year it all started, 1929 ('5690'), is encoded in the same place.

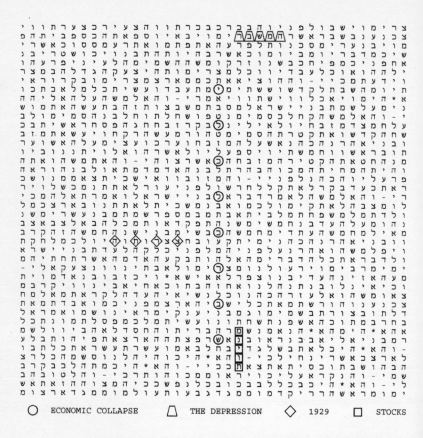

○ ECONOMIC COLLAPSE   △ THE DEPRESSION   ◇ 1929   □ STOCKS

But man's triumphs, like the Moon landing, are also encoded. 'Man on Moon' appears with 'spaceship' and 'Apollo 11.' Even the date Neil Armstrong first stepped on the lunar surface, 20 July 1969, is in the Bible.

Armstrong's words, 'One small step for a man, one giant leap for mankind,' are echoed by the hidden text of the Bible. Where the date he set foot on the Moon is encoded, the words that cross 'Moon' in the Bible are, 'Done by mankind, done by a man.'

It is all encoded in Genesis with 'Apollo 11,' at the point where God tells Abraham, 'Look now toward Heaven, and count the stars, if thou be able to number them.'

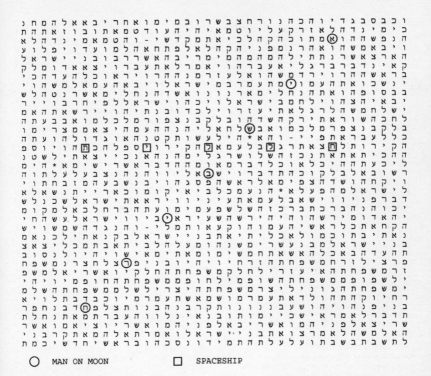

○ MAN ON MOON   □ SPACESHIP

In the years following my first trip to Israel, I kept searching the Bible code on my own, not as a mathematician, but as an investigative reporter, checking the facts.

What is subject to proof, what can be pinned down in addition to the math, is information about the recent past, and the near future. Two years into my investigation I found something cosmic predicted in the code – and then watched it happen in the real world.

In July 1994, the world witnessed the biggest explosion ever seen in our solar system. A comet bombarded Jupiter with the force of more than a billion megatons, creating fireballs the size of the Earth.

I had found the Jupiter / comet encoding in the Bible myself, two months before the collision, using a computer program written for me in Israel, based on Rips' mathematical model.

The collision was encoded twice, once in the Book of Genesis

אלוטוידבראלחתניולקחיבנתירויאמרקומוצאומנחמקומזהכימשחיתי-והאתהעיריהיכמצחקבע
זכברואתכלישביהערימוצמחמחאדמהותבטאשתמאחריוןתהיצציבכמלאתיסעמשמאברהמכברקראלהמקןמאש
הצעירהגמהוןץדהבנותקראשמובנעמיהואביבןיעמונעדחיומיסעמשמאברצאתהנגביישבני
אמראמברמכיאמרתירקאיךניראתא*חיכמבמקומהזהחרוראג*יעלדבראשתירוממאמנחאתחייבתאכ
אברחמהידניקהבניכרהדחיכיןלדהזיבנלוקןכירויויגדלהידלדירימלויעושמאברחחממשתהתגדולביימחגמלאתי
לאאתחחמממומושקאמתהנערויהיא*חיראתהנערדגלייבבדברויהירבהקשתחירדיבלערוומ
ירגבראברחמבארצפלשתחלתמרמימיארכמיארתהרדברימאחלהולהדאתנא*חימצבהאתחאברחמיארמאליואבר
לשטאתאבנוירקראלמלכיו-ומחנשחמימיאמראברתהמאברחמימאימרחמניירימאראלתלשלחדיתלחלאלחת
לחילדרימלכבהלחלנחראתחיחאיאברתהמופילגשוישמחראומהותילדלאגמרואאתשבניואאחמומאתחמועכמלחרי
מחארצלאאמראכאמאתהן*ץמעניתתיכספהשדהקחממנקיראקבצרתהאתמהדשמהיעעןדעפרואתאתחבראתהמלארל
הארצאראשירצאתמאטמשוריאמראליואברחמאםרלכביכפטותישיבאותהבניישמחי-והא*חיהשממאימשרלקחנימיבתאב
לדחעינחתהמלאכדלתהותעלראיתצמחבדלקראתהתורואמריא*ניכמאמעועשראלמעירדכומאברתהאתתמשתהדאניותמחר
ינליאמראמבאורוכי-וחלמתמעמדבוחזואואכיכפניתכטיתמוקחמלגמליומניבאאתהשהיתחיופתחרה
ממדכואמראמראליכמאתחשתחהנותעירמשתהחכליכמאברתהלכואברואשרתשרחתכתיחי-וחלבנציאיא*נטרמאכלהלדבראל
שבחנעראתניויאמראימאועשריואחראחתלכויאברמראלהמאלמאלהאחדראתתירי-וחתצלירחדרדכישלחתנירורבלחלאזני
ישבנראתחרתדנובכיוידדינחיואשרדמולטוישמתרכלאמדמומאוברמאעתונלנעוצפחואמרבנוירמבי*ליי-וחאתמעממוי־אמתהחלחמאמ
מתירסאפפבלאאלמירואויישכנומחןון*םהעדשוראשירעלפנצירמבצחכאתחאשרורתחעלפבניכלראחי-וכלאפלואלאלהאאדלדת
זכברתכלירךיאמרהעשרוהנאתכנכיחולוכלכלמותולמדהזהלירבכרחוי אמריקצבעאמריעקבהשבהעליכיכימומי שבעלוירומכרא
די*אמראלירויצחקיקאמרתיפנאמתועלחיתירוראחמיאימ*כ-יני נאמעועקבשכ בכאאדתאעאמרמאמשאתחדוחברב
לנופרינובארצור יעלמשמבמאברשבעוירויראליו-וחבליד לחחהאוראימראמנכיא*חיא ברחמאבכאלחתירא
כחיעניכניורימראתירקראאתאשעבורנהאדליריאמראליובניראימראלייכ ה וכנויי יאמרהנחנאזקנתירלאידע
אתיעקבבבנחהתקטואתארתגדיייחזירמחלביימשהלעירדידיירועלחלחקצאריאריונ יאמרהממעטעמימומי אתהתחתחמאש
ומברכזכברוכויה התאושנטמשאתארעקבעלמשבעעקבבראתחחו יעקביאכיצאקאקשאחתפתניצקשתבמאתפני-וכטבי
לצואחרכי-ושטמשואתני אתיעקבעלמשנואתילעמרלאמתאתחחמאשמהמבהזונתכנגנ-ותמר-יושמעי אעקאעתאתדרכ ראחתרגהאתחירע
לומשמאמשהבבבר כוביאתנויצ ואעלי לואמרלואתתחקחאשחמבנה במבבחכנעינ ותכהאעמעיעקאבכשכאחדאחיגהשאהי-וקכ
רשממרא אשחירדיי שמעמאתחמצח בז יקשמעורעלערכ יא אמריקקראשמ מהלזההנא חחוא לאהנ א אמרלא לבנא חיאמרשינ-ות
האנאנאכר לאבכיהכ ר עתחכאשראתכ אתער קבעלחיעבאתריךאחמריאמרמאמרוו נ יאמרהנחנא זקנתי לאידעכומ אתיום
שואלחמנחהאתחכהוכחהנ ותלחמת מגמהנ ח עבדכ יבדכימחעמ ש עכבעבראמר קבעל חיעבח ריאמורמאמ-ותראמאמ-ותיאמרעקבי-חי
לעשר א מצאאכמאתוו אמרתהמ גמ הנ עבדכיעבד כיעקבבאחריכ- כ יא אכפרח פנ יו מבבמנ חתה ה לכתלפנ יא חירקנ אר
בענעמאות חאשי וחצ אמלתת וע למ בח ר ועל ראחתירת שמאתת חש פ נחותו-ות ראמ א שע פ נ ילי דיר הנ ראששנ א תא
לתחמלחכאשרלפנ ירלרג חלתי המעמד אשראבאלאא לדיישע מירחירא י אמראשרי אמ רגתחנ א עמ עיואיצ ישעי אר מא יי
קתנשפשי בתבקמתני ואתתנ א בתתה נ וחבנ וכ לוראתב תח א תבתהנ וותשנ ש י מ למשבחתנ וראשרי ב מם דמ במ נ קנמ ן
ונתנלמהאכבזעאתהי וארכ לניוחאנ נ י שנ ימ לשבתח אנ ו תלעמ אחד בממ לו לנ וד ל ה זי יאבבש אכר ע כאא ש מפ חב מ ן
אלחיכנ כ רכ ראשרבכ תבכם ברח ותחכ הנ ות וחל לפ ופ שמ ל תכומ ולח נ ע ל ה ה ד א*ואעש השממ בא חל א*הע נ נ שב כב
תאבנ ירי סכעליחכ סכ ור יצ קלעי חש מ נ ואי קר אישמ אב א בת עקבבא ש מ קמ מ ה ק מ ראשר דב רא תחי*חבמ י בת א
עשוחא ד מש עד מ של קחאת נש י ומ ב נ ותי כ נ עא תד ח כ בתאבת הב לנ ו נ חח ק ק אתא חל י ה ב מ ב עען ה ב כ ע ה בת אצא ז ד
ואשראלו פ ב מ כאל ומ ב ל פ אפ ג מ א הל וק ש כאל ו פ ק ר חח א ל ו פ ג ם עמלא ל ו פ מ לאל ה א ל יפ מ א ל ה ד
זבנ זקנמ חראלוושחמ ל וכ נ וש חתפ סמ יומ ראאחיורכ יא תאה א ב ב אב א מ מ כ לא חירוי שנ או ת ו ל א יכ ל ו ד ב ר
וישאלהחאחיוחשלאמר מ מ תהב ק שוירמ ראתאתהמ א נ כ יא ב מק כ ם ב פ ח ה ת ר מ י וא מ רא מ א כ ל נ ו זמ ז ח
אלחי נ כ רא שרבת כ כ מ עד טרוי ח ל פ ו שמ ל ת כ וול מו ק וח ב עאל ה ב א ל וא ע ש ה שמ מ ב ח ל א*חע נ נ שב כ ב
תאבנ יר י סכ על יח כ סו ריצ ק ל עי חשמ ן ומ י ק ר א יש מ אב ב תע ק בב א ש מ ק מ ה ה ק מ ר א שר דב ר א ת ח י*חב מ י בת
עשוה ו ד משעם ד מ של קחאת נ ש יומ ב נ ו תיכנ עא תד ו ה כ ב תא בת הב ל נ ו נ ח ח ק ק א תא ח ל י ה ב מ ב ע ע נ ה ב ך ע ה ב ת א צ א ז ד
ואשרא ל ו פ ב מ כ א ל ומ ב ל פ א פ ג מ א ה ל ו ק ש כ א ל ו פ ק ר ח ח א ל ו פ ג ם ע מ ל א ל ו פ מ ל א ל ה א ל י פ מ א ל ה ד
אל ח ד נ ז ק נ מ ח ר א לו וש ח מ ל וכ נ ו ש ח ת פ ס מ יו מ ר א א ח י ו ר כ י א ת א ה א ב ב א ב א מ מ כ ל א ח י ר ו י ש נ א ת ו ל א י כ ל ו ד ב ר
יבנ ז ק נ מ ח ר א ל ו ו ש ח מ ל ו כ ל ה ב א ב א ה א ח י א ה א ב א ב א ב כ ל ה מ כ כ ל א ח י ר ו י ש נ א ו ת ו ל א י כ ל ו ד ב ר
וישאל ח ח א ח י ו ח ש ל א מ ר מ מ ת ה ב ק ש ו י א מ ר א ת א ת ה מ א נ כ י א ב מ ק כ ם ב פ ח ה ת ר מ י ו א מ ר א מ א כ ל נ ו ז מ ז ח

SHOEMAKER-LEVY   JUPITER

and again in the Book of Isaiah. The comet, 'Shoemaker-Levy,'
appeared both times with its full name – the names of the astronomers who discovered it in 1993 – and its impact with 'Jupiter' was
graphically presented. In the Bible code, the name of the planet and
the name of the comet intersect twice. In Isaiah, the exact date of
the impact was stated in advance, 16 July.

```
שחי-והצבא!תלכלהעמימבהרחזהמשתהתהשמרימשמנימממחימשמריממזקקימובלעבהרחזהפנ
מויסירמעעלכלהארצצלי-זּ-והדבוראמרבימחהראהתאה*חאה*חנזוזחקקי-כלולורישיענזזהי-וחקקי-כלולנ
שריפרשהשחחלשהרתה۩ש۩ילצּאהתועמאארבותהדירוומבצמרמשגבחומתחכשחחּשּפילהחגיעלּאּראצּעּפנשבּריו
טמרכתצרשלומשלומכיבכבּ۩۩בטחוּבי-והדייעדכיביחּי-וחצורעולמימכיחשחמישּבימּרומקריהנשאגב
לסאפ אר חמ פשטיכּי-וחקוי-וכלּ۩۩דּלזּּּברכתאּהתנפשנשׁישיארי תכזבליל האפ ברחי בקרביאשחּהתּכּכיכּאש
זּ ורנכחז וריבשרנקּנאתּעמאאשּצר כתהּ۩۩۩מסּ-ותּהשפּהשּלּרנּ כּי-גמכלמעשיינופעלתלנרוי-וחּאּ*חיג
תלגוריי-וחיספפהּלגּ۩۩כאּ ּאּרּ۩۩כלכקצי-רּ۩۩חהּ۩۩פ۩۩כאּ۩۩ נלחשמויסרכלכמוכמהרהתקריבּלּלּד
יומתיכנבּלתייקומוחקיצוורנּ ו/שכני-עפברכיּ۩۩ורתטלכואר רפ אי מ תּ פי ללכעמיׄ۩באבחׄדרייכוסגרד
אתכּסתחעּ ו דעהרוג יחבייומחהתּוּא~יפקּרי-והבחרבבוהקשׁ۩۩גּדלּלהרוחחיקהעללוי-ותנכּנשׁ ברחּ ועללוי-תחנז
ירמאצארנחחמאהכנּלימי-תּ  גיּ שמרישֹי תּ במל סּ מחהאּשּשעעּ הצ בּ האּ۩۩נ תחדּ אּ רּ חזבּ בּ מּ עּ זּ י-י עּ שֹ הּ שֹ ל וּ מּ ל יֹ שֹ ל
אתבּ שּ לּהתחתּ רי בנ חההג ּ ּ ברו חהת קשׁ הבּ י-מ קּ רּ ימּ כלּ כּ נּ בּ א תּ כבבּ פ א רע ול נ יּ עּ קּ בּ ז זּ הּ כלּ פרי-חּ סּ ר טּ אתּ אּ הּ בּ שֹ א נ וּ בּ כּ לּ אבּ
צ וּ כלּ הּ סּ עעבּ פ יּ חֹ בּ יּ בּ שֹ קצ יּ רּ התּ השבּ רּ נ חֹ נ שֹ י מּ בּ א וּ תּ מּ אמּ י-רּ וּ תּ א אּ וּ תּ חֹ כ יּ-לּ א אמּ בּ יּ נ וּ תּ הּ א ע עּ לּ בּ נ כּ לּ א ירּ ר חמּ נ זּ י-ו עֹ שֹ מ הּ ו וּ יּ צ
```

○ SHOEMAKER-LEVY   ◇ WILL POUND JUPITER   ▭ 8th AV (JULY 16, 1994)

The event that astronomers were able to predict a few months
ahead of time, the Bible code predicted just as precisely 3000 years
before it happened.

It was one of those finds that was so dramatic it caused me to
believe all over again. Through two years of investigation, I kept
asking myself, Could this really be true? Had some non-human
intelligence actually encoded the Bible? Each morning I woke up
doubting it all, despite the overwhelming evidence.

Could this be a hoax? Not a new revelation, but another Hitler
diary, a cosmic Clifford Irving?

The rabbis and the professors have never agreed on the origins
of the Bible. The religious authorities say that the first five books,
Genesis through Deuteronomy, were written more than 3000 years
ago by Moses. The academic authorities say they were written by
many hands over many hundreds of years. The argument turns out
to be irrelevant.

Every Hebrew Bible that now exists is the same letter for letter.
A Torah – the first five books – cannot be used if even one letter is
missing or out of place. And the Bible code uses that now universally
accepted Hebrew text.

Details of today's world are encoded in a text that has been set in stone for hundreds of years, and has existed for thousands of years. There is a complete version from 1008 AD that is nearly the same, and fragments of all but one book of the entire Old Testament have been found among the Dead Sea Scrolls, which are more than 2000 years old.

So the text used in the computer program – the one in which I found the exact date of the collision of the comet with Jupiter, 16 July 1994 – was written long before any man looked at the skies through a telescope.

A hoax is simply ruled out because it would have required a forger who could see the future. No forger had encoded the Jupiter collision, not 2000 years ago, not 200 years ago, not two months before it happened. Once more, I felt certain.

I went to see Rips at Columbia University. He was there as a visiting professor, occupying the same office in the mathematics building that was once occupied by the president of the American Mathematical Society, Lipman Bers, who organized the worldwide campaign that freed Rips from a Soviet prison twenty-six years ago.

Back in the Soviet Union as a young graduate student, Rips was arrested for demonstrating against the 1968 invasion of Czechoslovakia. He spent the next two years as a political prisoner. It was only through the intercession of mathematicians in the West that Rips was ultimately freed and allowed to emigrate to Israel.

Now a professor at Hebrew University in Jerusalem, Rips has also taught at the University of Chicago and Berkeley, and is respected throughout the world of mathematics.

In his office at Columbia, Rips looked at my print-out of the Jupiter collision. 'This is exciting,' he said, like myself sometimes still awed by the precision of the Bible code.

Astronomers knew the comet would hit Jupiter because they could trace its trajectory, they knew when because they could measure its speed. But whoever encoded the Bible had the same information thousands of years before that was possible, thousands of years before Shoemaker and Levy discovered the comet, so how could the Bible encode the date of the impact?

It was, of course, the big question – how could the future be known?

I went with Rips to see one of Harvard's top mathematicians, David Kazhdan. Kazhdan told me he believes that the Bible code is real, but he could not explain how it works.

'It does appear that the Bible was encoded 3000 years ago with information about future events,' said Kazhdan. 'I've seen the results. There are no scientific grounds to challenge it. I think it is real.'

'How does it work?' I asked.

'We don't know,' said Kazhdan. 'But we recognized the existence of electricity a hundred years before we could explain it.'

I asked Rips and Kazhdan how anyone, man or God, could see what does not yet exist. I had always assumed that the future does not exist until it happens.

Rips replied first with a theological answer. 'The world was created,' he said. 'The Creator is not confined by time or space. For us the future is non-existent. For the Creator, the whole universe from beginning to end was seen in one stroke.'

Kazhdan gave a Newtonian explanation. 'Science accepts that if we know the position of every molecule and atom, we can foresee everything,' he said. 'In the mechanical world, if we know the position and velocity of an object – a bullet or a rocket to Mars – then we could also know precisely when and where it will arrive. So there's no problem in that sense about knowing the future.'

'But if you ask me if I am surprised that the future is encoded in the Bible,' added Kazhdan, 'of course I am.'

I. Piatetski-Shapiro, a leading mathematician at Yale, also confirms the Bible code, but is equally amazed by its revelation of events that took place long after the Bible was written.

'I believe the code is real,' said Piatetski-Shapiro. 'I saw the results, and they were quite surprising. Predictions of the future, of Hitler and the Holocaust.'

The Israeli who works with Rips, Doron Witztum, had done an extensive search for 'the Holocaust' in the Bible code, and found it spelled out in extraordinary detail.

'Hitler' and 'Nazi' were encoded together with 'slaughter.' 'In Germany' was encoded with 'Nazis' and 'Berlin.' And the man who actually ran the concentration camps, 'Eichmann,' was encoded with 'the ovens' and 'extermination.'

'In Auschwitz' was encoded where the plain text of the Bible decrees 'an end to all flesh.' Even the technical details of the 'final solution' were there. The gas used to kill the Jews, 'Zyklon B,' was encoded with 'Eichmann.'

Piatetski-Shapiro had seen these findings and he was startled. 'As a mathematician,' he said, 'my instinct is that there is something real here.'

But the Yale professor cannot explain how it was done. 'There is no way within the known laws of mathematics to explain seeing the future,' he said. 'Newtonian physics is too simple to explain a set of predictions this complex and detailed. Quantum physics is also not enough. What we're talking about here is some intelligence that stands outside.'

The mathematician paused for a moment, then spoke: 'I think that is the only answer – that God exists.'

'Do you think one day we will be able to explain it in purely scientific terms?' I asked.

'I doubt it,' said Piatetski-Shapiro. 'Maybe part of it, but always some part will remain unknown.'

'It is possible, theoretically, to believe in the Bible code without believing in God,' he added. 'But if you assume God exists, you don't have to answer the question, Who can see the future?'

If the future can be foreseen, can it also be changed?

If we had known about Hitler in advance could we have prevented World War II?

Could Rabin or Kennedy have been saved from an assassin's bullet?

Even if Amir or Oswald had been found in the Bible code in advance, could they have been stopped? Was there an alternative probability – that the gunmen would be caught, that Rabin or Kennedy would live?

The question is whether the Bible code tells us what will happen or may happen, presents one pre-determined future, or predicts all the possible futures.

Physicists have been locked in the same debate ever since Werner Heisenberg formulated his famous Uncertainty Principle. Stephen Hawking defined it in layman's terms: 'One certainly cannot predict future events exactly if one cannot even measure the present state of the universe exactly!'

Most scientists believe that the Uncertainty Principle is a fundamental, inescapable property of the world. And it states that there is not one future, but many possible futures.

Hawking put it this way: 'Quantum mechanics does not predict a single definite result for an observation. Instead, it predicts a number of different possible outcomes, and tells us how likely each of these is.'

Does the Bible code, like quantum physics, present all the probabilities? Or, are the encoded predictions set in stone? Some, like the Rabin assassination, clearly do happen. Did all the predictions come true?

We don't yet have enough experience with the Bible code to know, but even the apparently iron-clad rule of the Uncertainty Principle might not apply to the code.

In the end, all conventional science, indeed all conventional concepts of reality, may be irrelevant. If some being that stands outside the system, outside our three dimensions, outside of time, encoded the Bible, the code may not obey any of our laws, scientific or otherwise.

Even Hawking admits that the rules of chance may not apply to God: 'We could still imagine that there is a set of laws that determines events completely for some supernatural being.'

Once we admit that we are not alone – that there is some intelligence beyond our own – everything else must be re-examined.

And the greatest scientist of our time, Einstein, never accepted that the universe was governed by chance.

'Quantum mechanics is certainly imposing,' said Einstein. 'But an inner voice tells me that it is not yet the real thing. The theory says a lot, but does not really bring us any closer to the secret of the "Old One."

'God,' said Einstein, 'does not play dice.'

Can there really be a code in the Bible that recorded events thousands of years before they happened, that told our history ahead of time, that might now reveal a future that for us does not yet exist?

I went to see Israel's most famous mathematician, Robert J. Aumann. He is one of the world's experts in game theory, and a member of both the Israeli and the US National Academy of Science.

'The Bible code is simply a fact,' said Aumann.

'The science is impeccable,' he continued. 'Rips' results are wildly significant, beyond anything usually seen in science. I've read his material thoroughly, and the results are straightforward and clear.'

'Statistically it is far beyond what is normally required. The most stringent standard ever applied is 1 in a 1000. Rips' results are significant at least at the level of 1 in a 100,000. You just don't see results like that in ordinary scientific experiments.'

'It's very important to treat this like any other scientific experiment – very cold, very methodical, you test it, and you look at the results. As far as I can see, the Bible code is simply a fact.'

'I'm talking as an accountant. I've checked the books, and it's Kosher,' said Aumann. 'It's not just Kosher, it's Glatt Kosher.'

Aumann had been skeptical. At first he could not believe that a code in the Bible revealed the future. 'It goes contrary to all my training as a mathematician, and even the religious thinking I've come to be comfortable with,' he said. 'It's so different from anything known to science. There has been nothing like it in all the hundreds of years of modern science.'

Aumann talked to leading mathematicians in Israel, in the United States, all over the world. No one could find a flaw in the math. He followed Rips' work for years, and he continued to investigate it for months.

Finally, on 19 March 1996, the most famous mathematician in Israel told the Israeli Academy of Science, 'The Bible code is an established fact.'

There is still a great deal no one knows about the Bible code. Rips, who knows more than anyone, says it's like a giant jigsaw puzzle with thousands of pieces, and we only have a few hundred.

'When the Bible code becomes widely known, and people try to use it to predict the future, they should know it's complicated,' says Rips. 'All probabilities may be there, and what we do may determine what actually happens. Maybe it was done this way to preserve free will.

'The worst thing that could happen is that some people might interpret what they find in the Bible code as commandments, as telling them what to do – and it's not that, it is only information, and it may only be probabilities.'

But if all probabilities are in the Bible code, it only raises the big question to a new level. How can each moment in human history be encoded? In the broad sweep of history, even the Rabin assassination and the Moon landing and Watergate are all just moments. How can they all be encoded in one book?

I asked Rips if there was any limit to the information that was in the code, how much of our history was hidden in the Bible.

'Everything,' said the mathematician. He quoted again the statement he had read to me when we first met, the words of the eighteenth-century sage, the Genius of Vilna: 'All that was, is, and will be unto the end of time is included in the Torah.'

How could that be possible, the original text of the Old Testament was only 304,805 letters long?

'Theoretically there is no limit to the amount of information that could be encoded,' said Rips. He took my legal pad and started writing down an equation. 'If we have a finite set, we can look for the power set, and the set of all its subjects,' he said. 'And each element of each set can be on and off.' On the notepad he had written down a formula: $S, P(S), P(P(S)) = P^2(S) \ldots, P^k(S)$.

I couldn't understand the math, but I got the point. Even with a limited data base, there could be an endless number of combinations and permutations.

'At least 10 or 20 billion,' said Rips. He explained the meaning of that number: 'If you start counting from 1 and never stop day or night, it will take you 100 years to count up to 3 billion.' In other words, the Bible code contains more information than we could even count, let alone find, in several lifetimes. And that doesn't take into account the 'crossword puzzles' created when 2 or 3 or 10 different words are linked together. In the end, says Rips, the amount of information is incalculable, and probably infinite.

And that is only the first, crudest level of the Bible code.

We have always thought of the Bible as a book. We now know that was only its first incarnation. It is also a computer program. Not merely a book that Rips typed into a computer, but something that its original author actually designed to be interactive and ever-changing.

The Bible code may be a timed series of revelations, each designed for the technology of its age.

It may be some form of information we cannot yet fully imagine, something that would be as strange to us now as a computer would have been to desert nomads 3000 years ago.

'It is almost certainly many more levels deep, but we do not yet have a powerful enough mathematical model to reach it,' says Rips. 'It is probably less like a crossword puzzle, and more like a hologram. We are only looking at two-dimensional arrays, and we probably should be looking in at least three dimensions, but we don't know how to.'

And no one can explain how the code was created.

Every scientist, every mathematician and physicist who understands the code, agrees that not even the fastest super-computers we have today – not all the Crays in the war room of the Pentagon, or all of the main-frames at IBM, not all of the computers now in the world working together – could have encoded the Bible in the way it was done 3000 years ago.

'I can't even imagine how it would be done, how anyone could have done it,' says Rips. 'It is a mind beyond our imagination.'

The computer program that reveals the Bible code is almost certainly not the last form the Bible will take. Its next incarnation probably already exists, waiting for us to invent the machine that will reveal it.

'But even what we do know how to find, we can probably never finish decoding,' says Rips. 'Even on that level, the information is probably infinite.'

No one yet knows if each of us, and all of our past and all of our future, is in some still unknown higher-level code in the Bible, if it is in fact some Book of Life. But apparently every major figure, every major event in world history, can be found with the level of encoding we already do know.

All of the leaders in World War II – 'Roosevelt,' 'Churchill,' 'Stalin,' 'Hitler' – are there. 'America' and 'revolution' and 1776 ('5536') appear together. 'Napoleon' is encoded with 'France,' but also with 'Waterloo' and 'Elba.' The revolution that changed the 20th century, the communist 'revolution' in 'Russia,' is encoded with the year it triumphed, 1917 ('5678').

Great artists and writers, inventors and scientists from ancient to modern times are also encoded in the Bible. 'Homer' is identified as the 'Greek poet.' 'Shakespeare' is foretold in a single code sequence that spells out not only his name but his deeds: 'Shakespeare' – 'presented on stage' – 'Hamlet' – 'Macbeth.'

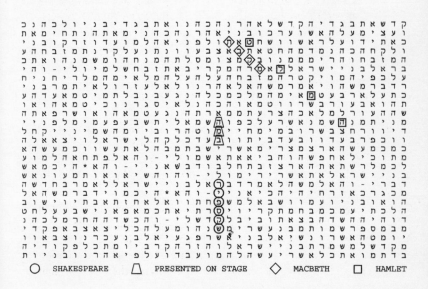

○ SHAKESPEARE   △ PRESENTED ON STAGE   ◇ MACBETH   □ HAMLET

'Beethoven' and 'Johann Bach' are both encoded as 'German composers,' and 'Mozart' is identified as a 'composer' of 'music.' 'Rembrandt' is encoded with 'Dutch' and 'painter.' 'Picasso' is called 'the artist.'

Every major advance in modern technology appears to be recorded. The 'Wright Brothers' are encoded with 'airplane.' 'Edison' is encoded with both 'electricity' and 'lightbulb.' 'Marconi' is encoded with 'radio.'

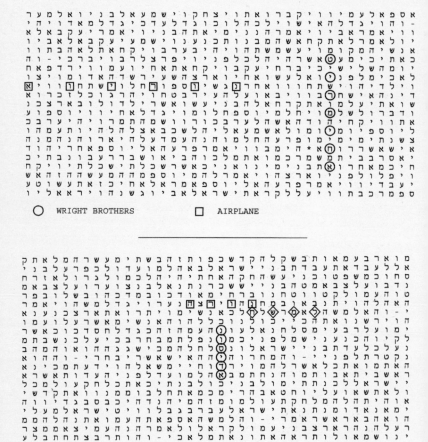

○ WRIGHT BROTHERS   □ AIRPLANE

○ EDISON   ◇ ELECTRICITY   □ LIGHT BULB

The two scientists who defined the universe for the modern world, 'Newton' and 'Einstein,' are both encoded in the Bible, each with his major discovery.

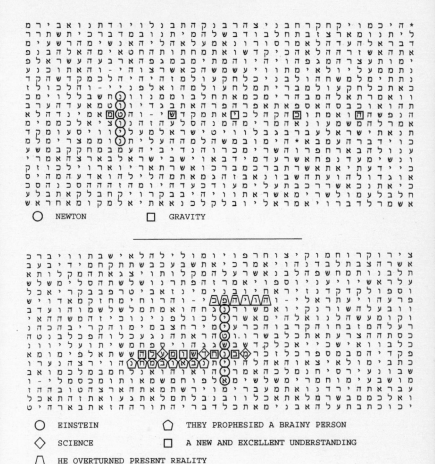

NEWTON ○   **GRAVITY** □

EINSTEIN ○   **THEY PROPHESIED A BRAINY PERSON** ⬠

SCIENCE ◇   **A NEW AND EXCELLENT UNDERSTANDING** □

HE OVERTURNED PRESENT REALITY △

'Newton,' who explained the mechanics of our solar system, how the planets are held in place by the force of gravity, appears with 'gravity.' Even Newton's own search for a code in the Bible that would reveal the future is encoded in the Bible. 'Bible code' also appears with 'Newton.'

'Einstein' is encoded once. 'They prophesied a brainy person' appears in the same place. The word 'science,' overlapped by the words 'a new and excellent understanding,' cross his name. And right above 'Einstein' the hidden text states, 'He overturned present reality.'

His 'theory of relativity' is also encoded. In fact, the full understanding of the universe that eluded Einstein, the Unified Field Theory, may also have been encoded in the Bible 3000 years ago. With his name, the one time it appears, and again with the theory of relativity, the code gives the same clue: 'Add a fifth part.'

Apparently the answer that Einstein was seeking will be found not in our three dimensions of space, or in his fourth dimension of time, but in the fifth dimension that all quantum physicists now agree exists.

'The most ancient religious texts,' noted Rips, 'also state that there is a fifth dimension. They call it "a depth of good and a depth of evil."'

Heaven and Hell? It's the kind of question that once preoccupied the world, but that few scientists, and fewer reporters, take seriously anymore. But the Bible code forces us to ask the biggest questions.

Does it prove there is a God?

For Eli Rips, the answer is yes. 'The Bible code is firm scientific proof,' the mathematician states. But Rips believed in God before he found the evidence.

Many others will also say that we now have the first secular evidence of His existence. I am persuaded only that no human could have encoded the Bible in this way.

We do have the first scientific proof that some intelligence outside our own does exist, or at least did exist at the time the Bible was written.

I do not know if it is God. I only know that no human being could have encoded the Bible 3000 years ago, and accurately foretold the future.

If the Rabin assassination, and the Gulf War, and the collision of a comet with Jupiter are all encoded, and they clearly are, then some intelligence very different from our own did it.

The Bible code demands that we accept what the Bible itself can only ask us to believe – that we are not alone.

But the code does not exist simply to announce the existence of the encoder. The Bible was encoded to sound a warning.

CHAPTER TWO

ATOMIC HOLOCAUST

The plain words of both the Old and New Testaments predict that the 'Final Battle' will begin in Israel, with an attack on the Holy City, Jerusalem, and finally engulf the entire world.

In Revelation, it is told this way: 'Satan shall be loosed out of his prison, and shall go out to deceive the nations which are in the four quarters of the Earth, Gog and Magog, to gather them together to battle. They surrounded the camp of God's people, the city he loves. But fire came down from Heaven, and devoured them.'

In the Bible code, only one world capital matches either 'World War' or 'atomic holocaust' – 'Jerusalem.'

On the day Rabin was killed I found the words 'all his people to war' encoded in the Bible. The warning of total war was hidden in the same code matrix that predicted the assassination.

'All his people to war' appeared right above 'assassin will assassinate,' in the same place as 'Yitzhak Rabin.'

I immediately flew back to Israel.

The Rabin assassination changed everything. It was the first moment that the Bible code seemed entirely real to me, the moment when what was encoded became life and death fact. And now the code warned that the entire country was in danger.

While Israel mourned Rabin, I worked with Eli Rips at his home outside Jerusalem. We tried to decode the details of the new prediction – 'all his people to war.'

Rips and I searched the Bible code for signs of a catastrophic conflict. We didn't yet know that the code warned of an atomic attack on Jerusalem. We had not yet found 'World War.'

But in the first computer run we did find the words 'Holocaust of Israel.' The 'holocaust' was encoded one time, starting in a verse of

○ YITZHAK RABIN   ☐ ASSASSIN WILL ASSASSINATE

◇ ALL HIS PEOPLE TO WAR

Genesis where the patriarch Jacob tells his sons what will befall Israel in the 'End of Days.'

'The first question is when,' said Rips, and he immediately checked the next five years, every year in the rest of the century. Suddenly he paled, and showed me the results.

The current Hebrew year, 5756 – the end of 1995 and most of 1996 in the modern calendar – appeared in the same place as the predicted new 'holocaust.'

○ HOLOCAUST OF ISRAEL   ☐ 5756 / 1995-96

It was a starkly frightening table. The year actually joined 'Holocaust of Israel.' It was a perfect match. '5756' was spelled out in a verse of the Bible where the 'holocaust' was encoded.

The year 2000, 5760 in the ancient calendar, was also a very good match. But the last year of the century seemed distant at that moment. In the second week of November 1995, in the days following the Rabin assassination, the overwhelming fact was the clear encoding of the 'holocaust' with the current year.

'What are the odds?' I asked Rips. 'A thousand to one,' he said.

'What could cause a holocaust in modern Israel?' I asked. The only thing we could imagine was a nuclear attack. We now found it encoded in the Bible, a startling statement of modern danger in the ancient text – 'atomic holocaust.'

'Atomic holocaust' appeared only once. Three years in the next five were encoded in the same place – 1996, 1997, and the year 2000. But again the year that caught our attention was the current year, 5756: 'In 5756' was encoded just below 'atomic holocaust.'

'What are the odds that could happen twice by chance?' I asked. 'A thousand times a thousand,' said Rips.

○ ATOMIC HOLOCAUST   □ IN 5756 / 1995-96

There were indications of danger all through the rest of the century, and beyond. If the Bible code was right, Israel would be in unprecedented danger for at least five years.

But only one other year was as clearly encoded with 'atomic holocaust' as 1996 – 1945, the year of Hiroshima.

We looked again at the phrase 'all his people to war,' the statement that appeared with the Rabin assassination. The same words 'all his people to war' – were also encoded with 'atomic holocaust.' In fact, those words appeared three times in the plain text of the Bible, and were encoded twice with 'atomic holocaust.'

Rips again calculated the odds. Again, they were at least a thousand to one.

I asked Rips how likely it was that each element of the predicted danger − the war, the holocaust, the atomic attack − would be encoded against such high odds. 'We have no way to calculate it,' said Rips. 'But it's in the range of many millions to one.'

The Bible code seemed to be predicting a new holocaust, the destruction of an entire country. If a nuclear war broke out in the Middle East, it would almost certainly trigger a global conflict, perhaps a World War.

And the events forecast were actually happening as predicted. A Prime Minister was already dead. I could not simply wait to see if the next prediction also came true.

We had information that might have saved Rabin, but failed to prevent his murder. Now we had information that might prevent a war. It was, for me, a truly bizarre situation. I had by chance stumbled onto a code in the Bible that clearly did reveal future events. But I was not religious, I didn't believe in God, and it all made no sense to me.

I had been a reporter at the Washington Post and the Wall Street Journal, I had written a book based on ten thousand documents, I was used to hard facts in our three dimensions. I was not a Bible scholar. I did not even speak Hebrew, the language of the Bible and the code. I had to learn it from scratch.

But I had found Rabin's assassination encoded in the Bible. Hardly anyone else knew that the code even existed. Only Rips knew that it also seemed to predict an atomic attack, another holocaust, perhaps a World War. And he was a mathematician, not a reporter. He had no experience dealing with government leaders. He had not been willing to warn Rabin. He was not ready to tell the new Prime Minister, Shimon Peres.

All of my reporter's instincts said that this new danger could not be real. All the Arab leaders had just come to Rabin's funeral. The peace seemed more secure than ever in late 1995.

'All his people to war' seemed a very remote threat. There had been no real war since Israel defeated Egypt and Syria in 1973. There had been no internal uprising since the Intifada ended with the Rabin-Arafat handshake in 1993. There had not even been a major terrorist attack in three years. Israel was more at peace than it had ever been since the modern state was established after World War II.

An 'atomic holocaust' seemed more than unlikely. A 'World War' seemed beyond belief. But I also had never really believed that Rabin would be killed. I just knew that his murder was encoded. And now Rabin was dead. He was killed, exactly as predicted, in 5756, the Hebrew year that began in September 1995.

I looked again at the new computer print-outs. 'The next war' was encoded once in the Bible. 'It will be after the death of the Prime Minister,' stated the hidden text. The names 'Yitzhak' and 'Rabin' were encoded in the same verse.

○   THE NEXT WAR

□   IT WILL BE AFTER THE DEATH (OF) PRIME MINISTER   ◇   YITZHAK

I was now certain that the Bible code did reveal the future. But I still did not know if every prediction came true. And I still did not know if the future could be changed.

As I lay awake wondering how I would get to Shimon Peres, and what I would tell him, the answer to the bigger question suddenly hit me.

In Hebrew, every letter in the alphabet is also a number. Dates and years can be written with letters, and in the Bible code always appear that way. The same letters that spelled out the current year, 5756, also formed a question.

The letters that stood for the numbers 5756, the year of the predicted holocaust, clearly spelled out a challenge for us all – 'Will you change it?'

ו נ ש ת ה   =   5756   =   WILL YOU CHANGE IT?

Less than a week after Rabin's death, I sent a letter to the new Prime Minister, Shimon Peres, alerting him to the new danger encoded in the Bible.

My letter to Peres stated:

'There is a hidden code in the Bible that revealed the murder of Rabin a year before it happened.

'I am writing to you now because the Bible code states a new danger to Israel – an "atomic holocaust."

'The information about the threatened "atomic holocaust" of Israel is detailed. The source of the danger is named, and it is predicted for this Hebrew year, 5756.

'I believe the danger can be averted, if it is understood. This is not religion. The solution is entirely secular.'

The Prime Minister's first reaction was disbelief. 'Astrologers and fortune-tellers are contacting me all the time with one warning or another,' Peres told his long-time friend, a prominent member of the Labor party, Elhanan Yishai, when he delivered my letter on 9 November.

Less than a week had passed since Rabin was killed. Peres had no time for predictions in a Bible code.

The Prime Minister's press secretary, Eliza Goren, was equally skeptical. She had been standing next to Rabin when he was shot, she had seen the letter I sent him a year earlier warning of the assassination, and still she could not believe the code was real.

'We're all rational people here, Michael,' she said. 'This is the twentieth century.'

I am a reporter, not a fortune-teller. I did not want to make predictions. I did not want to be the man who flew around the world saying, 'Beware the Ides of March.'

And I had no idea if the danger of an 'atomic holocaust' existed outside of the Bible code. But American nuclear terrorism experts told me that it was more than plausible. In fact, they said it was a near miracle it hadn't happened yet. The former Soviet Union was an open market, the radical Arab states were the most likely buyers, and Israel was the obvious target.

'Never before has an empire disintegrated while in possession of 30,000 nuclear weapons, 40,000 tons of chemical weapons, tons of fissile materials, and tens of thousands of scientists and technicians who know how to make these weapons, but do not know how to make a living,' a US Senate report on the Soviet black market stated.

A Russian official who investigated the theft of enriched uranium from a nuclear submarine base in Murmansk put it more simply: 'Even potatoes are much better guarded.'

I didn't have to talk to the experts to know that the danger was real. I had been in Moscow in September 1991, just weeks after the failed coup against Gorbachev, when the Soviet Union seemed to collapse overnight. Everything was up for sale.

I remembered meeting with a group of Russian military scientists, including some of the top nuclear weapons experts. None could afford a decent shirt. The cuffs of their sleeves and their collars were all torn and frayed. The senior scientist present, who had designed a major Soviet missile system, took me aside and offered to sell it to me. Obviously, Arab terrorists would have no trouble buying a bomb.

The danger stated in the Bible code might be real. But I had no way to confirm it, and no way to prevent it.

Several days after I arrived back in the United States, I finally reached the deputy chief of Israeli intelligence, Gen. Jacob Amidror. I expected him, like Peres, to dismiss the Bible code. The upper ranks of the Israeli government were then defiantly secular, and the military and intelligence officials were more secular than anyone.

I immediately assured Gen. Amidror that this was intelligence, not religion. 'I'm not religious,' I told him. 'I'm an investigative reporter. To me, the Bible code is information, not religion.'

'How can you say that?' replied Amidror. 'How can you say it's not God? This was encoded in the Bible 3000 years ago.'

Amidror, it turned out, was religious. He not only accepted the code as real, he accepted it as the word of God. In the almost totally secular higher ranks of Israeli intelligence, I had reached the one man who needed no assurance of the Bible code.

But Amidror said he could find no evidence of the stated danger in the real world. 'If there's a danger, it's from the other realm,' he said. 'In that case, all we can do is pray.'

Just after New Year's day in 1996 Peres' top military advisor, Gen. Danny Yatom, called me in New York. 'The Prime Minister read your letter, and he read your letter to Rabin,' said Yatom. 'He wants to meet with you.'

I flew back to Israel, and to prepare for my meeting with Peres, went back to work with Eli Rips.

We re-checked all the math. Rips typed 'holocaust of Israel' and the current Hebrew year '5756' into his computer. They matched. The odds were a thousand to one. He typed in 'atomic holocaust' and the year. Again they matched. The odds were more than a thousand to one, 8 in 9800.

Who would launch an atomic attack against Israel? Who was the enemy? Crossing 'atomic holocaust' were the words 'from Libya.' And 'Libya' appeared two more times on the same table.

The name of Libya's leader, 'Kaddafi,' was encoded in the last book of the Bible, in a verse that stated: 'The Lord shall bring a nation against thee from afar, which will swoop down like a vulture.'

And the words 'Libyan artillery' were also encoded, again with the current year, '5756.' The odds that the weapon would be encoded with the year were again at least a thousand to one.

'Atomic artilleryman' was also encoded in the Bible, and the exact location seemed to be stated. It was 'the Pisgah,' a mountain range in Jordan, the same mountains Moses climbed to see the Promised Land.

When I checked the plain text of the Bible, the first verse that mentioned the Pisgah also stated, almost openly, 'Weapon here, in this place, camouflaged.'

It seemed beyond belief that the actual words of the Old Testament, written 3000 years ago, would reveal the location of an atomic weapon about to be fired against Israel. And yet, if the danger was real, if a 'holocaust of Israel,' if an 'atomic holocaust' was imminent, then it was perfectly logical.

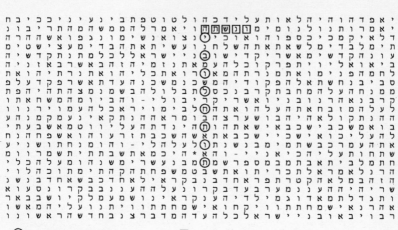

○ LIBYAN ARTILLERY   □ 5756 / 1996

If there really was a code in the Bible, if it really did tell the future, then of course this very moment when the land of the Bible might be obliterated, when the people of the Bible might be wiped out, would be the warning that was most clearly encoded, important enough even to be stated in the plain text.

'It's very consistent,' said Rips. 'It's clearly intentional.'

Rips confirmed that the atomic attack was clearly encoded, against very long odds, that mathematically it was beyond chance. But he was nervous about my meeting with Peres.

'The Almighty may have guarded the future from the eyes of anyone not intended to see it,' said Rips.

On 26 January 1996, I met with Shimon Peres at the Prime Minister's office in Jerusalem, and warned him of the encoded atomic attack.

At our meeting, the Prime Minister asked only one question: 'If it's predicted, what can we do?'

'It's a warning, not a prediction,' I answered. I told him I believed that the Bible encodes probabilities, that nothing was pre-determined. 'What we do determines the outcome,' I said.

I gave Peres two computer print-outs from the Bible code. One showed the words 'holocaust of Israel' encoded with the current Hebrew year, 5756. On the other, the words 'atomic holocaust' appeared, again with the current year. I told him that the odds of that happening by chance were at least 1000 to 1.

Peres interrupted: 'A thousand to one it will happen?'

No one could state the odds of the holocaust actually happening, I explained. No one yet understood the code well enough to do that. But the odds against 1996 twice matching the danger in the code were at least 1000 to 1. Mathematically, it was beyond chance.

'If the Bible code is right, Israel will be in danger for the rest of this century, for the next five years,' I told the Prime Minister. 'But this year may be critical.'

The source of the danger appeared to be Libya. I showed Peres that in the code 'Libya' crossed 'atomic holocaust.'

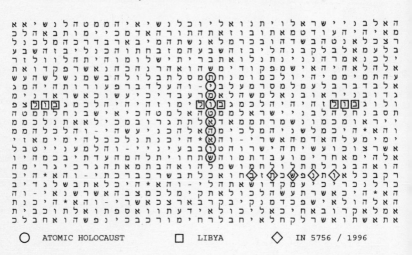

○ ATOMIC HOLOCAUST　　□ LIBYA　　◇ IN 5756 / 1996

'I don't know if that means an attack will be launched from Libya, or from elsewhere by terrorists supported by Libya,' I said. 'My own guess is that Kaddafi will buy an atomic device from one of the former Soviet republics, and that terrorists will use it against Israel.'

Peres took it all in quietly.

It was clear that he had carefully read my letter to him, and that he had not forgotten the letter I sent Rabin a year before the assassination.

He asked no deep philosophical questions about the Bible code.

He never mentioned God. He did not ask if his own name was encoded, a natural question after Rabin was killed. He had only one thing on his mind, the stated danger to Israel.

He did not seem surprised by the threat of an atomic attack. Peres had been in charge of creating Israel's own nuclear weapons at a top secret military base in Dimona. He knew how easily a nuclear device could be converted to terrorist use.

'I don't know if Israel is in any actual danger,' I told the Prime Minister before I left. 'I only know that it is encoded in the Bible.'

The next day, 27 January 1996, Libya's leader Muammar Kaddafi made a rare public statement. He called on all Arab countries to acquire nuclear weapons.

'The Arabs, who are threatened by Israel, have a right to buy nuclear weapons in any way possible,' he said.

When Kaddafi issued his statement, I was on top of Mount Nebo in Jordan, the peak of the Pisgah mountains that Moses climbed to see the Promised Land, the range of mountains above the Dead Sea that the Bible code identified as the launch site for an atomic attack.

There seemed to be an almost open statement in the Bible code that the weapon was here. 'Under the slopes of the Pisgah' crossed 'atomic artilleryman.'

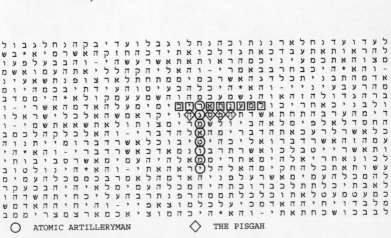

○ ATOMIC ARTILLERYMAN   ◇ THE PISGAH

□ IN ORDER THAT YOU PROLONG (THY DAYS) = ADDRESS, DATE

And the line right above that was like the X on a map.

There, the original verse of the Bible read, 'In order that you prolong thy days on Earth.' It was a curious passage to cross 'atomic artillery,' and the same verse also crossed 'atomic holocaust.'

It seemed to offer hope that the attack could be prevented. A hidden message in that verse of the Bible told how.

In Hebrew the same letters that spell out 'in order that you prolong' also spell the words 'address' and 'date.' The address was clear. It was the mountain range in Jordan, 'the Pisgah,' the location of the atomic weapon that appeared right below 'address.'

But we could not find the date. We knew where to look, but not when. Nonetheless I went there, and that's where I was standing when Kaddafi made his threat, the day after I met with Peres.

There were three miles of barren hills and desert wadis 'under the slopes of the Pisgah,' any one of which could conceal an artillery piece, or missile launcher. Nuclear terrorism experts back in the US had told me that an atomic artillery shell could be carried in a backpack by one strong man, easily by two men. And there were thousands of atomic artillery shells scattered throughout the former Soviet Union, each capable of destroying an entire city.

It was eerie to stand there, where Moses might have stood, and look across the Dead Sea at Israel, within plain sight on the other side of the water, knowing that somewhere in the surrounding hills and wadis Libyan terrorists might be preparing to launch a nuclear warhead against Tel Aviv or Jerusalem.

I was back in Jerusalem one day later to meet with Danny Yatom, the General who set up my meeting with Peres and who was about to be named chief of Israel's famed intelligence agency, the Mossad.

Yatom was just back from the failed Washington peace talks with Syria, but he had already talked to Peres about our meeting.

'Did he take it seriously?' I asked Yatom.

'He met with you,' said the General.

We discussed in more detail the danger of an 'atomic holocaust' encoded in the Bible. Yatom wanted to know when and where. I told him what was indicated, but added, 'The place, the date may be only probabilities. We might be wrong about every detail, but right about the overall danger.'

Yatom asked me the same question Peres had asked – 'If it's encoded what can we do?'

'You can't stop a comet from striking Jupiter,' I said. 'But you can certainly stop Libya from attacking Israel.'

Three days later, in a speech in Jerusalem, Peres for the first time said in public that the greatest danger facing the world was that nuclear weapons would 'fall into the hands of irresponsible countries, and be carried on the shoulders of fanatics.'

It was a clear re-statement of the warning in the Bible code – that Kaddafi would buy an atomic device, and that Libyan-backed terrorists would use it against Israel.

But if the Bible code was right, Peres was wrong. It was not the greatest danger facing the world.

'If this is real at all,' I told Gen. Yatom, 'it's the beginning of the danger, not the end.'

CHAPTER THREE

ALL HIS PEOPLE TO WAR

On Sunday morning 25 February 1996, Israel was hit by the worst terrorist attack in three years. A Palestinian suicide bomber blew up a bus at the rush hour in Jerusalem, killing 23 people.

Over the next nine days two more terrorist bombings in Jerusalem and Tel Aviv brought the death toll to 61, shattered the peace in the Middle East, and plunged Israel back into a state of war.

I had known the day the wave of terror would begin since the day Rabin died. Right above 'assassin will assassinate' there was a second prediction – 'all his people to war.'

Those same words appeared twice more in the Bible, both times with a date: 'From 5th Adar, all his people to war.' Adar 5th was the same date in the ancient Hebrew calendar as 25 February 1996.

The ominous warning of the Bible code – 'all his people to war' – had come true on the exact day the code predicted.

Again, as when Rabin was killed, I was shaken. The bombings actually shook me less than the new proof that the Bible code was real.

Four months earlier, when Israel was at peace, when the peace seemed so secure that leaders of the Arab world came to Rabin's funeral, the Bible code had predicted that by the end of February Israel would be at war.

One month earlier, when I met with Prime Minister Peres, that prediction still seemed so unlikely that I was afraid to tell him, and undermine my warning of an 'atomic holocaust.'

And now, on the very day the Bible had predicted 3000 years ago, the war had started, and Peres himself declared that Israel was at war, 'a war in every sense of the word.'

It was a chilling confirmation of the Bible code's accuracy, and all the details of the three suicide attacks were also encoded.

'Autobus' and 'Jerusalem' and 'bombing' all appeared together. Even the street where Palestinian terrorists twice blew up buses, two Sundays in a row, was named in the Bible – 'Jaffa Road.' The month and year, 'Adar 5756,' the Hebrew date equivalent to February and March 1996, was encoded with the exact location of the attacks, and the word 'terror.'

| ○ | AUTOBUS | □ | EXPLOSION | ◇ | JERUSALEM | ▭ | ISRAEL |

In fact, in the hidden text of the Bible where 'autobus' is encoded there was a complete description of the early morning attacks: 'fire, great noise, they awoke early, and they will ride, and there will be terror.'

The final terrorist attack, a suicide bombing in the heart of Tel Aviv that brought the death toll to 61, on 4 March 1996, was also detailed in the Bible code.

The name of the shopping center, 'Dizengoff,' appears with 'Tel Aviv' and 'terrorist.' 'Terrorist bombing' and 'Tel Aviv' were also encoded together.

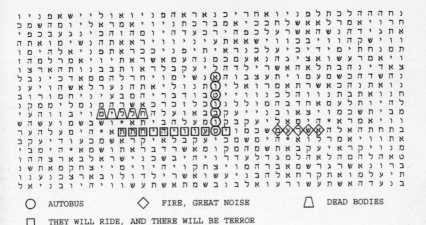

○ AUTOBUS   ◇ FIRE, GREAT NOISE   △ DEAD BODIES

□ THEY WILL RIDE, AND THERE WILL BE TERROR

The name of the terrorist group behind the attacks was encoded in the Bible with the weapon – 'Hamas bomb' – and running through it was the year, '5756.'

The carnage in Jerusalem and Tel Aviv, the horrible image day after day of bodies torn to pieces, split Israel in half, divided the Arabs and the Jews, and brought a sudden bloody end to a peace that had seemed so certain. Twisted metal and torn flesh replaced the image of the famous handshake between the now slain Israeli Prime Minister Rabin and the Palestinian leader Arafat.

When Rabin was killed, there was only the shock of his death, and of the Bible code's reality. When the bombings began on the exact date the code predicted, the shock was greater. Because I now knew that the code also predicted an 'atomic holocaust,' a 'holocaust of Israel,' a 'World War.'.

And the ominous warning – 'all his people to war' – that was encoded with the Rabin assassination, the warning that so accurately predicted the exact date the new wave of terrorism would begin, also predicted a far greater danger.

Two times those same words – 'all his people to war' – appeared in the Bible code with 'atomic holocaust.'

On the last day of April 1996, after Prime Minister Peres met with President Clinton, I met again with Gen. Danny Yatom at the Israeli Embassy in Washington.

Yatom had just been appointed chief of the Mossad, Israel's secret intelligence agency. He came out from a diplomatic reception to meet with me.

We stood alone outside the Embassy gate, apart from the crowd of dignitaries in the courtyard. Around the entire perimeter, legions of police, Secret Service agents with night-vision scopes, and Israeli security men with guard dogs were on patrol.

I gave Yatom a map of ancient Israel, highlighting the mountain where Moses stood in Jordan to view the Promised Land.

'If one staging area for an atomic attack on Israel seems most likely, this is it,' I told him. Yatom tore open the envelope. 'If the danger is real at all, it might be immediate,' I said. 'May 6th, at night, is indicated.'

In fact, we had not yet been able to find any date clearly encoded. 'May 6th' was indicated, but the letter combination that spelled it in Hebrew came up so often in the Bible that it had no clear meaning. Mathematically, it was meaningless.

Still, it was the only apparent date, and it was now just a week away.

'I don't know if that date has any real meaning,' I told Yatom. 'But the Bible code did predict the exact date of the first bus bombing. You may have only one week to check this out.'

May 6th came and went without incident. Yatom found no weapon. Israel was not attacked.

But just when I was ready to doubt the Bible code, it once more came true.

A week before Israel's historic 29 May 1996 election – a vote that would decide if it pursued the peace sealed by the handshake between Rabin and Arafat – I found the outcome predicted in the Bible code.

'Prime Minister Netanyahu' was encoded in the Old Testament, and the word 'elected' crossed his name. On the same line, in the same verse of the Bible, was his nickname, 'Bibi.'

○ PRIME MINISTER NETANYAHU   □ ELECTED   ◇ BIBI

I did not believe it would happen. Benjamin Netanyahu was the proclaimed opponent of the peace plan. Shimon Peres was its architect, and the rightful heir to Yitzhak Rabin. I was sure that Israel would not turn back, even after the wave of terrorist bombings.

I was certain that Peres would be re-elected. All the polls agreed. No one expected Netanyahu to win.

The day before the vote, I called Eli Rips and told him that I had found 'Prime Minister Netanyahu' encoded in the Bible. It was Rips who discovered that 'elected' ran across his name. Statistically, it was beyond chance. The odds were better than 200 to 1.

If Netanyahu did win, the Bible code seemed to predict that he would soon die. 'Surely he will be killed' actually ran right across 'Prime Minister Netanyahu' in the Bible.

On the next line, again running across his name, was the Biblical threat of premature death: 'his soul will be cut off.' It is the phrase used specifically to describe the death of a man before he reaches age 50. Netanyahu was 46.

His death was not as clearly predicted as Rabin's. The odds that it would be encoded with his name were 100 to 1. The Rabin assassination was encoded against odds of 3000 to 1.

But there was death all over the table that predicted Netanyahu's election. 'Murdered' appeared twice. The code also seemed to state that he might die in a war. The full hidden text predicting his death said: 'his soul will be cut off in a battle.'

The note I made to myself the day before the election stated, 'If I were going only by the Bible code, I would have to say that Netanyahu, if elected, will not live out his term of office.'

But I was not worried. I did not believe the Bible code could be right this time. I did not believe that Netanyahu would die. I was certain that Netanyahu would not even win the election.

On 29 May 1996, as the Bible code had predicted, Benjamin Netanyahu was elected Prime Minister of Israel.

The vote was so close – 50.4 to 49.6 percent – that the outcome was not certain until two days after the election. It was a dead heat finally determined by absentee ballots.

And yet it was encoded in the Bible 3000 years ago.

The White House, the PLO, the pollsters, and the entire Israeli press were all caught by surprise. No one expected Netanyahu to win. Like everyone else, I went to sleep the night of the election thinking Peres had won, and woke up to discover that Netanyahu was the new Prime Minister.

Again, I was shocked. I had the same sense of horror I felt when Rabin was assassinated, and when the wave of terror began on the predicted date. The big surprise was not Netanyahu's upset of Peres, but the fact that it had been foreseen 3000 years ago.

Once more, the Bible code was right, and I was wrong. It was not merely confirming my own instincts, or predicting the obvious. It was, instead, consistently revealing in advance things no one expected to happen.

The danger of an 'atomic holocaust' suddenly seemed very real again.

It was not only that the Bible code itself seemed real again, but also that 'Netanyahu' was encoded with the entire sweep of events that led to the horror, starting with the Rabin assassination and ending with an atomic attack.

It was like the pieces of a puzzle coming together, slowly, inexorably completing some horrible picture.

'Netanyahu' fit into place right between 'Yitzhak Rabin' and his assassin 'Amir,' right above the words I had found the day Rabin was shot, 'All his people to war.'

And I now saw that running across the name 'Amir' were the words 'he changed the nation, he will make them evil.' It was as if the crazed gunman had replaced the peacemaker Rabin with the

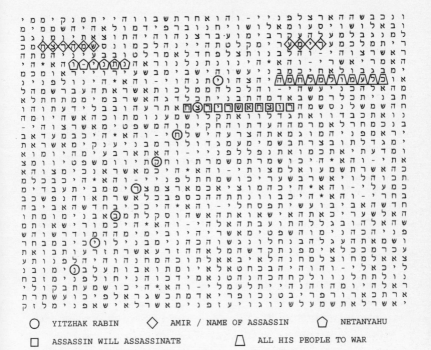

| ○ | YITZHAK RABIN | ◇ | AMIR / NAME OF ASSASSIN | ⬠ | NETANYAHU |
| □ | ASSASSIN WILL ASSASSINATE | | △ | ALL HIS PEOPLE TO WAR |

man who would now lead 'all his people to war,' Netanyahu.

And with 'Netanyahu' appeared words of Biblical terror – 'for the great horror, Netanyahu.' Those same words, suggesting an event so awful it has no equivalent outside of the cosmic scale of the Bible, appear again with the prediction of his election, the only time 'Prime Minister Netanyahu' is encoded.

And the same words – 'for the great horror, Netanyahu' – appeared a third time. They were encoded with 'atomic holocaust.'

The day after the new Prime Minister made his victory speech, I called his father in Jerusalem.

Ben-Zion Netanyahu is one of his son's closest advisors, the elder of an old Zionist family, whose own father upon coming to Israel changed the family name to a word that in Hebrew means 'given by God.' Professor Netanyahu is a scholar of the Inquisition, of the ancient origins of the assault on the Jews that led to Hitler's Holocaust.

Bibi meets with him every Saturday. But when Ben-Zion Net-anyahu received my letter Friday morning, he didn't wait. He gave it to the Prime Minister the same day. My letter stated:

'I have asked your father to give you this letter, because I have information suggesting a threat to Israel that you must understand personally to confront.

'The threat is revealed by a hidden code in the Bible that has accurately foretold events that happened thousands of years after the Bible was written.

'It predicted the Rabin assassination, it predicted the exact date the terrorist bombings this year would begin, and it also predicted your election.

'Now it warns of an "atomic holocaust."

'I do not know if Israel is actually in danger. I only know that the danger is encoded in the Bible.

'I take it seriously, because it predicted that Rabin would die in 5756, that terrorists would strike on February 25th, and that you would be Prime Minister.

'If the threat of an "atomic holocaust" is also real, there may be only a short time to prevent it. We have found new information that may reveal a date.'

We had finally found the day that Israel might be attacked – the last day of the Hebrew year 5756, 13 September 1996.

'Holocaust of Israel' was encoded with '29 Elul' – the date in the ancient Hebrew calendar equivalent to 13 September. 'Atomic weapon' was also encoded with '29 Elul.' '

It was exactly three years from the day of the famous handshake between Yitzhak Rabin and Yasir Arafat on the White House lawn. If 13 September 1993 was the beginning of peace after 4000 years of war between Arabs and Jews, then 13 September 1996, might be the final horrible blow in that endless battle.

Six weeks before the predicted date of the 'atomic holocaust,' I flew back to Israel. No meeting with the new Prime Minister had yet been arranged.

In Israel, I first went to see Eli Rips. The Prime Minister's father had already called him, and while I was there Rips returned Ben-Zion Netanyahu's phone call.

The mathematician told him that the Bible code did appear to state that Israel faced an atomic attack. He said that it was clearly encoded against very great odds. But he also said that no one knew if there was any real danger.

'There is a code in the Bible,' said Rips. 'But we do not know if it is always predictive.'

'The words "atomic holocaust" and "holocaust of Israel" do appear with the current year,' he added. 'But no one knows if that means the danger is immediate, or inevitable, or if there is any actual danger at all.'

'What is clear,' Rips told the Prime Minister's father, 'is that the words stating the danger are intentionally encoded.'

'He'll meet with you,' said Rips when he got off the phone. 'He expressed amazement, but he said he would meet with you.'

'If this is real, then I will believe in God, not only God, but the God of Israel, and I will have to become religious,' said Ben-Zion Netanyahu as I entered his living room.

It was a large statement for the defiantly secular Zionist, one of the Jews who relied on guns, not God, to create the new nation after World War II. I told him that I did not believe in God, and was not religious.

'How can you say that?' demanded Netanyahu. 'It has to be supernatural. No man did this. If there is a code in the Bible, then it is 2000 or 3000 years old. And it reveals what happens now. If it's real, there is a God.'

'So, why have you come to see me?' he asked, without pausing.

'Because the Bible code states that Israel is in unprecedented danger, and the Prime Minister needs to know,' I said.

'The Prime Minister already knows that,' he said. 'I know that. We don't need a code in the Bible to tell us that.'

'But the code states that Israel faces an "atomic holocaust," possibly this year,' I said.

I showed him the Bible code print-outs. The prediction of the Rabin assassination. The prediction of his son's election. The two predictions of a 'holocaust of Israel' and an 'atomic holocaust.'

'If this is really encoded, then it was encoded by a supernatural being so much more advanced than us, that we are ants. How can we stop it?' asked Netanyahu.

Netanyahu and Rips, indeed everyone I met with, seemed to assume that if the code was real, it must be from God. I did not.

I could easily believe that it was from someone good, who wanted to save us, but was not our Creator. Clearly it was not someone omnipotent, or he would simply prevent the danger, instead of encoding a warning.

All I said to the Prime Minister's father, however, was that nothing was pre-determined, that what we did would decide the outcome.

'I will talk to my son,' said Netanyahu. 'I will try to set up a meeting.'

While I waited to hear back from the Prime Minister, I looked at the evidence in the Bible code that Israel was in danger.

The only encoding of 'the next war' again caught my attention. When I first found it, it had seemed clear confirmation of a link between the Rabin assassination and the threatened atomic holo-caust.

Right above 'the next war' the hidden text of the Bible stated, 'It will be after the death of the Prime Minister.' In the same verse the names 'Yitzhak' and 'Rabin' were also encoded.

But now, when I looked again, I saw that same hidden text made a second prediction – 'another will die.'

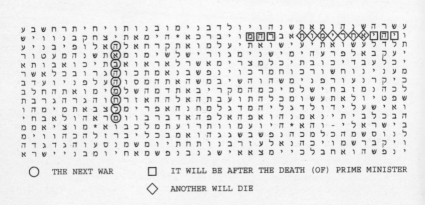

○ THE NEXT WAR   □ IT WILL BE AFTER THE DEATH (OF) PRIME MINISTER

◇ ANOTHER WILL DIE

It was striking confirmation that Netanyahu also might be in danger, and it linked his predicted death to 'the next war.'

I went back to see his father, to tell him the one thing I had held back at our first meeting: the same code that predicted his son's election, also seemed to predict that he would die in office.

Ben-Zion Netanyahu had already lost one son. The Prime Minister's brother, Jonathan, had been killed while leading the famous commando raid on Entebbe that freed hundreds of hostages on 4 July 1976. In Israel, he was a national hero.

I did not want to tell the elder Netanyahu that his other son was now in danger. But if anyone could get through to the Prime Minister, it was the old man I now showed the new set of Bible code print-outs.

'Prime Minister Netanyahu' was encoded once in the Bible. The word 'elected' ran across his name. 'We found that a week before your son was elected,' I said.

I showed him a second print-out. The word 'Cairo' appeared with 'Prime Minister Netanyahu.' It was the first Arab capital he visited. The third print-out showed the words 'to Amman,' again in the same place as 'Prime Minister Netanyahu.' His trip to Jordan's capital was set for the following week.

'The first three predictions have already come true,' I said. 'I think we must also take the fourth prediction seriously.'

I handed the Prime Minister's father the fourth print-out. The words 'surely he will be killed' crossed 'Prime Minister Netanyahu.'

| ○ PRIME MINISTER NETANYAHU | △ SURELY HE WILL BE KILLED |
| □ HIS SOUL WAS CUT OFF | ◇ MURDERED |

The code made it seem inevitable. I assured the elder Netanyahu that it was only a probability, not a determined fact.

He asked to see again the prediction of Rabin's assassination, and looked at it silently for a moment.

And he said again that he would talk to his son.

'I saw my son this evening,' Ben-Zion Netanyahu told me the day before I was scheduled to leave Israel. 'He doesn't want to meet.'

'Bibi is not a mystic, he's very practical, very hard-headed, and he just doesn't believe this,' his father said.

It was hauntingly like the words Rabin's friend used, when I tried to warn him of the predicted assassination: 'He won't believe you. He's not at all a mystic. And he is a fatalist.'

And now Rabin was dead.

I flew back to New York and sent a final letter to Prime Minister Netanyahu. He received it just before the Hebrew New Year. My letter stated:

'According to the code, Israel will be in danger for the next four years, but this year may be critical, and the days just before Rosh Hashanah may be the moment.'

The final countdown now began. The Bible code had yet again been proven real, accurately predicting an Israeli election that every poll called wrong, just as it had accurately predicted the day a wave of terror would begin, just as it had accurately predicted the year Rabin would be killed.

But as 13 September 1996, the day of the predicted holocaust, drew near, the new Prime Minister refused to heed the warning.

It was three years from the day of the Rabin-Arafat handshake. Rabin was now dead, as the Bible code predicted. The peace was now dead, as the Bible code predicted. Peres, the architect of the peace, had been replaced by Netanyahu, the opponent of the peace, as the Bible code predicted.

Everything stated for 5756, the year of the predicted 'atomic holocaust,' had come true. As the year came to an end I could not forget the question spelled out by the Hebrew letters that also spelled the year, the challenge seemingly addressed to us now – 'Will you change it?'

And then I found that 5756 was also encoded with the 'End of Days.'

CHAPTER FOUR

THE SEALED BOOK

The two great Biblical Apocalypses, the Book of Daniel in the Old Testament and the Book of Revelation in the New Testament, are predictions of unprecedented horror, to be fully revealed when a secret book is opened at the 'End of Days.'

In Revelation, it is the book sealed by 'seven seals' that can be opened only by the Messiah: 'And I saw in the right hand of him that sat on the throne a book written within and on the backside, sealed with seven seals. And no man in Heaven, nor in Earth, neither under the Earth, was able to open the book, neither to look thereon.'

In Daniel, which is the original version of the same story, an angel reveals the ultimate future to the Hebrew prophet, and then tells him, 'But thou, O Daniel, shut up the words, and seal the book until the time of the End.'

It was these two verses that caused Isaac Newton to look for a code in the Bible.

The End is foretold four times in the original five books. I checked the first, where the patriarch Jacob tells his twelve sons 'what will befall you in the End of Days.'

In the Bible code, '5756' appeared in the same place.

'In 5756' ran right across 'in the End of Days.' It is the year in the ancient Hebrew calendar that began in September 1995 and ended in September 1996. No other year in the next ten matched. The odds that the current year would be encoded with the 'End of Days' by chance were 100 to 1.

I could not believe that the Apocalypse started now.

I checked the second statement of the End Time in the Bible. Here Moses tells the people of Israel 'all the things that will come upon thee at the End of Days.' It was encoded with the Rabin assassination.

[Hebrew letter matrix]

○ IN 5756 / 1995-96   □ IN THE END OF DAYS

I checked the third. Just before Moses died, in his final speech to the ancient Israelites, he again warned that 'evil will befall you in the End of Days.' That was also encoded with the Rabin assassination.

I checked the fourth, where the mysterious sorcerer Balaam tells an ancient enemy of Israel 'what this people shall do to thy people in the End of Days.'

His Apocalyptic vision had a frightening ring of reality. It foretold a great battle in the Middle East, a future war between Israel and the Arabs, a terrible conflict that would bring many nations 'everlasting ruin.'

'I see it, but not now,' said Balaam 3000 years ago. 'I behold it, but it is not near.'

In the Bible code, that prediction of the 'End of Days' matched 'atomic holocaust' and 'World War.'

There was one other way the 'End of Days' was foretold in the Bible. It was in the very last words of the Book of Daniel, right after the angel refuses to tell the prophet the details of an Apocalypse he says will last three and a half years.

'Go thy way, Daniel, for the words are closed up and sealed till the time of the End,' says the angel. 'You will stand up for thy inheritance at the End of Days.'

I checked this final Biblical expression of the End Time in the Bible code. It also matched the current year, 1996. The odds that 'in

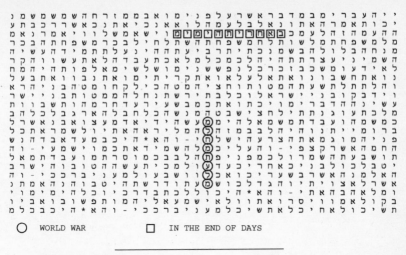

○ WORLD WAR   □ IN THE END OF DAYS

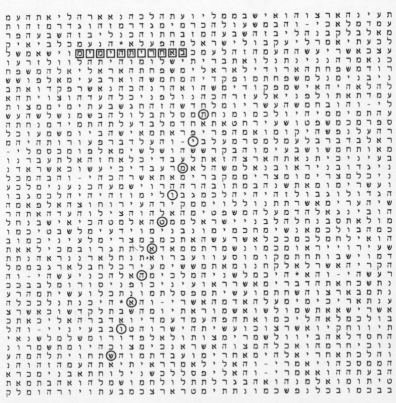

○ ATOMIC HOLOCAUST   □ IN THE END OF DAYS

5756' and 'End of Days' would again appear together by chance
were more than 200 to 1.

○ END OF DAYS   ◇ IN 5756 / 1995-96

I did a computer run of more than a hundred years. No other
year in the next century matched both Biblical prophecies of the
'End of Days.'

The Bible code clearly stated that the End started now – that the
current year, the year that in the modern calendar began in late 1995
and ended in late 1996, was the beginning of the long-prophesied
Apocalypse.

But the code did not say when the 'End of Days' would end.

I looked again at the last chapter of Daniel, where the secret book
is sealed shut. There it is stated that the 'sealed book' will reveal the
details of a greater horror than the world has ever seen: 'And there
shall be a time of trouble, such as never was since there was a nation.'

The Bible code did appear to be a warning of the ultimate catas-
trophe. It was not clear when it would happen, but the code did
seem to state that there would be a third 'World War,' an 'atomic
holocaust,' the real Armageddon.

For more than four years I had been investigating the Bible code,
and from the beginning I had known that both of the two major
predictions of the End Time said that it would be fully revealed
when a secret book was opened.

But until this moment I never realized that the Bible code might
be the secret book.

Yet, if the Bible code was real, it could have only one purpose –
to warn the world of an unprecedented danger.

Nothing short of that could explain a 3000-year-old code in the one book most central to the world. And the danger must be right upon us, or we would not be finding the Bible code now.

Some intelligence that could see the future encoded the Bible. It knew when the danger would exist. It designed the code to be found by a technology that would not exist until then.

Could the Bible code be the 'sealed book'? It was sealed, with a kind of time-lock, that could not be opened until the computer was invented.

Had we really opened the 'sealed book'? Could this really be the 'End of Days'?

I remembered Eli Rips' caution that the Bible code was like a giant jigsaw puzzle with thousands of pieces, and we had only a handful. A picture was clearly emerging, but it was too large, and too horrifying to believe.

I flew back to Israel, and met again with Rips at his home in Jerusalem.

We looked together at the place in the Bible where the two Biblical statements of the 'End of Days' were encoded together, and where they both were encoded with the current year.

'Can you believe this is real?' I asked Rips.

'Yes,' he said quietly.

'Do you think that the Bible code might be the "sealed book"?' I asked.

The mathematician who discovered the Bible code had also never realized that the code might be the prophesied 'sealed book,' the secret text that the Bible itself states will be opened as a final revelation in the 'End of Days.'

'Obviously, if the danger that is encoded is real, if there is an "atomic holocaust," it would fulfill the prophecy in Daniel,' said Rips.

He opened his Bible, and read aloud the famous words: 'And there shall be a time of trouble, such as never was since there was a nation.'

The secret book, Rips agreed, had been designed to be opened now. 'That is why Isaac Newton could not do it,' said Rips. 'It was "sealed until the time of the End." It had to be opened with a computer.'

I told Rips that I did not really believe that there would be an 'End of Days,' much less that it would begin now.

'I am convinced that the ancient commentary is true,' said Rips. 'It states that there will be a terrible time before the coming of the Messiah.'

I told Rips that I could not believe in a supernatural salvation. I was certain that the only help that we were going to get was the Bible code itself. I could hardly believe even that.

I looked again at the place where the 'End of Days' was encoded with 'in 5756.' Two other words stood out in that code matrix. The name of Rabin's assassin, 'Amir.' And the word 'war.'

'Amir' was spelled out in the same skip sequence as 'End of Days,' right where it crossed the year Rabin was killed. And right below the year was the word 'war.'

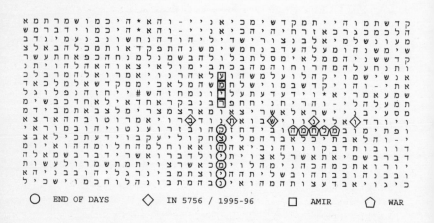

O END OF DAYS   ◇ IN 5756 / 1995-96   □ AMIR   ⬠ WAR

It was not clear when the predicted 'war' would begin, but it was clear that the code was intended for this moment in time.

The 'End of Days' was no longer some mythical event in the distant future. According to the Bible code, it had already begun. This was the beginning of the long-prophesied Apocalypse.

But both the danger and its prevention seemed to be encoded. 'Plague' was there, but also 'peace,' and a word that could be read either as a plea or a command – 'Save!'

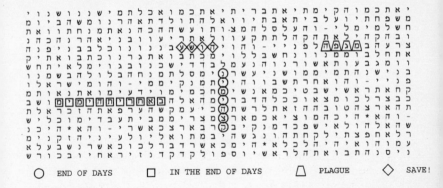

| ◯ END OF DAYS | ▢ IN THE END OF DAYS | △ PLAGUE | ◇ SAVE! |

Rips opened his Bible to Daniel again, and pointed to the words that immediately followed the prediction of an unprecedented 'time of trouble' – 'And at that time thy people shall be rescued, everyone who shall be found written in the book.'

Had the 'sealed book' been opened, perhaps just in time, to warn us of the ultimate danger, the long-threatened 'End of Days'?

I could not believe it.

I never believed there would be an Apocalypse. I had always assumed that it was an empty threat, the club all religions used to keep people in line.

All through history doomsayers thought they saw in the Bible predictions that the world would end in their own times. They read the words of Daniel and Revelation and were sure it was a picture of the present moment.

The keepers of the Dead Sea Scrolls, the zealots who hid copies of nearly all the books of the Bible in caves above the Dead Sea more than 2000 years ago, were certain that the Final Battle was right upon them.

The early Christians believed that the New Testament clearly stated that the End would come in their own lifetimes. Did not Christ warn, 'This generation shall not pass till all these things have happened'?

In every succeeding age someone arose to say the End was now. At the first millennium, in the year 1000 AD. At every time of war and crisis. And they always quoted the Bible, and they were always certain that they had pierced the veil, seen through the symbolic language and knew exactly when the End was coming.

And they were always wrong.

But no serious scientist had ever before found a computerized code in the Bible, a mathematically proven fact that had been confirmed by every other scientist who actually examined it.

And no one had ever found a code that accurately predicted real events in the real world. No one before had found names and dates in advance. No one before had found the name of a comet and the day it would strike Jupiter. No one before had found the name of a Prime Minister, and the name of his assassin, and the year he would be killed. No one before had found the exact day a war would begin.

The Bible code was different.

If the Bible code was a warning to this world, where did it come from? Who could look 3000 years ahead, and encode the future into the Bible?

The Bible itself, of course, says that God is the author, that he dictated the original five books to Moses on Mount Sinai: 'And the Lord said to Moses, Come up to me to the mountain, and I will give thee the tablets of stone, and the Torah.'

It was, according to the Bible, a startling encounter.

In the pre-dawn stillness of the desert, there was suddenly a terrible thunder, and the black mountain towering above was illuminated by an explosive flash of lightning. Great flames shot out from the mountain top, as if the peak itself had been set afire, and in the growing light, the vast expanse of desert around it began to quake.

Startled awake by the thunder and the lightning, and the shaking of the ground beneath them, 600,000 men, women, and children rushed out of their tents, and stared up in terror at the mountain that now shook violently and smoked like a furnace. A ram's horn sounded above the thunder, and one man stepped forward toward the mountain.

Suddenly a voice called out to him from nowhere: 'Moses, come up to the top of the mountain.'

It was 1200 BC. According to the Bible, on the top of Mount Sinai Moses heard the voice we call 'God.' And that voice gave him the ten laws that defined Western civilization, the Ten Commandments, and it dictated to him the book that we call the Bible.

But when God says, 'Behold, I make a covenant: before all thy people I will work miracles,' the code says 'computer.'

The word 'computer' appears six times in the plain text of the Bible, hidden within the Hebrew word for 'thought.' Four of the six anachronistic appearances of 'computer' are in the verses of Exodus that describe the building of the Ark of the Covenant, the famous 'Lost Ark' that carried the Ten Commandments.

The code suggests that even the writing of the laws on the two stone tablets may have been computer-generated. 'And the tablets were the work of God, and the writing was the writing of God, engraved on the tablets,' states Exodus 32:16. But encoded in that same verse is a hidden message: 'it was made by computer.'

○   IT WAS MADE BY COMPUTER

☐   THE WRITING OF GOD ENGRAVED ON THE TABLETS

The code must be describing a device far beyond any we have yet developed. The New York Times recently reported that mankind may be ready to take the next leap, to harness the world inside atoms and create 'an information-processing method so powerful that it would be to ordinary computing what nuclear energy is to fire.' This 'quantum computer,' said the Times, could perform in minutes calculations that would take the fastest super computers we now have hundreds of millions of years to complete.

The astronomer Carl Sagan once noted that if there was other intelligent life in the universe some of it would have certainly evolved far earlier than we did, and had thousands, or hundreds of thousands, or millions, or hundreds of millions of years to develop the advanced technology that we are only now beginning to develop.

'After billions of years of biological evolution – on their planet and ours – an alien civilization cannot be in technological lockstep with us,' wrote Sagan.

'There have been humans for more than twenty thousand centuries, but we've had radio only for about one century,' wrote Sagan. 'If alien civilizations are behind us, they're likely to be too far behind us to have radio. And if they're ahead of us, they're likely to be far ahead of us. Think of the technical advances on our world over just the last few centuries. What is for us technologically difficult or impossible, what might seem to us like magic, might for them be trivially easy.'

The author of *2001*, Arthur C. Clarke – who envisioned a mysterious black monolith that reappears at successive stages of human evolution, each time we are ready to be taken to a higher level – made a similar observation: 'Any sufficiently advanced technology is indistinguishable from magic.'

What the Bible code suggests is that behind the 'miracles' of the Old Testament there was an advanced technology.

The code calls it a 'computer.' But it may only be using the language we can understand. 'History suggests that each age appeals to its most impressive technology as a metaphor for the cosmos, or even God,' states the Australian physicist Paul Davies in his book *The Mind of God*.

Since the root of the same word that means 'computer' in Hebrew also means 'thought,' when the Bible code reveals a 'computer' behind the 'miracles' it may actually be revealing a 'mind.'

But not a mind like ours, anymore than a computer like ours.

The one basic shared belief of all major religions is the existence of an outside, non-human intelligence, God.

If the Bible code proves one thing, it is that a non-human intelligence really does exist, or at least did exist at the time the Bible was written. No human could have looked thousands of years ahead, and encoded in that ancient book the details of today's world.

We have forgotten that the Bible is our best known story of a close encounter. The long-awaited contact from another intelligence actually took place long ago.

According to the Bible, it happened when a voice spoke out of nowhere to Abraham, and again when it spoke to Moses from a burning bush.

The Bible code is, in fact, an alternative form of contact scientists searching for intelligent life beyond this planet have suggested: 'the discovery of an alien artifact or message on or near Earth.'

Physicist Davies theorized that the 'alien artifact' might be 'programmed to manifest itself only when civilization on Earth crossed a certain threshold of advancement.' That perfectly describes the Bible code. It had a time-lock. It could only be opened once computers had been invented.

The rest of Davies' vision is again a precise description of the Bible code: 'The artifact could then be interrogated directly, as with a modern interactive computer terminal, and a type of dialogue immediately established. Such a device – in effect, an extraterrestrial time capsule – could store vast amounts of important information for us.'

Davies, winner of the Templeton prize for science and religion, imagines 'coming across the artifact on the Moon or on Mars' or 'discovering it suddenly on the Earth's surface when the time is right.'

In fact, we have always had it. It is the best known book in the world. We have just never recognized what it really was.

What Moses actually received on Mt Sinai was an interactive data base, which until now we could not fully access.

The Bible that 'God' dictated to Moses was really a computer program. First it was carved in stone and written on parchment scrolls. Then it was bound into a book. But in the code it is called 'the ancient computer program.'

Now the computer program can be played back, and reveal the hidden truth about our past and our future.

The 'Bible code' itself is encoded in the Bible, and the same words also mean, 'He hid, concealed the Bible.' The suggestion is that there is another Bible encoded within the story that is openly told in the Old Testament.

The computerized code clearly confirms that it is the 'seal,' the time-lock that until now has protected the hidden secrets. 'Sealed before God' actually crosses 'Bible code.'

○ BIBLE CODE   □ SEALED BEFORE GOD

And 'computer' is encoded in the last chapter of Daniel, starting in the very verse that commands the prophet to 'shut up the words and seal the book, until the time of the End.'

○ COMPUTER   □ TO SHUT UP THE WORDS AND SEAL THE BOOK UNTIL THE END

The Bible code is the secret 'sealed book.'

Prophecy, of course, is not unique to the code. It happens all through the Bible. The patriarch Jacob tells his twelve sons what will happen in the distant future. Moses reveals two possible futures to the ancient Israelites.

In fact, Jack Miles in his Pulitzer Prize-winning biography of God states, 'It is the miracle of prediction – fortune-telling at the international level – rather than any battlefield miracle that is expected to bring everyone to the worship of the true God.'

But the Bible code for the first time gives us a direct line to the future. Instead of relying on prophets who see visions and interpret dreams, we can now access by computer an ancient code hidden in the Bible.

The code's existence is actually revealed in two well-known stories of ancient prophecy.

The best known fortune-teller in the Bible is Joseph. Sold into slavery by his jealous brothers, he rose to become the virtual ruler of Egypt, by telling the Pharaoh the future.

Joseph alone knew that the Pharaoh's dream of seven fat cows and seven lean cows foretold a great famine. His prediction saved all of Egypt from starvation.

'Can there be another person who has God's spirit in him as this man does?' the Pharaoh asks his court. And he says to Joseph, 'Since God has shown you all this there is none so wise; according to thy word shall all my people be ruled.'

The Pharaoh makes Joseph his regent and gives him a new name: 'Zaphenath-Paneah.'

It is always written that way, in every translation of the Bible, and, even in the original Hebrew, always treated as a name. Over the millennia, there have been many learned speculations on its meaning. Some say it is the Hebrew translation of an Egyptian name originally written in hieroglyphics. Scholars have guessed that it means 'revealer of secrets.' Others say it means, 'the god speaks, and lives.'

But, in fact, the supposed name has a very clear meaning in Hebrew: 'decoder of the code.' Perhaps no one has seen it before, because no one knew there was a code in the Bible.

So, the Bible calls Joseph 'decoder of the code.' An alternate translation suggests that he created the code for us to find now: 'Joseph encoded, you will decode.'

But Joseph cannot be the encoder. The Bible did not even exist until 'God' dictated it to Moses on Mount Sinai hundreds of years after Joseph was dead.

Joseph's name in Hebrew means 'it will be added.' The full hidden text in Genesis 41:45 therefore really reads, 'The code will be added, you will decode it.'

Again in the Book of Daniel, what seems to be a story of ancient prophecy is really a revelation of the Bible code.

There, too, God awes the greatest ruler on Earth, the King of Babylon, by revealing the future. He foretells the rise and fall of ancient kingdoms.

'Truly your God must be the God of gods and the Lord of kings, and the revealer of secrets, to have enabled you to reveal this secret,' the King tells Daniel.

But the same words that in Hebrew mean 'revealer of secrets' also mean 'secret scroll.' And the full hidden text states: 'He revealed the secrets enough that you were able to reveal this secret scroll.'

The Bible code is the 'secret scroll.'

Is the same 'God' who revealed the future to Joseph, who revealed the future to Daniel, now through the Bible code also revealing the future to us?

It seemed to be once more, as Miles put it, 'fortune-telling at the international level.'

The Rabin assassination, and the year it would happen, were revealed in advance. The Gulf War, and the date it would start, were precisely foretold. But I did not yet know if the predictions of a third 'World War,' of an 'atomic holocaust,' of the 'End of Days' were also accurate.

And I wondered why 'God' would reveal the danger, rather than simply prevent it.

'The God who is assisting Joseph,' notes Miles, 'was great enough to know what was going on, but not great enough to determine what would go on.'

The same might be true of whoever encoded the Bible. He could see the future, but he could not change it. He could only hide in the Bible a warning.

The Book of Daniel, suggests Miles, presents human history as 'a vast reel of film whose contents can be known before it is projected.' God can 'provide a preview.'

The question was whether we by seeing the movie could change it, whether we by opening the 'sealed book' could only know the horror of the 'End of Days,' or also prevent it.

'Even within a world created by an all-powerful and benevolent God, there can be a struggle between good and evil, whose outcome is uncertain,' says Eli Rips.

The Bible code may be a set of probabilities. The sealed book might hold all our possible futures. Each predicted event appears to be encoded with at least two possible outcomes.

Rips agrees that the Bible code might have a positive and a negative strand, two opposing statements of reality intertwined: 'As in court, an Advocate, and an Accuser.'

'Possibly there are two opposing statements always encoded to preserve our free will, and it may be that the Bible code is written as a debate,' said Rips. 'According to the Midrash, the world was created twice – it was first conceived from the point of view of absolute judgement, right and wrong. Then God saw that the world could not exist this way, that there was no room for human imperfection, and he added mercy.

'But it's not like mixing hot and cold water and getting lukewarm, it's like mixing fire and snow and each preserves its separate existence. That may be the two strands in the Bible code.'

Rips, however, does not believe that there are two encoders. 'The Bible must have been encoded all at once by one mind,' he insisted. 'But it may encode two different points of view.'

He opened the Bible to Isaiah 45:7, and read it to me: 'I am the Lord and there is none else, I form the light, and create darkness; I make peace and create evil; I, the Lord, do all these things.'

For Rips, as a mathematician and as a devout Jew, there is no need to ask the question, Who is the encoder?

The answer is obvious. The encoder, the Advocate and the Accuser are all one. It is God.

For me, it was not that simple. I had proof there was a code, but not proof there was a God. If the Bible code came from an all-powerful God, he would not need to tell us the future. He could change it himself.

The code seemed, instead, to be from someone good, but not all-powerful, who wanted to warn us of a terrible danger so we could prevent it ourselves.

The Book of Revelation states that the Final Battle will come by surprise, like a thief in the night. In fact, the words that come right before Armageddon are, 'Behold, I come as a thief.'

The Bible is a warning of sudden and inevitable doom.

But the real message of the Bible code is just the opposite. A warning is encoded in the Bible so that we can prevent the threatened Apocalypse.

The truth is hidden in the last chapter of Daniel, the verses that describe the 'sealed book.'

They reveal that the secret book was designed to be found now. This year, 1997, in the ancient Hebrew calendar 5757, is encoded with the words, 'He sealed the book until the time of the End.' Right above that the hidden text states, 'for you, the hidden secrets.' And crossing '5757,' again those same words, which also mean 'for you, it was encoded.'

But who was the encoder?

The last words spoken to Daniel – 'Go thy way till the end be, for thou shalt rest, and stand up for thy inheritance at the End of Days' – have a second meaning.

They also tell the story of someone who has been struggling all through time to prevent a foreseen disaster, and bring history to a good end:

'You will persevere for the fate of everyone to the End of Days.'

Someone hid in the Bible a warning – the information we need to prevent the destruction of this world.

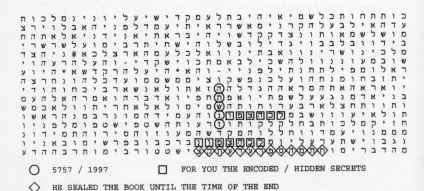

O   5757 / 1997   □   FOR YOU THE ENCODED / HIDDEN SECRETS

◇   HE SEALED THE BOOK UNTIL THE TIME OF THE END

CHAPTER FIVE

THE RECENT PAST

'To see the future you must look backwards,' states the Book of Isaiah.

So when I found that the Bible code stated that the Apocalypse was now – that the 'End of Days' had already begun, that the real Armageddon might start with an atomic attack on Israel – since I had no way of investigating the future, I began to investigate the past.

The closest this world ever came to an Apocalypse, at least since the Flood, was World War II.

'World War,' 'Hitler,' and 'Holocaust' are all encoded together in the Bible, in the last book of the Old Testament. 'This world devastated, World War' is spelled out in a single code sequence, the only time 'World War' appears.

The names of all the World War II leaders – 'Roosevelt,' 'Churchill,' and 'Stalin,' in addition to 'Hitler' – are in the Bible code. All the major combatants, 'Germany,' 'England,' 'France,' 'Russia,' 'Japan,' and the 'United States,' are also encoded with 'World War.'

The year the war began, 1939, is encoded with both 'World War' and 'A. Hitler,' and the word 'Nazi' appears in the same place. 'The Holocaust' is encoded with 1942, the year that the 'final solution,' the mass extermination of all the Jews in Europe, was ordered.

America's sudden entry into the war, when the Japanese struck Pearl Harbor, is vividly told in the Bible code.

Encoded with 'Roosevelt' is his title 'President,' and his 7 December 1941 declaration of war: 'He gave the order to strike on the day of the great defeat.'

'Pearl Harbor' is encoded, and the words 'destruction of the fortress' run across it. The naval base is identified as the location of

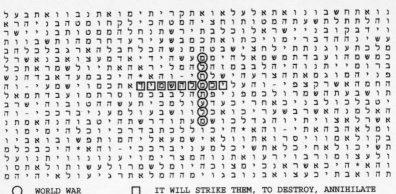

○ WORLD WAR   ☐ IT WILL STRIKE THEM, TO DESTROY, ANNIHILATE

○ ROOSEVELT   ◇ PRESIDENT

☐ HE GAVE THE ORDER TO STRIKE ON THE DAY OF THE GREAT DEFEAT

○ ATOMIC HOLOCAUST   ☐ 5705 / 1945   ◇ JAPAN

'the fleet.' It also appears with 'World War' and 7 December – and 'Hiroshima.'

'Hiroshima' is spelled out with a skip sequence of 1945, the same as the year that the bomb was dropped. The impact of that first atomic bomb is also described – 'Hiroshima to end shooting whole world' – at the point in Genesis where the plain text states, 'And it repented the Lord that he had made man upon the Earth and it grieved him at his heart.'

'Atomic holocaust' is encoded with '5705,' the Hebrew year equivalent to 1945. The year actually crosses 'atomic holocaust' the one time those words appear in the Bible.

The immediate danger never seemed more real. If the last World War was so accurately encoded, then it was impossible to ignore the Bible code's warning of the next war.

'The next war' was encoded in the Bible with a hidden text that stated, 'It will be after the death of the Prime Minister.'

All the assassinations that have changed the course of human history – the murders of Abraham Lincoln and Mahatma Gandhi, Anwar Sadat and Yitzhak Rabin, and both John and Robert Kennedy – were foreseen in the Bible.

The only time 'President Kennedy' appears, the next words in the same code sequence are 'to die.' The name of the city where he would be shot, 'Dallas,' was encoded in the same place.

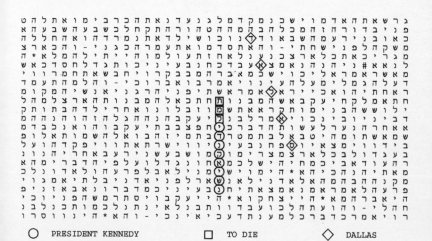

'Oswald' is encoded with 'name of the assassin who will assassinate.' The same words, from the same verse of the Bible, were encoded
with 'Yitzhak Rabin' and the name of his assassin, 'Amir.'

'Marksman' and 'sniper' are also encoded with 'Oswald,' and there
is even a precise description of how he would kill Kennedy – 'he
will strike in the head, death.'

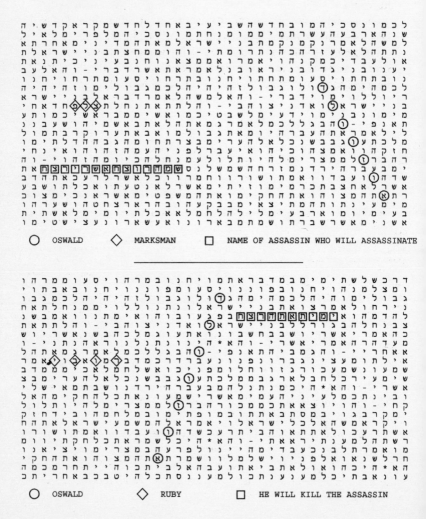

O OSWALD   ◇ MARKSMAN   ☐ NAME OF ASSASSIN WHO WILL ASSASSINATE

O OSWALD   ◇ RUBY   ☐ HE WILL KILL THE ASSASSIN

Oswald's own death is also foretold in the code. The name of the man who shot him, 'Ruby,' appears with 'Oswald,' and the hidden text says 'he will kill the assassin.'

The name of the slain President's brother, 'R.F. Kennedy,' also appears in the Bible. And the second Kennedy assassination was also predicted. In fact, the two murders are encoded together in the same place.

On a single table appear the words 'President Kennedy to die' – 'Dallas' – 'R.F. Kennedy' – 'second ruler will be killed.'

Crossing the name 'R.F. Kennedy' is the name of his assassin, 'S. Sirhan.' And it is at the exact point that 'Sirhan' and 'Kennedy' cross that the hidden text states, 'Second ruler will be killed.'

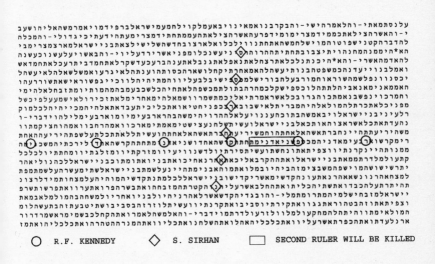

There is a striking pattern to assassinations in the modern world. It is the leaders who bring hope who are killed. And each of the murders is encoded in the Bible.

'A. Lincoln' is encoded twice, in Genesis and Deuteronomy. The name of his assassin, 'Booth,' appears three times in one verse of the Bible that crosses 'Lincoln.' And 'assassinated' crosses 'A. Lincoln' the only other time the name of the President who freed the slaves is encoded.

The man who led India's fight for freedom from colonial rule, Mahatma Gandhi, is encoded in the Book of Exodus. And his name, 'M. Gandhi,' is immediately followed in the Bible code by the words 'he will be killed.'

The murder of the other leader in the Middle East who, like Rabin, is best remembered for trying to bring peace, Egyptian President Anwar Sadat, is also encoded. His name, the name of his assassin, Chaled Islambuli, and the date of the assassination, 6 October 1981, all appear together.

'Chaled will shoot Sadat' is on one table, and 'he will assassinate' crosses 'Sadat' on another where the Hebrew date '8 Tishri' also appears. Even the location, a 'military parade,' is encoded in the Old Testament.

Three thousand years ago every major assassination of the past two centuries was foreseen, and accurately detailed in the Bible code.

It was what I tried to tell Prime Minister Rabin, a year before he was also killed: 'The only time your full name – Yitzhak Rabin – is encoded in the Bible, the words "assassin that will assassinate" cross your name.

'That should not be ignored, because the assassinations of Anwar Sadat and both John and Robert Kennedy are also encoded in the Bible.'

The code said Rabin would be killed 'in 5756,' the Hebrew year that started in September 1995. The year was encoded with 'Rabin assassination' and 'Tel Aviv.'

And now, Rabin was also dead, as predicted, where predicted, when predicted.

If the Bible code was right, the 'next war' would come after an assassination, but it would be triggered by an act of terrorism.

The Middle East was the center of world terrorism, and each of the bombings, the murders, the massacres, was encoded in the Bible.

The first attack I found was striking, because the 3000-year-old Bible code was ahead of the news. I was flying to Tel Aviv in December 1992, when the stewardess handed me the Jerusalem Post.

On the front page was a banner headline, 'Border Policeman Kidnapped.' I immediately ran his name, 'Toledano,' on the search program in my lap-top computer. It appeared only once, encoded in the Book of Genesis.

'Captivity of Toledano' stated the full code sequence. Adjoining the 'd' in 'Toledano' was the name of the city where he was kidnapped, 'Lod.' And the code also said, 'He will die.'

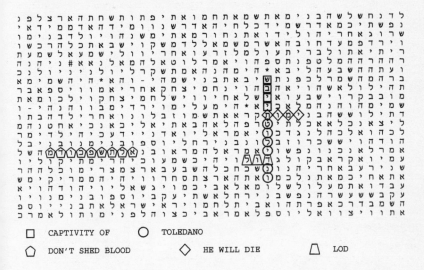

| ☐ | CAPTIVITY OF | ◯ | TOLEDANO |
| ⬠ | DON'T SHED BLOOD | ◇ | HE WILL DIE | △ | LOD |

The newspaper report said his fate was still unknown. The next day his body was found.

Later, when transcripts of the captured terrorists' confessions were published, one of the Palestinians recounted the moments following the kidnapping. He said that there was an argument among the three terrorists whether to kill the policeman, and claimed that he told the others, 'Don't shed blood.' Those same words appeared with 'Toledano' in the Bible code.

The Bible code also foresaw the worst act of reverse terrorism in modern Israel, the February 1994 massacre of thirty Arabs praying at a mosque.

The name of the killer, an Israeli doctor, 'Goldstein,' the name of the city where the murders took place, 'Hebron,' and the words 'man from the house of Israel who will slaughter' all appeared together in the Bible.

O GOLDSTEIN   ◇ HEBRON

☐ MAN FROM THE HOUSE OF ISRAEL WHO WILL SLAUGHTER

The site of the massacre reveals something about the ancient roots of the current danger in the Middle East, and how inextricably bound up it all is with the Bible.

The mosque was built on top of a temple, which was built on top of a tomb. It is believed to be the tomb where Abraham and Isaac and Jacob, the Biblical patriarchs, are buried.

It has long been a flashpoint in the Arab-Israeli conflict. In 1929, there was another massacre in Hebron. Palestinians rioted, and killed 67 Jews, driving the survivors from the city. That, too, was foreseen in the Bible code. 'Hebron' appears with the year of the riot ('5689'), and the full hidden text states, 'Hebron, that evicted them.'

Today, five hundred heavily armed Jews live in an enclave around the Tomb of the Patriarchs, and several hundred more in a nearby settlement called Kiryat-Arba, surrounded by 160,000 Arabs. The Israeli settlers refuse to leave. They quote the Bible to stake their claim. Chapter 23 of Genesis states it clearly: 'The field, and the cave that is in it, were deeded over to Abraham as a burying place.'

Abraham bought the land as a tomb for his wife, Sarah, and his family 4000 years ago. The Arabs don't contest the ancient deed. They just note that Abraham was, according to the Bible, also their father.

The original words of Genesis state, 'Sarah died in Kiryat-Arba, that is Hebron.' The hidden text of the same verse states, 'You will struggle in the city of the ambush, that is Hebron.'

But as the 20th century comes to a close, random murders, even massacres on the scale of Hebron, are not the real danger. Terrorists wielding weapons of mass destruction are the new threat.

That threat emerged suddenly in two totally unexpected places, Tokyo and Oklahoma City. Yet both attacks were encoded in the Bible.

On 20 March 1995, there was a poison gas attack on the Tokyo subway by a lunatic religious cult, Aum Shinrikyo.

Twelve people were killed and more than 5000 injured when the German nerve gas Sarin, developed by Nazi scientists, was released in subway trains during the morning rush hour.

'The cult,' noted a US Senate report, 'thus gained the distinction of becoming the first group, other than a nation during wartime, to use chemical weapons on a major scale.' The committee vice chairman, Senator Sam Nunn, stated, 'I believe this attack signals the world has entered into a new era.'

'Aum Shinrikyo' was encoded in the Bible with 'subway' and 'plague.' The word 'gas' was encoded twice in the same place.

When Japanese police raided the religious cult's headquarters they found enough poison gas to kill 10 million people, every man, woman, and child in Tokyo.

The Doomsday cult had world-wide connections, at least a billion dollars in assets, and in addition to the nerve gas had also stockpiled vast quantities of germ warfare agents, including anthrax. It had even sent a team to Zaire to collect the deadly Ebola virus, and also tried to acquire nuclear weapons.

What might have happened – if Aum Shinrikyo's leaders had not been caught, its plans discovered, and its weapons seized – was also encoded in the Bible.

'Tokyo will be evacuated' was the unfulfilled prophecy, the probability that was prevented.

Encoded with 'Tokyo, Japan' was the Biblical word for 'plagues,' the word used in the Bible for the Ten Plagues of Egypt, and the word right after that was 'flying weapon.'

'Airplane squadron' was also encoded with 'plagues,' and the poison gas 'cyanide' and the incurable virus 'Ebola' appeared in the same place.

Later, Japanese police reported that documents seized at Aum's headquarters showed that the cult was planning a massive assault on Tokyo, using manned and robot helicopters equipped to spray deadly biological and chemical agents.

The group's leader, Shoko Asahara, predicted that the world was coming to an end. Before he was arrested, Asahara set a new date for Armageddon: 1996.

The year encoded with 'Tokyo will be evacuated' was '5756,' the date in the ancient Hebrew calendar equivalent to 1996.

A plague of Biblical proportions had almost been unleashed on Tokyo, and what might have happened was encoded in the Bible.

One month later, at 9 AM, on 19 April 1995, a truck bomb blew up the Murrah Federal Building in Oklahoma City, killing 168 people, including 20 children. Within hours, the police arrested Timothy McVeigh, a former Army sergeant with ties to the militant right.

The Oklahoma bombing was the worst terrorist attack in American history. It was encoded in the Bible in nearly the same detail it was reported in TV news bulletins. 'Oklahoma' appeared with the words 'terrible, frightening death' and 'terror.'

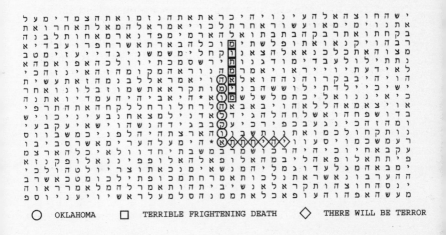

○ OKLAHOMA   □ TERRIBLE FRIGHTENING DEATH   ◇ THERE WILL BE TERROR

The target was named: 'Murrah Building.' And with it there was a description of the horror: 'death,' 'desolated,' 'slaughtered,' 'killed, torn to pieces.'

The chief suspect was identified: 'his name is Timothy McVeigh.' In fact, laid out like a crossword puzzle in the Book of Exodus were the charges filed against McVeigh in the 19 April 1995, massacre: 'His name is Timothy McVeigh – Day 19 – on the 9th hour – in the morning – he ambushed, he pounced, terror – two years from the death of Koresh.'

Government investigators claimed that McVeigh wanted to avenge the Koresh cult, an Apocalyptic religious group, most of whose members died in an inferno that ended their shoot-out with federal agents exactly two years earlier on 19 April 1993.

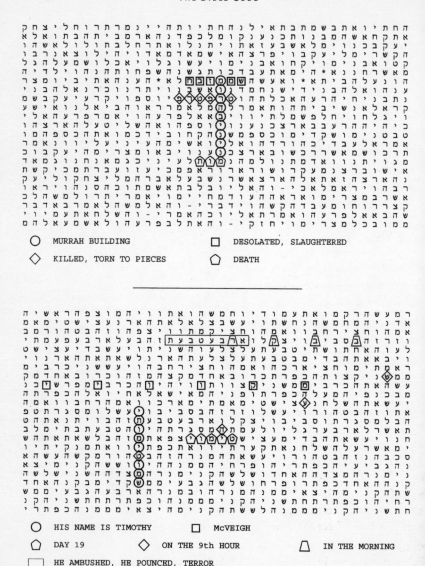

○ MURRAH BUILDING   □ DESOLATED, SLAUGHTERED

◇ KILLED, TORN TO PIECES   ⬠ DEATH

○ HIS NAME IS TIMOTHY   □ McVEIGH

⬠ DAY 19   ◇ ON THE 9th HOUR   △ IN THE MORNING

▭ HE AMBUSHED, HE POUNCED, TERROR

And there was a disturbing echo of that cult's insanity in the verse of the Bible where the Oklahoma tragedy was encoded: 'the terror of God was upon the cities that were around them.'

The recent past was encoded in extraordinary detail.

But the two questions that I had from the beginning – Could we find the details of events before they happened? and, Could we change the future? – were still unanswered.

Timothy McVeigh had remained hidden in the Bible for 3000 years, and was found in the code only after he was charged with killing 168 people in Oklahoma. Yigal Amir could not be found in advance even though the Rabin assassination was predicted. Aum Shinrikyo's alleged plot against Tokyo was unknown until its leaders were arrested.

So the big question still remained – If this really was the beginning of the 'End of Days,' what could we do about it? It was no longer just a philosophical musing.

If the Bible code was right, and its record re: the recent past suggested it could be, this world might be about to face both man-made and natural disasters on a scale it had never seen before, events so terrible that nothing prepared us for it, except the long-known prophecies in the Bible.

CHAPTER SIX

ARMAGEDDON

More than 2000 years ago, a Messianic cult hid out in the hills above the Dead Sea, waiting to be joined by angels for the final battle against evil, preparing for the 'War of Sons of Light with the Sons of Darkness.'

Fearing the Romans would destroy the last remaining copies of the Bible, this small group of ancient Israelites hid hundreds of parchment scrolls in the caves of the sheer desert cliffs.

In 1947, a Bedouin shepherd boy threw a stone into one of the caves, and heard the sound of pottery breaking. Inside the broken urn he found the oldest known copy of any book of the Bible.

I climbed those cliffs days after I first learned that the Bible, proven by the Dead Sea Scrolls to be at least 2000 years old, concealed a computerized code that foretold events that happened thousands of years after the Bible was written.

I sat for hours at the top of the barren mountain, looking out over the bleak landscape that had not changed in the millennia since the cult encamped there waiting for the End.

The next day, I went to the Shrine of the Book in Jerusalem, and saw on display the most ancient prophecy of the Apocalypse, the 2500-year-old Isaiah scroll.

The entire original text of Isaiah, found intact in those caves above the Dead Sea, was now wrapped end-to-end around a huge drum that stood on a pedestal, over a deep open well in the center of the domed museum.

Why, I wondered, was the scroll displayed in this unique way? I called Armand Bartos, the architect who designed the museum that now housed the Dead Sea Scrolls.

'It was originally designed so that the drum could automatically retract, go down to the level below, and be covered over by steel plates,' said Bartos.

'Why?' I asked.

'It was done to protect the earliest copy of the Bible known to the world,' he said.

'From what?' I asked.

'Nuclear war.'

No one yet knew that in the ancient scroll, wrapped around the huge drum, mounted on a device designed to withstand an atomic bomb, was a hidden warning that Jerusalem might, in fact, be destroyed in a nuclear attack, an 'atomic holocaust' that might trigger a 'World War,' the real Armageddon.

The secret was in a 'sealed book.'

Isaiah describes a terrible Apocalypse yet to come, a truly frightening vision of a future war, and then states: 'For you this whole vision is nothing but words sealed in a book.'

It is the first reference to the secret 'sealed book' in the Bible. It is a vision of our future that was hidden, first in a cave, and then in a code that no one could decipher until the computer was invented.

At first, states Isaiah, no one would be able to open the 'sealed book': 'And if you give the book to someone who can read, and say to him, "Read this, please," he will answer, "I can't, it is sealed."'

But finally, Isaiah predicts, the 'sealed book' will be opened: 'On that day the deaf will hear the words of the book, and from the gloom and the darkness the eyes of the blind will see it.'

And in the hidden text, the same verses of Isaiah reveal that the sealed book is the Bible code: 'He recognized the words, they will be computerized, his report they heard on this day, the secrets, the magical words of the book.'

The 2500-year-old warning of a nuclear war could be found only with a computer. And now the Bible code revealed when and where the real Apocalypse might begin.

I checked every year in the next hundred years. Only two years, 2000 and 2006, were clearly encoded with 'World War.'

The same two years were also encoded with 'atomic holocaust.' They were the only two years in the next hundred encoded with both 'atomic holocaust' and 'World War.'

There is no way to know whether the code is predicting a war in 2000 or 2006. The year 2000 is encoded twice, but 2006 is mathematically the best match. And there is, of course, no way to know if the danger is real.

But if the Bible code is right, a third World War by the end of the century is at least possible, and a World War within the next ten years is a probability we cannot ignore.

'Atomic holocaust' and 'World War' are encoded together. The next war, according to the code, will be fought with weapons of mass destruction the world has never seen used in battle before. World War II ended with Hiroshima, but now there are at least 50,000 nuclear weapons, from atomic artillery shells to multi-warhead ballistic missiles. Each can destroy a whole city. The whole world could be obliterated within a few hours.

World War III would literally be Armageddon.

⭕ WORLD WAR   ◇ 5760 / 2000

יעזרויגבהחהואתביתמרההואתביתהרנערימבצרורגדרתצאנונבירואובנבנאותאתהאלעאואתקר
בוישמשהאתבניייישראלאלאמרזאתהארצאשארתתנחלואתהבגורלואשרצותי- והלתתלתשעהמטותוחצימט
יינהלנמולאתמסבנחלהלהלבניייישראלממטהלמטהכיאישבנחלתמטהאבתיוידבקובניייישראלכלבמטהירש
זדורותעלוההרהחויישצאהאמרייכישבהרבהחהואקלקראתהמדפואתהכמכאשאריתעשהאושעישובכתואתהלבשמב
לארכנוחצחרהגלעדועריינתתיראובניולגדיולתרתהגלעדולדהבשנמכלתעובנותנתי־ותל־ותלהבטהה
מדרונופיצי־והאתוכמבעמיולוושמשאמתממתהמספרבגוימאשרנתחי־והאתממעבודבתמשמאלהמשה
יאמרי־והאלישמעתעויבנתאתקןוברדרחעעהמהחזאשארוברואלכחיכישעתתבונ־האתהבנאמכהחמכמאבלול
טו*יתאהוחובשבאזאכי־וחא-חוכב*יכני־ושעה־והא־־חיכשכללעהעעמימאשראהאחכ-ואמפנימאמתה גמאתראעראעתהחעדה־ו
לחשמאתכמאשרחטאתהמלעשותהרלואבגנ׳־ייוחלתכעההחבעבאפ־וחמאמחמאשרקפצי־ וחעלי־ומשח
ו בכ*הולמלקוושורתדרנכותואמצכ־וצוצותחרכנ־וחתכעשוצבאודכלחאתה עשתהמעמר ל־וכמפנ־חתדלב
וחא*הירכוחשראתאלשמשמ־ורשמעאתבאתכלהדברי־מהעהללעמלעהענאזכצמצלכ־וטבלכ־ולבנ־כאהרי־כעה־על־ום
שנחהרוהואתהנחתמבשע־וכ־וכוכב־והאלו־וכיא־וכ־ונלחחולע העתחמעלכעורוהחה־ותומ אהלמואלעזרבהשעהרעבו־ל
חול־וכ־ולכ־יעבדאתהלמאאמר־ומ־ושתהמלומלו־ושאו־ולירחאו ולכלצבאשה־ומ־ומאשראלעאצ־וחתח־וח־והא* הכ־ולבל
רצאשר דברלתלתליאבתכ־וכ־יתאמרמאתאתלהלמ אתהאת־חתהאע ־וחא*ך־ומ ־ח־ואעאנכ־וחל ים
יתאנוחלום שפאטהטהזבר־וחכ־י־וחהלאהי־ושבנאסור־ור־ומורא־וחא־ ־ו ־ונ־ושמעאעבקרור־וח־יעל־ואב־י־וב־יקר־ולאמר ־יסר־ואתרתואל־יאשמע
א*חכאמא־וחמלאשא־וכ־ולאהח־וכשכ בכסש־ונשאהאכלצ־ושכבכלדראשר־ושכלקעכחשרתעבכל־וכוכלאלה־וחד־יכ כ־לאתשמענ־יב
י־וחא*הלכאראמ־אבדארמ־ ־וכ־ידמד ירצ־־מהע־יחת ־יכ נ־וחעהעמבמטעומ־יע־והר ישמלד־וכ־וגד־ול־וע־ורע־י־ורעאוזאתנומנמצר
נכ־־וחלראישואל־אל־וכזנבוח ־ית־ירקלמ־יעלהמעלהולאהחתכהלמטהכ־ית ־וחא*חע־וא א־וכא־ושרנ א־וכ־יצוכ־מ־וכ־ום

○ WORLD WAR   ◇ IN 5760 (2000) / IN 5766 (2006)

־ומלחמתהזהחחגשבעתעתימ־ממתאכלב־ומחדראשונ־אנמכ פראקדשכלמלאכתעבדדהדלאתתעש־ורהקרבתמאשמהעעלחל
־ומנ־ת־חמפ־סתבלבול־ותהבשמ־ונשלשמהערשנ־נ־ומלפרשנ־י־ימל פלא־ואחדאשרוה־י־ימל פלאחח־אחדאשרונ־נלכבשמהתאכחב־ושב־י
חטאתאהאדמ־למלדל־תעדלתהתמ־מ־דמ−־זחתה−ענ־נסכ־יהחבו־ו־ומחחשב־יפ־ר−־ומעהעבנ −עתהא־וע־ירפ־ימ−־ומ−־ובכ ־יננ שנ−־ונאה בעה־והבנ
מחפ־ר־יפראתהממ אשחב־ו־ו−ומשמע−ועכ מ לומ−־ואצאשהמו־ונ דר־וה ־ול ־אס רוח−ילל ־אס רנ−־־פ שה−ימ א ־ישהת−ה פרנ־רמ−−ו ־חנ−־יס ל−ה ת ה−כ־ל נ
רמע ל־ל ־וח ־ועל־ל ב רפ ע־ורנ ות ־ח ח ממ ·ג פ ה−נ ב ע ד ות ·−־וחעא ·נ ·ח פ−ב ־ו−ו עה−ול ·ו ר ב טפ ·ב ־כל א ·א ·שהר ־ין ·ד עאתהע מ ·ד עהעל מ שלמ א ·ו ־ז כ ·ה ר כ ה ר ·ג ·ז
הבכ −רשה־ים א ·א ל ·מ ל א א · ·ח־ד א ·חת א ·ע ל ·ת ערנ ו ־וא תה −ר דנ ו ·−ימ א ר מ ·ר נ ·מ ·ש ה ל ·ב נ ·ו ·י ·ג ד ·ול ד ·ב נ ·ו ·ר א ·ו בנ ·ק מ ·כ ·מ ·כ ·ב א ·ו ל מ ל ח מ ה ר א ·ת נ ·ת מ
ל ·מ ש ה ·ל ·ד ·ע ·ד ·ע ·כ ·י ·ש ·מ ·ע ·כ ·א ·ש ·א ·ר ·ד ·ע ·ד ·ו ·ח ·ט ·ו ·ש ·ת ·כ ·מ ·ק ·נ ·ו ·נ ·כ ·ל ·ב ·מ ·ה ·נ ·כ ·י ·ר ·ה ·ה ·ו ·ש ·מ ·ב ·ע ·ר ·ה ·י ·ה ·ג ·ל ·ע ·ד ·ו ·ע ·ל ·כ ·י ·ע ·ב

○ ATOMIC HOLOCAUST   ◇ IN 5760 (2000) / IN 5766 (2006)

The warning of when and where and how our world might face the real Armageddon, a nuclear World War, was hidden in the most sacred verses of the Bible 3000 years ago.

When we opened the 'sealed book' to search for World War III, we discovered that the year it might begin was foretold in a twenty-two-line scroll that is central to the Bible.

The scroll is called the 'Mezuzah.' It contains the 170 words that from all the 304,805 letters of the original five books of the Bible God commanded be kept in a separate scroll, and posted at the entrance of every home.

'In 5760' and 'in 5766,' the years 2000 and 2006, are encoded in those 170 words.

'World War' – the only time it is encoded in the entire Bible – appears in the same place, and crosses one of the sacred verses.

'Atomic holocaust' – the only time it is encoded in the Bible – also appears with the same two years in the same two verses of the scroll.

The Mezuzah contains fifteen verses, and begins with the most important commandment: 'Hear, O Israel, the Lord our God, the Lord is one.' Twice within those few verses God tells exactly how the words must be preserved:

'And these words, which I command thee this day, shall be in thy heart; and thou shalt teach them diligently to thy children, and shalt talk of them when thou sittest in thy house, and when thou walkest by the way, and when thou liest down, and when thou risest up. And thou shalt bind them for a sign upon thy arm, and between thy eyes. And thou shalt write them upon the doorposts of thy house, and on thy gates.'

The years World War III might begin were revealed in the most carefully saved words of the Old Testament.

And where the years 2000 and 2006 are encoded, the hidden text of the sacred scroll warns of war: 'It will bombard your country, terror, devastation, it is being launched.'

It could not be by chance that the warning of when the world might face a nuclear war was encoded in two of the fifteen verses of the Bible that God twice commands be memorized, taught to the children, and recited every day and every night.

It could not be by chance that the years most clearly encoded with 'World War' were both hidden in the 170 words that were saved in a separate scroll for 3000 years, and are still today fastened on the doorway of nearly every home in Israel.

If even one letter is missing, a Mezuzah cannot be used. Someone wanted to make absolutely certain, no matter what happened to the rest of the Bible, that these words, this scroll was preserved, exactly as originally written, with its hidden code intact.

And that ancient code, which now predicted that World War III could start within a decade, also had predicted that World War II would start 'in 5700' – in the modern calendar 1939–40.

'In 5700, the cremator came,' states the full hidden text, predicting not only the war, but the ovens of the Holocaust.

Armageddon in the years 2000–2006 was the warning encoded in the same sacred verses of the Bible, the carefully preserved code in the Mezuzah that so accurately foretold the last World War.

Instead of a nuclear war between superpowers, the world may now face a new threat – terrorists armed with nuclear weapons.

'Terrorism' is encoded with 'World War,' and right below 'third' appear the words 'war to the knife.' It suggests a war of total annihilation. It is clearly encoded with 'atomic holocaust.'

The sudden collapse of the Soviet Union changed the world. It removed America's chief adversary, but made the world's biggest stockpile of nuclear weapons available to terrorists.

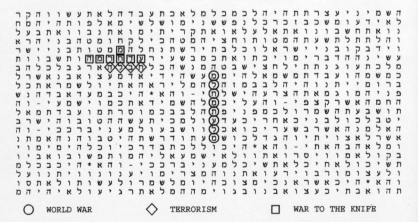

○ WORLD WAR   ◇ TERRORISM   ☐ WAR TO THE KNIFE

A US Senate committee last year confirmed the danger: 'Never before has an empire disintegrated while in possession of 30,000 nuclear weapons,' the vice chairman, Senator Sam Nunn, stated.

Calling the former Soviet Union a 'vast potential supermarket of nuclear, chemical, and biological weapons,' Senator Richard Lugar warned that 'the probability that one, two or a dozen weapons of mass destruction detonating in Russia, or Europe, or the Middle East, or even the United States, has increased.'

'The fall of communism' was foretold in the Bible code. The only time the word 'communism' appears at all, 'the fall of' and 'Russian' are encoded with it.

'China' is encoded just below. Intertwined with 'in China' is a prediction – 'next.'

To many in the West, the collapse of the Soviet Union was seen as a victory. The end of communism in China would be seen as a final triumph. But chaos in another nuclear power would also increase the risk that weapons that can destroy whole cities might be sold to, or stolen by terrorists.

If the Bible code is right, nuclear terrorists may trigger the next World War. It may begin as Prime Minister Peres suggested a few days after I met with him, when a nuclear weapon 'falls into the hands of irresponsible countries, and is carried on the shoulders of fanatics.'

World War II ended with an atomic bomb. World War III may start that way.

◇ FALL OF   ○ COMMUNISM   ☐ RUSSIAN   △ IN CHINA NEXT

Jerusalem, the most fought-over city in history – from the time King David conquered it, and the Babylonians burned it, and the Romans destroyed it, and the Crusaders besieged it, down through 3000 years of bloody conflict that did not end when the Israelis took it back in the 1967 war – is clearly encoded in the Bible as the target of the predicted nuclear attack.

Only one world capital is encoded anywhere in the Bible with either 'atomic holocaust' or 'World War' – 'Jerusalem.'

The name of the city is hidden in a single verse of the Bible. 'Jerusalem' is encoded within God's threat to punish Israel down through history – 'I, the Lord your God, am a jealous God, punishing the children for the sins of the fathers to the third and fourth generation of those who hate me.'

'Your city to be destroyed by an act of terrorism' crosses 'atomic holocaust.'

And the target is confirmed in the most ancient prophecy of the Apocalypse, the one found intact among the Dead Sea Scrolls, the 2500-year-old Book of Isaiah.

'Woe to you, Ariel, Ariel, the city where David settled!' warns Isaiah, using an old Biblical name for Jerusalem. The siege that reduces the Holy City to 'dust' is described in words that are vividly Apocalyptic:

'Suddenly, in an instant, the Lord Almighty will come with thunder and earthquake and great noise, with windstorm and tempest and flames of a devouring fire.'

It is an extraordinarily accurate vision of an 'atomic holocaust,' as foreseen thousands of years ago, expressed in the only words an ancient seer could use to describe it.

Compare it to a modern description of the atomic bombing of Hiroshima:

'The whole city was ruined instantly. The center of the city was flattened. Half an hour after the blast fires set by the thermal pulse began to coalesce into a firestorm, which lasted six hours. For four hours at midday, a violent whirlwind, born of the strange meteorological conditions produced by the explosion, further devastated the city.'

The words that seem to echo Isaiah are from Jonathan Schell's classic account of the 1945 bombing in *The Fate of the Earth*.

No one in Hiroshima heard the explosion. The blast created a vacuum. But miles away there was a tremendous noise, a terrible 'thunder' unlike anything heard before.

The Hiroshima bomb was exploded in the air, almost 2000 feet above the city. If a nuclear bomb were exploded on the ground, as it would likely be in any terrorist attack, the horror would be even greater.

The entire population of a city would instantly be reduced to dust. Again, from Schell: 'Any human being in the area would be reduced to smoke and ashes; they would simply disappear. The incinerated population, now radioactive dust, would rise up into the mushroom cloud, then fall back to the ground.'

Now listen again to Isaiah: 'Brought low, you will speak from the ground, your speech will mumble out of the dust, your voice will come ghostlike from the Earth, out of the dust you will whisper. And your many enemies will become like fine dust, the ruthless hordes like blown chaff. It will happen suddenly, in an instant.'

It is an odd description of an ancient siege, but a perfect vision of the aftermath of a nuclear strike and counter-strike.

And then there is the curious, cryptic passage: 'For you this whole vision is nothing but words sealed in a book.'

They remained sealed, until now, revealed by a code that may exist to warn us at the critical moment of the impending atomic attack.

'Atomic weapon' is encoded in Isaiah. The 'm' in 'atomic' is also the 'm' in 'Jerusalem.' Where 'Jerusalem' crosses 'atomic weapon,' so does the word 'scroll.' And overlapping 'scroll' are the words 'he opened it.'

○ ATOMIC WEAPON   □ JERUSALEM   ◇ SCROLL / HE OPENED IT

And the ancient name for Jerusalem, 'Ariel,' the name used in Isaiah's warning of the Apocalypse, is encoded with 'World War.'

The long-known Biblical prophecy of Armageddon seemed to be confirmed by the Bible code. Jerusalem, the center of the Western world's three major religions, the fabled city where David ruled, where Jesus died, where Mohammed ascended to Heaven, might be obliterated in a final battle brought on by religious hatred.

The real Armageddon could be a nuclear World War.

○ WORLD WAR   □ ARIEL / JERUSALEM

I had never believed the Apocalyptic prophecies of the Bible. I never believed that God or the Devil would destroy the world, or that the forces of good and evil would clash in a Final Battle.

But the Bible code's statement that the final battle, Armageddon, could begin in the Middle East with an act of nuclear terrorism seemed all too real.

The word 'Armageddon' comes from the last book of the New Testament, in a verse that seems fanciful: 'The spirits of devils, working miracles, go forth onto the Kings of the Earth and of the whole world, to gather them to the battle of that great day of God Almighty. And he gathered them together into a place called in the Hebrew tongue Armageddon.'

But Armageddon is a real place. It is the Greek name for an ancient city in Israel, Megiddo. In Hebrew, 'Mount Megiddo' is 'Harmegiddo.' 'Armageddon' is simply the Greek transliteration of that name.

I went there late one night. I was driving back to Jerusalem, and saw a green and white highway sign with a name that I had seen before only in the Bible, 'Megiddo.' It was past midnight, but I stopped to see the ruins of the fortified city. It seemed inconceivable that this remote place would ever really be the site of a major battle.

But near Megiddo, hidden to tourists, is one of Israel's most important Air Force bases, Ramat David. It is in the north, facing Israel's implacable foe, Syria. It would be on the front lines of any real war in the modern Middle East.

'Armageddon' is encoded in the Bible with the name of Syria's leader, Hafez Asad. In fact, the name of the actual site of the long-prophesied Final Battle appears with his name in a single skip sequence: 'Armageddon, Asad holocaust.'

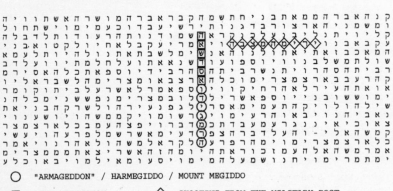

○ "ARMAGEDDON" / HARMEGIDDO / MOUNT MEGIDDO

□ ASAD HOLOCAUST   ◇ SHOOTING FROM THE MILITARY POST

'Syria' is encoded with 'World War.' It is the country that stands out, because it is not expected. 'Russia' and 'China' and 'USA' all also appear with 'World War.' But they are the three superpowers most likely to be involved. 'Syria' is the surprise.

But if Armageddon is real, it may begin the way it is prophesied in the plain text of the Bible.

The last book of the New Testament predicts a final war of unprecedented fury: 'Satan shall be loosed out of his prison, and shall go out to deceive the nations in the four quarters of the Earth, Gog and Magog, to gather them together to battle.'

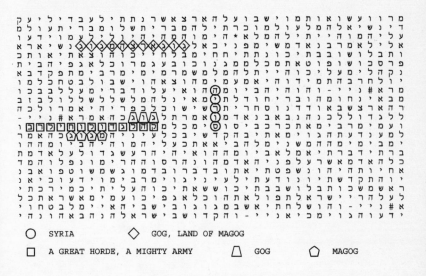

○ SYRIA   ◇ GOG, LAND OF MAGOG

□ A GREAT HORDE, A MIGHTY ARMY   △ GOG   ⬠ MAGOG

No one knows where the ancient 'Gog and Magog' were located. But the original prophecy of the Final Battle, told in Ezekiel, is that Israel will be invaded from the North: 'You will come from your place in the far north, you and many nations with you, a great horde, a mighty army.'

The only modern enemy north of Israel is Syria.

'Syria' is encoded in Ezekiel, starting in the verse that predicts the invasion. Syria's allies are named: 'Persia' and 'Phut,' countries that are now called Iran and Libya.

The plain text of Ezekiel predicts a terrible battle between Israel and the surrounding Arab nations, 'a great slaughter on the mountains of Israel.'

According to the Bible code, that is how World War III might begin – with an atomic attack on Jerusalem, followed by an invasion of Israel.

At the same museum in Jerusalem where the Dead Sea Scrolls are on display, where the original vision of the Apocalypse was mounted on a device designed to withstand an atomic attack, there is another exhibit.

The original manuscript of Einstein's Theory of Relativity, and the equation that changed the world, that started the atomic age – $E = mc^2$ – is shown there in the scientist's own handwriting.

But what really caught my attention was something else Einstein had said: 'I do not know with what weapons World War III will be fought, but World War IV will be fought with sticks and stones.'

At the close of the twentieth century, we are threatened with a kind of chaos that the world has never faced before. We have built weapons that can destroy human civilization in a single day, and those weapons may now be on the loose.

The predictions in the Bible code seem to fulfill the open prophecy of the Bible, and the horror is now given a face and a time and a place – a nuclear World War, perhaps by the year 2000 or 2006, the real Armageddon, perhaps within a decade.

And that is not the end of the predicted danger.

APOCALYPSE

In every vision of the Apocalypse, the final blow is a massive earthquake.

In Revelation, the last book of the New Testament, it is the seventh plague from the seventh angel: 'And there was a great earthquake, such as was not since men were upon the Earth, so mighty an earthquake, and so great. And every island fled away, and the mountains were not found.'

Ezekiel actually predicts that the final war with 'Gog and Magog' will end that way: 'On that day there shall be a great earthquake in the land of Israel. All the people on the face of the Earth shall tremble at my presence. The mountains will be overturned, the cliffs will crumble and every wall will fall to the ground.'

The destruction of this world by a huge earthquake is constantly threatened and foretold in the plain words of the Bible.

'I will make the heavens tremble, and the Earth will shake from its place,' God warns in Isaiah. 'Men will flee to caves in the rocks and to holes in the ground from dread of the Lord when he rises to shake the Earth.'

And hidden in the last verse of the original Bible, the words that close the story the Bible says God dictated to Moses on Mount Sinai, is the same warning:

'To annihilate, totally destroy, he hurled a violent force, and for everyone the great terror: fire, earthquake.'

It cannot be by chance that the last secret revealed in the Bible code is the final blow threatened in every open prophecy of the Apocalypse.

The code seems to warn that over the next hundred years there will be a series of 'great earthquakes' around the world. Three years

are clearly encoded with 'the great terror': 2000, 2014, and 2113.
The distant year is the best match.

○ IN 5873 / 2113   ◇ DESOLATED, EMPTY, DEPOPULATED
□ FOR EVERYONE, THE GREAT TERROR: FIRE, EARTHQUAKE

It is not clear if the code is stating a series of disasters, or a series
of delays. The first earthquakes, however, may come within the first
decade of the next century, perhaps even by the end of this century.

○ GREAT EARTHQUAKE   ◇ IN 5760 / 2000

○ GREAT EARTHQUAKE   ◇ IN 5760 (2000) / IN 5766 (2006)

The long-envisioned Apocalypse, if real, will begin not in some mythical, far-off land, but in real cities, in the real world.

The United States, China, Japan, and Israel are all encoded with 'great earthquake' and years in the near future.

The Bible code appears to predict that the next big earthquake in the US will strike California. All the major quakes that have already shaken that state were foreseen.

The biggest that ever struck the United States – the great San Francisco earthquake of 1906 – was encoded 3000 years ago. 'S.F. Calif.' and 1906 appear together. 'Fire, earthquake' is also encoded with the year, and the hidden text states 'city consumed, destroyed.'

The biggest recent earthquake to hit the US mainland, again in San Francisco, is also encoded. The year, 1989, the words 'fire, earthquake,' and 'S.F. Calif.' all appear in the same place.

But Los Angeles is mathematically the best match with 'great earthquake' of any major city in the world.

'L.A. Calif.' is encoded with 'great earthquake' against very high odds, and both 'America' and 'USA' also appear with the predicted cataclysm.

Seismologists agree that Southern California is the most likely area in the United States to face a major earthquake in the near future. The US Geological Survey in 1995 stated that there is an '80 to 90% probability of a magnitude 7+ earthquake within Southern California before 2024.'

The experts who made that prediction missed the last big quake in the Los Angeles area, the one in January 1994 that killed 61 people in Northridge. It was not on a known fault line, and it was not foreseen.

Except in the Bible code. '5754,' in the modern calendar 1994, was encoded with 'great earthquake' and 'L.A. Calif.'

That was barely a tremor compared to the predicted cataclysm, and a year in the near future appears with Los Angeles in exactly the same place that the 1994 disaster was foreseen.

Crossing 'great earthquake,' right below 'L.A. Calif.,' is the year 2010. And the same year, '5770' in the Hebrew calendar, is encoded again with the name of the city, actually overlapping 'fire, earthquake.'

○ GREAT EARTHQUAKE   ◇ L.A. CALIF.   △ IN 5770 / 2010   □ 5754/19

○ L.A. CALIF.   □ FIRE, EARTHQUAKE   ◇ 5770 / 2010

It is only a probability. Both the code and the seismologists may be wrong. But the Bible code seems to predict that the big earthquake will hit Los Angeles in 2010.

Three other areas of the world are also encoded with 'great earthquake.'

All are encoded with the same two years, 2000 and 2006. There is no way to know which might actually be struck in the next decade.

'Great earthquake' is encoded with 'China.' It was the scene of the worst earthquake in world history, the 1976 cataclysm that killed 800,000 Chinese. That year, '5736,' crosses 'earthquake' right above 'China.'

○ GREAT EARTHQUAKE   □ CHINA   △ 5736 / 1976   ◇ 5760 / 2000

But China may be hit again. Just above 1976 there is another date, 'in 5760,' the year 2000. 'China' appears three times with 'great earthquake,' again with 2000 and also with 2006.

Israel, which has not suffered a major earthquake this century, is the place most prominently stated in the plain text of the Bible. Ezekiel openly predicts 'a great earthquake in the land of Israel.'

'Israel' also appears four times with 'great earthquake' in the Bible code, but Israel appears so often in the Bible that there is no way to calculate the mathematical significance.

Israel is, however, located on what may be the world's greatest fault line, the Red Sea rift that in prehistorical times shifted so violently it separated Africa from Asia.

But the one country most likely in danger, according to the Bible code, is Japan.

When I first met him, my publisher asked me to predict one world event. I declined.

'I don't know a thing about tomorrow,' I told him. 'I just know what's encoded in the Bible.'

But he kept insisting, and finally I told him that if one thing seemed likely, it was that Japan was going to suffer a series of major earthquakes.

Three months later, Japan had the worst earthquake in over thirty years. It happened in a remote area, so few were killed, but on the Richter scale it was a major event.

I checked it in the Bible code. The exact epicenter of the quake was encoded, 'Okushiri,' an island so small that even many Japanese didn't know it existed until the earthquake.

The full matrix read, 'Okushiri July will be shaken.' The earthquake struck on 12 July 1993.

I found that just before a scheduled trip to Japan. I felt compelled to share what I knew. If the Okushiri quake was so accurately encoded, then the other predicted earthquakes might also be real.

I went to see the Japanese Cabinet Minister in charge of earthquake preparedness, Wakako Hirōnaka. Her husband is a famous mathematician, and she was interested but perplexed.

'What can I do?' she asked me. 'Evacuate Tokyo?'

In fact, 'Tokyo will be evacuated' was encoded in the Bible. But not when, or why.

A year later, the port city of Kobe was devastated by a massive earthquake that killed 5000. That, too, had been foreseen in the Old Testament. 'Kobe, Japan' was encoded. With it were the words, 'fire,' 'earthquake,' 'the big one.' And the year it happened, 1995 ('5755') crossed 'fire, earthquake.'

'Japan' is also the country most clearly encoded with a future 'great earthquake.' The years 2000 and 2006 appear in the same place.

Again, there is no way to know if the stated danger is real. But there seems to be an Apocalyptic urgency to the warning about Japan, just as there is about Israel. In fact, in the Bible code, there seems to be an almost eerie link between the two countries.

Both are repeatedly stated to be in unprecedented danger.

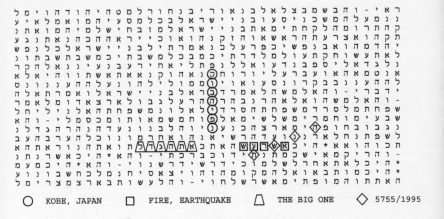

○ KOBE, JAPAN   □ FIRE, EARTHQUAKE   △ THE BIG ONE   ◇ 5755/1995

'Japan' and 'Israel' appear together with the two Biblical statements of the 'End of Days.' 'Japan' is encoded with 'holocaust of Israel.' 'Israel and Japan' are again together in the hidden text of the Bible as a single phrase, and the names of the two countries cross the only encoding of 'year of the plague.' And 'Japan' is the only country in addition to Israel encoded with 'Final Battle.'

○ YEAR OF THE PLAGUE   ◇ ISRAEL AND JAPAN

A disaster of Biblical proportions seems to be threatened throughout the Bible code for both countries. In Israel, the immediate danger appears to be nuclear war. In Japan, the immediate danger appears to be a catastrophic earthquake.

And if the entire world might be endangered by the war the Bible code predicts will start in Israel, the entire world might also be shaken by an earthquake that strikes Japan.

דניכיאממאנאתהלשלחהאתהעמיהכנינימביאמחראברהבהגבבלכוכסהאתהעינהארצולאיוכללראתאתהאראצוא
יעהההאחחשמנאהוישריממאמהרורהבאהרגעמאהאמחחיריעההאחחממדאהאהחלכלהריריעתהחמשחרייעתחהיינחב
שתיטבעתזהבריתנעלהעלשתיכתפהתאפהדמלמטהממלפניולעממתמחברתמרמעעללחשבהאפדונ⟨ר⟩⟨ב⟩כסואתהשש
ומנאשרעעלכפהכחכיתנעל⟨א⟩ראשהחטטהרניכפרעלייהקׁ⟦ז⟧⟨ב⟩⟨ב⟩⟨י⟩ – והועשהחכהנאתהחטאתוכפֹע⟦ע⟧⟦ל⟧המטהרמט
⟨א⟩כהנאתהמ⟨ס⟩⟨א⟩חערככע⟨ש⟩⟨א⟩תהיבלו⟨א⟩ש⟨א⟩תהאערכ⟨ב⟩⟨ב⟩ומההויאקדשלי – והבשנחתריובליושוב⟨ה⟩הלאשרקנ
ושההאביהירכֹרקבֹפניהחלהאתכלמשבעתהעתימיהמתסגרשבעתהבעתיכמיהמתסגרשבעתה⟨ד⟩יובלאלהאספרנטו⟨ה⟩ריממאחו
קדיהחמהחשהוארביעיאמכלאפרושהשמאראתהאלהבניילדולמשהפשתמתהמלשריחממשפתהחמשריחמיאלהמשפתהֹ⟨ב⟩למשהחתמ
ספֹעולהחדבראשאראנכיאמצוהאתהאכמולהאתהגרעוממנולשמאראתמרמאתמצותי – והא*חיכמאראנכיֹ⟨ב⟩ׁמאֹ⟨ב⟩אתכמעאיני
ממרלאהאסכלשמעעמאהתהֹקולי – והא*חי⟦ר⟧אתההאשהגדלהחהזאהתהלאהאראתהוראימרי – והֹ⟨ב⟩⟦ל⟧היהטֹיבואו
יושכנלוליוׁסֹפאמרמבֹרכתי – והארצומהֹדשמיממֹטלומתהומרֹצתהֹתתתממֹהוממֹזדתבואתהֹשמשהוממֹגדגרישיר

⭕ GREAT EARTHQUAKE   ☐ JAPAN   ◇ IN 5760-66 / 2000-2006

⭕ ECONOMIC COLLAPSE   ☐ FIRE, EARTHQUAKE STRUCK JAPAN

'Economic collapse' is encoded one time in the Bible. The year the last Great Depression started, 1929, is encoded in the same place. And 'economic collapse' is also encoded with the words 'earthquake struck Japan.'

Japan is now so central to the global economy that any great disaster in that country would impact the whole world. The true global upheaval may be a great 'economic collapse' rather than a 'great earthquake.'

But the ultimate danger we face may be the greatest natural disaster mankind has ever witnessed.

Sixty-five million years ago an asteroid bigger than Mount Everest struck the Earth, exploding with the force of 300 million hydrogen bombs, and killed all the dinosaurs.

'Asteroid' and 'dinosaur' are encoded together in the Bible. The Biblical name for the first creatures God created on Earth is also encoded in the same place.

'And God created the great Tanin,' states the first chapter of Genesis. The word means 'dragons' or 'monsters.' It describes some huge animal that no longer exists.

And 'dragon' is encoded across 'dinosaur,' just above 'asteroid.' With them is encoded the name of the dragon that, according to legend, God slayed before Creation.

It is surely intentional that the name of the dragon the Bible says God fought – 'Rahab' – appears in the Bible code exactly where the 'asteroid' hits the 'dinosaur.'

In fact, the full hidden text states, 'It will strike Rahab.'

It suggests that the extinction of the dinosaurs was the real slaying of the dragon, the cosmic event recalled by Isaiah: 'Was it not you who cut Rahab in pieces, and pierced through the dragon?'

Scientists now agree that mankind would never have evolved unless the dinosaurs had been wiped out by the asteroid.

But they also wonder whether mankind may face a similar fate, if we too will be wiped out by a rock hurtling in from outer space.

A leading American astronomer, Brian Marsden, director of the Smithsonian Observatory in Cambridge, Mass., first sounded the alarm in 1992.

He calculated that a comet named Swift-Tuttle that had just been sighted would reappear 134 years later in 2126. And he said that it might then collide with the Earth.

The comet was at least as big as the asteroid that killed the dinosaurs. Marsden's very low-key warning – 'a change by +15 days could cause the comet to hit the Earth in 2126' – was a Dooms-day alert. It was front-page news around the world.

'The International Astronomical Union, the world astronomy authority, has for the first time issued a warning of a potential collision between Earth and a speeding object from the fringes of the solar system,' the New York Times reported. 'The size of the

רצלרבויברכי-והאתכלרכלגליועתהתמתיאעשהאגמאנכילבתיתיריאמראמהאתנלכוריאמריעקבלבאלתתגליכמאו
קאישעמועדעלדותהשחרוריראכיאיכללוניגעגבכפירכורותקעכפירכיעקבבהבאבקועמוריאמרשלחניכי
בןיאחליבמהבתעןנהבתצבעוןאשתעשורות*הרעשואתעישואתישאועלמואתקתרחאלהאלפיזבייעשורבןיאלי
ללייספוייחיברכתי-רהבכלאשרישלובביתבובשדהויעזבכלאשרלובידיוספולאידעאתמואמומחכיאמה
ובכלמארצמרימהחלמהותרעבכלארצמצרימארצמצענמכאאתאגמאשרנמצאהאגביעברדוריאמר
נדברומחנצטדקהא*חיממזאאתאתתאוןנעדרכנחבכיעודריםאלדבכיגמאכנחנוגמאשרנמצאהאגביעברדוריאמר
גומקיכמואתהלכמבבמקניכמאאמאפסכסספייבאיאתאמקניהמאליוספוייתנלהמייוספלהמבסוסימומבמק
אובהתאבוויחייוספמאאחייעשרשניניראיוספלאפרימביישלשלימגמאבניומכירבנמנשהילדעלברכי
ישבאלירחתרחתןוויאמרלואלבחנאואשתיבהתלאלהאשראברמבמצרימוארחתנעוארחומיאמריתרלמשהתכל
חהנהאנכינגפאמתכלגברבלובכבפרדעדעהשראת*רצפרדעימועלועובאובזיכבולאבניבבריכבבעולפלמסתכוב
נשראבהאחדובכלגבולותמצרימורחתקי-והאתלבפרעהותלאשלהאאתבןיישראלירראמרי-והאלמשהתנהיד
נייהשראלמארצמרימיקהמשהאתעצמותיוספוהשבעהוהשביעבעתהשבעאתבןיישראלביתיהמאבי*חימא
ליצאאישמומקומביומהשביעייוישבותבתהועמעדיוומחשצעירכראובביתאויקראישמעראלמשהתתנואזכרועדעבראלבנ
פנימקבלבלתתחטאויהיעמדתהעמרמקונאחלמשהאלפואשמהא*חימאיאמרי-והאלמשהכתאממארלב
יהדמזרקלוהמזרחהחממאיעמדאשנרתויקספהחברתיויחמרוכלאשרדבר-וחזעשיהושנתהממרקממשהתהאת
תקדמהמזרחהחממאיעמדאשנרתויקספהתבעפדתימשלהשהראדניממשלהשהראדנישמל
חאשהלי-והעלהתמתרילדרתיכמפמתחאהלמועדלבראאליכשמואנעדתישמהלב
תנגנושלחתילפניכמלאכולגרשתיאאתכנענעיבהאמריוחתיוהפרזיוהחוייהבוסיואלהארצלהחלבזתלבודבש
חחנמהבלבוכלאיכלאשרנשותולבולקרבהלחמלאבאכתהלהתוריומשהאתהאתרומהשבעיהבריאובני
כליתדהתמשכנואתכליתדחתאחרצסבימונהנתחלכתואהרגמנותלעולהעשויישועישובגדישרהבקדשרעש
רבמערבעדערבתשבתוסיבבתכמיהודברי-והאלמשהלאמרדברבאלבניישראלממצררימההמעבדיעהמצרבחשמהעשרויומ
היולועלמאני-והא*חימאממשרצריימהמעברצמצראלבנייומשלהמאפומאתמרימלבביניאבונבילכואו
ישמנהיומחומעלהכלצאצאפקדיהמכלמשנמשנשיהממשלשלמיולשלמיהאלמפומאתמרימלבביניומתולדמלשמחתמלב
ובאאחריכובנירבסאשסעתהאמורונחירדואפרתפהמתהמסכו-חבהאתאתרנחהעדתנתכנועליוכסויעורותחשורפש
תועשחתהכחכאתמטפדיבולקחתיומונאחממהלאשרהאאואוגרשאשרבחאתמצרימולארשפתהמתאלמלבנותעלהלה
לפנ-יי-וחוסומכבולבניישראלומחזיפאתהראתהרצאתצלהליומזהיחזיפפפהלפנ-יי-והאמאתב
כמותבכולפני-יי-לא מרלמהזחיצאנומומצריומי אמרמשההשממאטאלפארגלי העמאשראנכיבקרבוראתהאמר
מאשרשלהמשהלתורא תהארצויכלוויכוייבחעלטההלהנר צואיבעתהדלהתאראצימלברתיאברתיישש
סררפברכפראלהעתנאיעדאדשראשרא תמ תערמעימויומהתערבעתהתבאהעיבנוהמהואבעהתנ עוחמל
זהתהארבעימשחחי-והא*חיבחיחכעתמהתבהיכ*חיכעמלדאשראמהביא*ןגובזחיעכאבומנכוובזוהירצהתהארצבהמא
ככיי-והא*חיכאשאכלהחתוהא*קנאכ*חיטלמ[ידלכנ]בןמובבני*מ[יהא*חיכלבחלתחלתולעלסגבלגחמזלהעמימאשר
סילימחתהרפונאשכועמקדישאתתהלי-והא*חיכבבכרהריאא*חיכבבזכרהיתלעלעמהסגבלגחמזלהעמימאשר
יברכדימיהרלואשו-ימארלבעימוומארבעמילימליאלהא-ולגמבעפעמהבלבהאלאלאאחכו-וחהשמהכוי
יי-והא*חיכמתלכוואתותואמצותיואתמצותיומשמרלבקלתלתשמערומרומועבדותואתדבקינותוברבקוויוזהאחהי
מאאנכלרכבכאהתהעגלהעגלונחללונגישוחכנ[ודגראבחריכי]במבחרי-והא*חיכלעברבברי
איזערעורםמושאמאתהעגלתההתעגלולנחלושחכנ[ו]נגשוחכנ[ו]לברכבשמי-וחעו
רכבי-והא*חי[גל]למעשהידכיכירתת[ב]טזו[ו]אתמפראאחריכלרלתומ[ן]אלמנואתריהכיהחו*חכחיכ-והב
בהמתהארצואינמחדידיכך-והובשחבינמצריונמבעפליומעמגרבוברבחרסאלהארלאתלתרהראפאכבכה-והב
רמי-יערבלוואלעבעברחימיקחתלעמנונוואתהנעשנכי-וחחכ-ואביאכבי-וחדברמראבפבפיבכלבזזבללעשדתו
מאתבני-ישראלאלפלפכימותיורי-יאמרי-וחמסינכיבאוזרחממשעייירמולהוחופיעמהרפאראוניאתהמרארבתבתקדשמימי

○ DINOSAUR   ◇ ASTEROID   ☐ DRAGON   ▭ IT WILL STRIKE RAHA

comet is in the range that scientists assume is sufficient to end civilization.'

'It comes screaming out of the sky like a Scud from Hell, bigger than a mountain and packed with more energy than the world's entire nuclear arsenal,' stated a lurid cover story in Newsweek, painting the frightening scenario.

Marsden later called off the alert. New calculations showed that the comet would pass safely at the end of July 2126. But if it came just two weeks later, in mid-August, the ten-mile-wide rock would crash into our planet.

No astronomer was within two weeks of predicting the actual 1992 appearance of Swift-Tuttle. Most were years off.

But the exact day the comet was spotted, Sunday, 27 September 1992, was encoded in the Bible 3000 years ago. It happened to be the eve of the Hebrew New Year. The Bible code foresaw the moment: 'Eve of New Year, Swift.'

'5753,' the Hebrew year of the 1992 appearance, was encoded with 'comet' and its full name 'Swift-Tuttle.'

And in the Bible code, 'Swift' is also encoded with '5886,' the year the comet is due to return, 2126.

The name of the comet intersects the year. And right above 2126 are the words, 'In the seventh month it came.' That suggests it will pass the Earth safely in July.

But a terrible warning is encoded in the Bible with the word 'comet.'

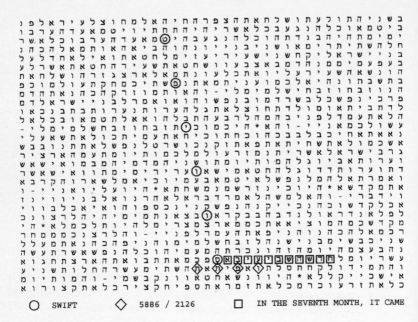

○ SWIFT   ◇ 5886 / 2126   ☐ IN THE SEVENTH MONTH, IT CAME

It was not until another comet collided with Jupiter in 1994 that our world recognized the true danger.

That impact created fireballs the size of the Earth, and left Jupiter scarred with massive black craters. It was the biggest explosion man ever witnessed in our solar system, and if it had happened here it would have wiped out the human race.

The Jupiter cataclysm was also foretold in the Bible code, found months before it happened. The name of the comet, 'Shoemaker-Levy,' was encoded with the name of the planet, 'Jupiter,' and the exact date of impact, 16 July 1994.

In 1995 the Pentagon and NASA began searching the skies for asteroids and comets that might slam into the Earth. 'We could face a surprise encounter,' said Dr Eleanor Helin, the US government scientist in charge of Near-Earth Asteroid Tracking.

She estimated that there are at least 1700 'Earth crossers,' asteroids and comets whose orbits intersect ours, and might be big enough to destroy all life on this planet. The odds of a collision are remote. It happens perhaps once every 300,000 years. But no one knows when the last one struck, or the next one will strike.

'It's sobering,' said Dr Helin, when the first organized effort to locate the 'Earth crossers' started. 'These things have been lurking out there all these years, but we've never seen them.'

The asteroid that killed the dinosaurs landed in what is now the Gulf of Mexico, blasting all of North America with a firestorm that apparently destroyed every living thing on the continent. The dust and ash and debris that shot up into the atmosphere then blotted out the Sun across the entire globe, causing world-wide extinctions.

It is estimated that two-thirds of all the species that ever walked, flew, or swam on Earth became extinct because of impacts from outer space. We are the first species that might be able to prevent it.

When Swift-Tuttle caused the first alarm, and the bombardment of Jupiter vividly demonstrated the danger we face, scientists began to plan the defense of the Earth.

The inventor of the hydrogen bomb, Edward Teller, said we could shoot down an asteroid with a massive nuclear-tipped rocket.

Other scientists suggested that simply exploding a nuclear device near a comet would melt the frozen gas, create jets that shot out like the thrusters on a rocket, and divert the comet from its collision course.

There was even a plan to land a spacecraft on any big rock heading towards Earth, attach rocket engines to it, and steer the comet or asteroid away from this planet.

But those are all untried schemes, at best sketchy diagrams and a few equations, and no one knows how much time, how much warning we might have.

'It may be only days or weeks,' says Gareth Williams, Marsden's colleague at the Smithsonian Observatory. 'If it's a comet on a very long orbit, it may catch us by surprise, it may be totally unknown.'

Until Shoemaker-Levy bombarded Jupiter, there was no organized effort even to track the rocks in outer space. There are still no concrete plans to stop one hurtling toward us.

The Bible code warns that a collision with the Earth may be a real danger.

There are a series of near encounters indicated, right up to the time Swift returns in 2126.

But the first year clearly encoded with 'comet' is only 10 years away – '5766,' in the modern calendar 2006.

Running across 2006 is a chilling statement: 'Its path struck their dwelling.' The warning that overlaps the year ends with the words 'starlike object.'

Right above 2006 is an apparent confirmation of the time: 'Year predicted for the world.'

○ COMET   ◇ IN 5766 / 2006   □ YEAR PREDICTED FOR WORLD

Other probabilities are encoded. Both '5770' and '5772' – the years 2010 and 2012 – also appear with 'comet.'

'Days of horror' runs across 2010. 'Darkness' and 'gloom' cross 'comet' right below.

'Earth annihilated' states the hidden text right above the year 2012.

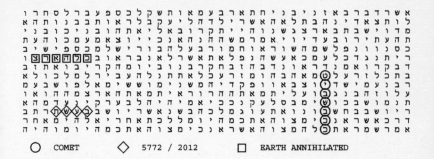

But where 2012 is encoded there is also a statement that the disaster will be prevented, that the comet will be blocked: 'It will be crumbled, driven out, I will tear it to pieces, 5772.'

That is very much what happened to the comet that hit Jupiter. Before it struck the planet it crumbled into 20 separate pieces. But then each of them bombarded Jupiter every day for a week.

There is an ancient tale, told in the Talmud, of a king who became angry with his son, and swore that he would hurl a massive stone at him. Later, he regretted it, but could not go back on his oath. So he ordered that the stone be broken up into small pebbles and that each of these be thrown, one by one, at his son.

The parable, played out on a cosmic scale with Jupiter, may also foretell the fate of man on Earth.

There is a theory that a collision by a comet in prehistoric times may have inspired later Apocalyptic tales in the Bible.

'Current studies indicate that there must have been at least one ten-gigaton impact within the past seventy thousand years,' wrote Timothy Ferris in the New Yorker, 'a horrific blast, which would have blacked out the sun, flooded much of the world, drenched the land with fire and the smell of brimstone, and otherwise brought down a whole Biblical Apocalypse.'

But a hundred million years may pass between impacts big enough to cause a global extinction, and a million years between explosions that could destroy a country, and thousands of years between comets that could level a city.

And at the time I discovered that this cosmic danger was encoded in the Bible, the predicted 'atomic holocaust,' the 'holocaust of Israel' that might trigger a World War, was only weeks away.

The countdown to what could be the real Armageddon was coming to an end.

CHAPTER EIGHT

THE FINAL DAYS

When I flew back to Israel at the end of July 1996, the threatened 'atomic holocaust' was just six weeks away.

On the flight, I read a report in the Jerusalem Post that Prime Minister Netanyahu was about to leave for a meeting with King Hussein in Amman, Jordan.

That, too, had been predicted in the Bible code. I found it a week before Netanyahu was elected, in the same place that his victory was predicted, more than two months before the just announced trip.

'July to Amman' appeared almost openly in the code, right next to 'Prime Minister Netanyahu.'

The newspaper report now confirmed his trip to Jordan. It was scheduled for 25 July 1996.

○ PRIME MINISTER NETANYAHU   ☐ JULY TO AMMAN

'Oh my God,' I said to myself, 'it is real.'

Once more the Bible code had been proven right. Three thousand years ago it had predicted that in July 1996 Netanyahu would go to

Amman. If the Bible code was right about that, if it was accurate down to the smallest details, then it was likely also right about the predicted 'atomic holocaust,' the 'holocaust of Israel,' and the 'World War.' The danger looked very real.

Then, at the last minute, Netanyahu's trip was suddenly delayed. The night before the Israeli leader was scheduled to leave for Amman, King Hussein fell ill. The Prime Minister did not go to Jordan until 5 August.

Was the Bible code wrong? 'Prime Minister Netanyahu' did go 'to Amman,' as predicted 3000 years ago. But he did not go in 'July,' as the code stated.

I went to see Eli Rips. I asked him if the Bible code might work like quantum physics. If it did, then it could not tell us both what and when. The Uncertainty Principle said it clearly – the more precisely you measured what, the less precisely you could measure when. That was why quantum mechanics predicted not one, but many possible futures.

Rips did not invoke the Uncertainty Principle. Instead, he pointed to the word in the Bible code right above 'July to Amman.' It said, 'Delayed.'

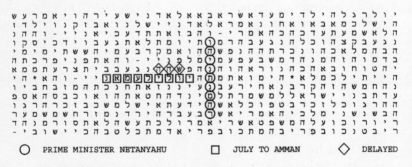

○ PRIME MINISTER NETANYAHU   □ JULY TO AMMAN   ◇ DELAYED

Could the Bible code be right about an event, but wrong about the date? The question had a special urgency in the final weeks of a countdown to a possible Armageddon.

Right up to 13 September 1996, the last day of 5756, the year of the predicted 'atomic holocaust,' I stayed in close contact with Israeli leaders.

Three days before the date encoded with 'holocaust of Israel,' I met in New York with the Prime Minister's national security advisor, Dore Gold. The next day, I sent a final message to Mossad chief Danny Yatom, and General Yatom sent back word that Israeli intelligence was on alert.

But nothing happened on 13 September 1996. There was no atomic attack. The Hebrew year 5756 came and went and Israel and the world were still at peace.

I was relieved, but puzzled. Was the Bible code simply wrong? Or, was the danger real, and only delayed? I thought about it all weekend, and on Monday sent Yatom a fax:

'One last word, and I'm out of the fortune-telling business.

'The atomic attack predicted for the last days of 5756 was obviously a probability that did not happen – but my guess is that the danger is not over.

'On several occasions we have seen things happen as predicted, but not when predicted. I urge you to remain alert to what is almost certainly a real danger.'

I could not be sure the danger was real, but now I had proof that the future was not set in stone.

Finally, there was an answer to the question posed by the Rabin assassination, debated by Einstein and Hawking, and raised by Peres when I warned him of the threatened atomic attack – 'If it's predicted, what can we do?'

The future was encoded in the Bible. Rabin's murder and the Gulf War proved that. But it was not pre-determined. It was a series of probabilities, and it could be changed.

The question spelled out by the same letters that spelled out the year 5756 – 'Will you change it?' – had been answered.

Did the Israelis, warned by the Bible code of an atomic attack, prevent it by being on alert at the time of the predicted danger?

Did Prime Minister Peres, by publicly stating the danger three days after I met with him, put a stop to a planned terrorist attack?

Or was it all changed only by chance, when Netanyahu at the last minute delayed a diplomatic trip to Jordan?

By delaying his trip, the Prime Minister may have saved his life.

'Death, July to Amman' stated the full hidden text that crossed his name. The word 'delayed' appeared right above. 'Delayed' appeared twice more with 'Prime Minister Netanyahu,' crossing the words 'his soul was cut off,' and crossing 'murdered.'

○	PRIME MINISTER NETANYAHU		
□	DEATH, JULY TO AMMAN	◇	DELAYED
△	HIS SOUL WAS CUT OFF	◇	DELAYED
⬠	MURDERED	◇	DELAYED

By saving his life, Netanyahu may have prevented, or delayed, a war.

'The next war' was encoded with a prediction: 'it will be after the death of the Prime Minister (another will die).' In fact, the full hidden text stated 'another will die, Av,' naming the Hebrew month equivalent to July.

○	THE NEXT WAR	□	ANOTHER WILL DIE, AV, PRIME MINISTER

And by forestalling a war in the Middle East, the delayed trip may have prevented a global conflict.

Both the plain words of the Bible and the code predict that a 'Final Battle,' a 'World War,' will start in Israel. So, the entire world may have been spared at least for a time by the suddenly cancelled trip.

Was it really possible that one small change, a trip that took place ten days late, could make such a huge difference? If it prevented an assassination, yes.

World War I was in fact triggered by an assassination. The Austrian Archduke Ferdinand was killed in June, 1914, setting off a conflict that within weeks swept all of Europe and Russia, and finally brought in the United States.

'A wrong turn by the Archduke's driver brought the heir to the Austrian throne face to face with [his assassin] Gavrilo Princip,' noted a PBS documentary, stating the immediate cause of World War I. 'In a flash, the whole continent was going to be at war.'

It is not difficult to imagine that in the already tense Middle East, the assassination of a second Israeli Prime Minister in less than a year, in an Arab capital, might set off a war. And an all-out war in the Middle East could quickly become global.

Physicists would call it the 'Butterfly Effect.' It is fundamental to Chaos Theory.

James Gleick, in his book *Chaos*, cites the 'Butterfly Effect' – 'The notion that a butterfly stirring the air today in Peking can transform storm systems next month in New York.'

Had Netanyahu merely by going to Jordan ten days late, stopped the count-down to Armageddon?

In the Bible code, just above 'World War' there is a date: '9th of Av is the day of the Third.'

It was the exact day of Netanyahu's scheduled trip to Jordan. 25 July 1996, was the 9th of Av, 5756, in the ancient Hebrew calendar.

It is a cursed date in Jewish history. It is the day that Jerusalem was destroyed by the Babylonians in 586 BC. It is the day that Jerusalem was destroyed by the Romans in 70 AD.

All through history, there have been a series of disasters that have befallen the Jews on that date, and it is so feared by the religious that they fast on the 9th of Av, and pray for mercy.

And now the Bible code stated that on the '9th of Av' a third
World War might start, with the third destruction of the Holy City,
a nuclear attack on Jerusalem.

The ancient name for Jerusalem, 'Ariel,' the name used in the
original warning of the Apocalypse, was in fact encoded between
'World War' and '9th of Av is the day of the Third.'

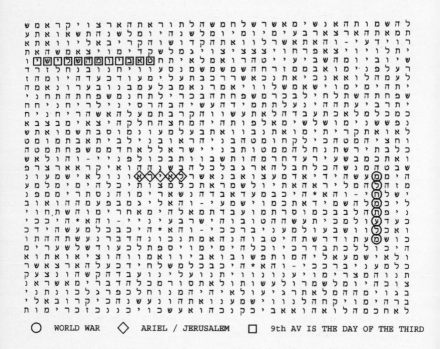

O WORLD WAR   ◇   ARIEL / JERUSALEM   □   9th AV IS THE DAY OF THE THIRD

But Netanyahu did not go to Amman, as scheduled, on the 9th of
Av. And 'delayed' is again encoded with both the date and the Prime
Minister's name.

In fact, both 'Bibi' and 'delayed' are encoded with '9th of Av,
5756.' In the same verse, there is an interwoven hidden text that
states, 'Five futures, five roads.'

ר ת ל י ש מ נ ד ר ע ת ח ת ק ו מ ל א מ ו ה ח א נ ה א ז ח צ ר ה א צ א ל א ב ב א ר צ מ ו

ה ו צ י א ו ה ר ת ח ת פ ה ר ו ח א ת צ א מ נ ה ח ה צ ר ת ז ה ת ו ש ו ב א ל ח מ י ל ל צ ר

ר א א ת ח ת ה ע ג ל ⓣ ל ר ש ש ר ח ל ח י ו ·ס פ ל ש א ת ו ת ח ת י ר ו ח י ל ק ע ב ק מ ב

ש ל ח ו ה ו נ ה א ⓗ ר ב ח · י כ ו ר כ ב כ נ ב ת א א ג ר ח · י ד ד ר כ ב מ ל ו נ ו י ·

מ ס ס כ ת ח ת ⓗ מ ש ו ת ה א ל ר ל ב ר כ · י ל כ ב ח · ה ר ב מ ל פ ט מ ב ר · י ע א מ ע ר

פ צ ע ח ב ו ר ⓗ ת ה ח ב ר ו ה ר · כ · י ח א ש ש ת ע ר י · ע ע ת א ו א ב ד ר א ו ח ת ת

ה ו ר מ מ מ א ל ⓗ ל מ א א ל ר ש ת א ש ש ו נ ו מ א מ כ ש ש ת ע ר ו ר י י ר ו נ ל ב ה ל

· כ ר ב ב · ז מ ⓣ ה ז י מ · ל א מ ש ש ק מ מ מ נ נ ו ל צ ק ת ר פ כ ה ת ו ח כ ב ת א ח ה

מ ז ב ח ו פ מ ז ⓣ ח ו ה י א ל ד ג ב א מ · ר ד ח א מ · מ ש ש ו ח ו מ ו ה צ א א א ה ת ה

נ ג ע ל א ל פ ס ⓧ ט ה ו א א ב ד ג ב ש ל ו · י ד ג ב נ ו פ א ח ת ו ה ר ה א ת ח ת ח ת ר א ו

ה מ מ ש ח ה ה ו מ א ל א א ת י ד ו ל ל ב ש א ת ה ה ב ד נ א פ מ ח ת ר א ש ל א י פ י ל נ ו

א ל ה ה ם מ ו · י ק ח מ א ש ש ה ו ל ל ו ל ד י · י מ א ל ו ל ל ב ש ר א ש ק ל נ כ ר ש י ש ב

ה א · מ ש ש י מ א · ל ם מ מ ה ו ת ה ל ת ד · מ נ א א ת ה ת נ ◇□□□□□□ ◇□ ◇ א נ ה ל

ל ה ע מ כ ו · א מ ר ב ל ע מ ה ה מ מ ש ש ה ל ת ר א ר צ ו ר · י ש ר ב ב ל · ◇◇ ◇ נ ל ע ל

ש ב ב א כ ל מ ר פ צ נ ב ל ק ב נ · מ ב ל ה א * א ל ה א מ ל א ע מ ב ל ק כ ב נ צ פ ר מ ל כ מ ו א ב ש

○ 9th AV, 5756 / JULY 25, 1996

◇ BIBI △ DELAYED □ FIVE FUTURES, FIVE ROADS

It was a clear statement that the future had been changed. It also seemed a clear statement that there were many possible futures, and that the Bible code revealed each of them.

Why didn't the Bible code just tell us the final outcome, the one real future?

'Everything is foreseen, but freedom of action is given,' states the Talmud, the ancient commentary on Biblical law.

For almost 2000 years sages have debated the apparent paradox – how can there be human free will if God knows everything in advance?

The Bible code makes that question real for the modern world. It forces us to ask the question Prime Minister Peres asked me – 'If it's predicted, what can we do?'

'It's a warning, not a prediction,' I told the Israeli leader. 'What we do determines the outcome.'

I tried to say it with total confidence, because I wanted to believe it, and I wanted him to believe it. But later, I discussed the apparent paradox with Eli Rips.

'I don't know if what is foreseen can be changed,' said Rips. 'I have thought about it a lot, and I once thought I knew the answer, but now I don't know.'

I told Rips that it seemed to me there were two ways to read the famous lines from the Talmud. First, that we have free will, but what we choose to do is known before we do it. Second, that although the entire future is foreseen, we can change it.

'I can't accept that we can change what was foreseen,' said Rips, 'because all the changes we make were also known to God in advance.'

'I used to think that our future was foreseen, period,' Rips continued. 'But the Bible code caused me to realize that there is another alternative – all our possible futures were foreseen, and we are choosing among them.'

That is why both 'July to Amman' and 'delayed' were encoded. That is why 1996 was encoded with 'atomic holocaust,' but the danger was also encoded with several other years. That is why the letters that spelled out the same year in the Hebrew calendar, 5756, also asked a question, 'Will you change it?'

Why didn't the Bible code just tell the one real future? The answer appears to be that there isn't just one real future, there are many possible futures.

'Delay' is written into the Bible and the code.

It is written in with 'holocaust of Israel,' just as it was written in with 'Prime Minister Netanyahu.'

'Holocaust of Israel' is encoded with the year 2000 as well as 1996, and the words 'you delayed' are encoded in the same place. '5756' posed a question, 'Will you change it?' The hidden text starting at the same letter that begins to spell out '5760' gives the answer, 'You delayed.'

'Delay' is written in with 'year of the plague.' Where 'Israel and Japan' cross those words, the same code sequence states, 'They delayed the year of the plague.'

'Delay' is written in with 'World War.' Where the years 2000 and 2006 are encoded, the hidden text states, 'I will delay the war.'

It is even written in with the 'End of Days.'

Every time the 'End of Days' appears in the plain text of the Bible, the word 'delayed' appears in the hidden text.

In Genesis 49:1–2, where Jacob tells his sons what will befall them 'in the End of Days,' the 'delay' is inherent in the very name of the Patriarch. In Hebrew the name 'Jacob' also means 'he will prevent' and 'he will delay.'

Has the End been 'prevented' or only 'delayed'?

When Moses tells the ancient Israelites what will happen in the

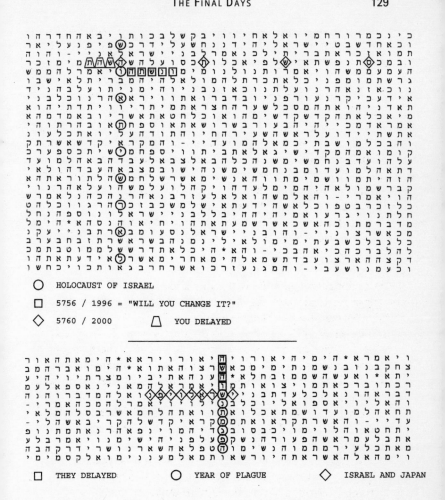

○ HOLOCAUST OF ISRAEL

□ 5756 / 1996 = "WILL YOU CHANGE IT?"

◇ 5760 / 2000   △ YOU DELAYED

□ THEY DELAYED   ○ YEAR OF PLAGUE   ◇ ISRAEL AND JAPAN

'End of Days,' the hidden text appears to say 'delayed.'

In Deuteronomy 31:29, Moses' warning that 'evil will befall you in the End of Days' is preceded by a hidden text that states, 'You knew it will be delayed.'

And in Numbers 24:14, where the sorcerer Balaam foretells the 'End of Days' – the words that are encoded with both 'atomic holocaust' and 'World War' – the hidden text states 'friend delayed.'

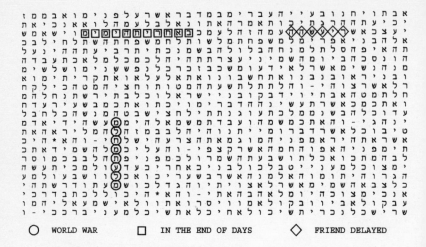

○ WORLD WAR   □ IN THE END OF DAYS   ◇ FRIEND DELAYED

'Friend delayed' overlaps 'fire shook the nation.' And the hidden text in the same verse also states 'I will advise you what' and 'I will advise when.'

The 'friend' is not identified. But he appears to be whoever encoded the Bible.

It is not yet clear if the End will come, when the stated delay will be over, but one thing is clear – 'delay' is written into all the original prophecies of the 'End of Days.'

Armageddon has not been prevented, according to the code, only delayed.

And there were many indications in the Bible code that the 'delay' might be very short.

'Prime Minister Netanyahu' is encoded with the current year, '5757.' And the Hebrew year that began in September 1996 and ends in October 1997 is also the year most clearly encoded with his adversary, the Palestinian leader 'Arafat.'

Just two weeks into the new year tensions in Israel once more exploded.

On Wednesday, 25 September 1996, open warfare broke out in Israel. For three days Palestinian police fought Israeli soldiers, who responded with helicopter gunships and sent tanks into the West

Bank for the first time since the 1967 Six Day War.

The death toll was 73, and hundreds were wounded.

What was most striking was how quickly the battle began, how suddenly apparent peace in Israel became a shooting war.

I called Eli Rips in Jerusalem. 'My own judgement is that the prospect of war is now a high probability,' said Rips. 'I'm not speaking now as a mathematician, or from the Bible code, but only as an Israeli observing the sudden outbreak of armed conflict.'

The immediate cause of the violence was the opening of a tunnel under the Temple Mount in Jerusalem, the site of both the Jews' holiest shrine, the Wailing Wall, the remains of the ancient Temple, and of Islam's third holiest shrine, the Dome of the Rock.

'Tunnel,' I discovered to my surprise, appeared in the code with 'holocaust of Israel.'

○ HOLOCAUST OF ISRAEL   □ TUNNEL

And when I checked 'atomic holocaust' I was shocked to see crossing 'atomic' the name of the West Bank city where the fighting began, 'Ramallah.' The full hidden text stated, 'Ramallah fulfilled a prophecy.'

Once more the Bible code seemed to be updating itself, almost as if the encoder were also following the constant turn of events in the Middle East. One location was encoded over the other, one crisis over another, one year over another, so that finally there was no way to be certain if the real danger was in 1996, or 1997, or the year 2000, or beyond.

But the overall danger was very clearly stated, and very clearly tied to the present moment. There was no question that the code was describing the people, the places, and the events in the current Arab-Israeli conflict.

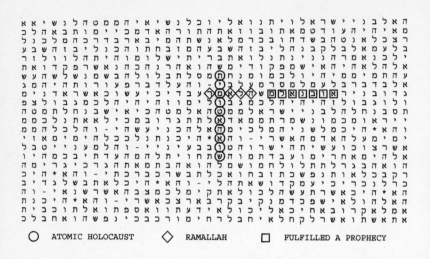

○ ATOMIC HOLOCAUST   ◇ RAMALLAH   □ FULFILLED A PROPHECY

I looked again at 'holocaust of Israel.' The word 'annexed' appeared twice in the same place, against very high odds. It was the word Israelis used to describe the two territories they captured from the Arabs in the 1967 war, the Golan Heights in the mountains facing Syria, and East Jerusalem.

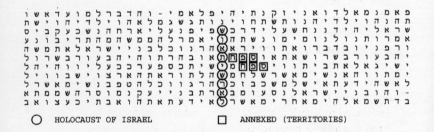

○ HOLOCAUST OF ISRAEL   □ ANNEXED (TERRITORIES)

Those were the two flashpoints in the modern Middle East.

'Arafat' also appeared in the hidden text of the Bible, encoded in the one place both Biblical statements of the 'End of Days' come together. It could not be by chance, and it was the clearest possible statement that the current conflict in the Middle East could actually boil over into Armageddon.

○ END OF DAYS   □ IN THE END OF DAYS   ◇ ARAFAT

'It is what is stated in the Midrash,' said Rips, referring to the ancient commentary on the Bible. 'It is perhaps the "exile under Ishmael" just before the "End of Days." Some of the Midrash say that at a time of Arab domination, 80% of the Israeli population will be killed.'

We were both silent for a moment. 'This may be what you are finding in the code,' said Rips.

I had not known of the ancient prophecy. Ishmael was the first son of the patriarch Abraham, the one he sent away. According to the Bible, he is the forebear of all Arabs. Abraham's second son, Isaac, was the chosen inheritor. He is the forebear of all Jews. The family feud had been going on for 4000 years, and was predicted to come to a terrible end.

In January 1997 Netanyahu and Arafat did shake hands on shared control of Hebron, the city where Abraham is said to be buried, and set a timetable for a broader settlement. But the most difficult issue, the final status of Jerusalem, which both the Israelis and the Palestinians claim as their capital, remained unresolved. And there was no way to know if the stiff handshake at 3 AM on 15 January would lead to a real peace, or a new outbreak of violence.

In March 1997 the peace began to unravel. Arafat rejected the first step in Israel's planned withdrawal from the occupied territories. Netanyahu announced that he would build a Jewish neighborhood in the heart of East Jerusalem, seen by the Palestinians as the capital of their future homeland.

'The saddest reality that has been dawning on me,' Jordan's King Hussein wrote Netanyahu as the tensions began to build, 'is that I do not find you by my side in working to fulfill God's will for the final reconciliation of all the descendants of the children of Abraham.'

And on 21 March, violence did erupt in Tel Aviv, Jerusalem, and Hebron. A Palestinian suicide bomber killed three and wounded forty at a Tel Aviv cafe, the first terrorist attack since Netanyahu was elected. On the same day, riots broke out in Hebron, and in Arab East Jerusalem at the site of the Jewish housing project, Har Homa.

'Har Homa' is encoded in the most sacred text of the Bible. It appears with no skips in the Mezuzah, the fifteen verses that were preserved in a separate scroll and posted on the door of every home in Israel.

And encoded with 'Har Homa' are the ominous words, 'All his people to war.'

'All his people to war,' the words in the Bible code originally found with the Rabin assassination, and found again with the wave of bombings in Jerusalem and Tel Aviv that shattered the peace Rabin had forged with Arafat, had once more in September 1996 and March 1997 become a reality. And those same words also appeared with the ultimate danger, 'atomic holocaust.'

Each spark that might set off the holocaust was foreseen, but until each crisis came to an end there was no way to know if it was just another skirmish in a 4000-year-old feud, or the beginning of Armageddon.

It may be impossible to know both what and when.

'Physics has given up,' said Richard P. Feynman, the Nobel laureate many consider the greatest scientist since Einstein. 'We do not know how to predict what will happen in a given circumstance. The only thing that can be predicted is the probability of different events. We can only predict the odds.'

And yet quantum physics is a highly successful branch of science. It works. Perhaps because it recognizes uncertainty as part of reality.

In the same way, the Bible code works. Again, because it recognizes uncertainty as part of reality.

'Our world is clearly reflected in it,' said Rips. 'It is as if we were looking into a mirror. Our efforts to see the future and to do something about it both probably play a role. I think that it is a very complicated, interactive event.'

Rips said that when he was working at his computer, searching for information in the code, he sometimes felt like he was on-line with another intelligence.

'The Bible code is not really responding now,' he explained, 'it just foresaw everything all at once, in advance.'

According to Rips, the whole Bible code had to be written at once, in a single flash. 'We experience it like we experience a hologram – it looks different when we look at it from a new angle – but the image, of course, is pre-recorded.'

It is the history of the human race recorded more than 3000 years ahead of time. It does not tell the story sequentially, but all at once. Modern events overlap ancient events, the future is encoded in verses that tell of the Biblical past. One verse might contain within it the stories of then and now and a hundred years from now.

'The problem is how we decipher it all,' said Rips. 'It is very clearly non-random, but it is as if we had an intelligence report in which we can read only one of every twenty words.'

Rips was, as always, cautious. 'This is the product of a higher intelligence,' he said. 'It may want us to understand, but it may not want us to understand. The code may not reveal the future to us unless we are worthy.'

I didn't agree. If the world was really in danger, it hardly mattered whether we were worthy. The encoder, if he was good, would surely warn us.

At the end, there was an unbridgeable gap. Rips was religious. I was not. For me there was always a question – who encoded the Bible, what was his motive, where was he now?

For Rips there was always an answer – God.

At the end of my five-year investigation I did find final proof that the Bible code itself is real. And chilling evidence that the world may have come closer to disaster in 1996 than we will ever know.

Our narrow escape in 1996 was clearly stated in the plain text of Isaiah, the first Apocalypse, the one book of the Bible found intact among the Dead Sea Scrolls, the one that seemed to predict an atomic attack on Jerusalem.

It was not hidden in a code. It was openly stated in the plain words of the 2500-year-old scroll.

The year was revealed in a unique verse, one that told the future backwards.

The foremost translator of ancient Hebrew texts, Rabbi Adin Steinsaltz, the man Time magazine called 'a once-in-a-millennium scholar,' pointed that verse out to me.

I went to see Steinsaltz when I first heard about the Bible code. The rabbi is also a scientist, and I wanted to see what he thought about a code in the Bible that predicted the future, foretold events that happened thousands of years after the Bible was written, reported in detail a future that did not yet exist.

'In the Bible time is reversed,' said Steinsaltz, noting an odd quirk in the original Hebrew text of the Old Testament. 'The future is always written in the past tense, and the past is always written in the future tense.'

'Why?' I asked.

'No one knows,' he said.

'We may be moving against the stream of time,' said Steinsaltz, noting that the laws of physics are 'time-symmetric,' that they run just as well backwards as forwards in time.

He opened his Bible, looking for a passage from the first of the prophets, Isaiah. 'Here, in Isaiah, it says that you need to look backwards to see the future,' he said.

'Where Isaiah says, "Tell the things that are to come hereafter," you can translate the same words to read, "They told the future backwards."

'In fact, you can translate the same words to read, "Tell the letters in reverse." It's like mirror writing.'

I looked at the letters backwards, but found no startling revelation. Only years later, after I discovered that Isaiah seemed to foretell an atomic attack, did I look at that same verse again.

Isaiah 41:23 states, 'Tell the things that are to come hereafter, and we will be dismayed, and behold it together.'

And now when I looked at the letters in reverse, the future told backwards, I saw that the mirror writing spelled out a year – '5756.'

It was not in a code. It was just there.

In the 2500-year-old verse that 'told the future backwards,' 1996, the year of the threatened 'atomic holocaust,' was plainly stated.

And so was the delay.

□ THEY TOLD THE FUTURE BACKWARDS   ○ 5756 / 1996 (BACKWARDS)

Overlapping '5756' the reverse text openly stated, 'They changed the time.'

□ THEY TOLD THE FUTURE BACKWARDS   ○ 5756 / 1996 (BACKWARDS)

◇ THEY CHANGED THE TIME (BACKWARDS)

The question asked by the same Hebrew letters that spell the year 5756 – 'Will you change it?' – had been answered decisively in the most ancient vision of the Apocalypse.

The answer was openly stated in the verse we are told to read backwards – 'You will change it.'

More than 2000 years ago, in the first Apocalypse, the first prophet, Isaiah, foretold the year of the real Armageddon, 1996, and also the delay.

One question remained unanswered – until when?

I saw Eli Rips one last time on New Year's Eve 1996. We looked again at the statistics for the two years most strongly linked to all the events of the Apocalypse.

The years 2000 and 2006, in the ancient calendar 5760 and 5766, were the only two years in the next hundred that matched both 'atomic holocaust' and 'World War.' All the dangers stated in the code – 'the End of Days,' 'holocaust of Israel,' even 'great earth-quake' – also matched 'in 5766.' Rips calculated the odds. They were at least a thousand to one.

'It is something exceptional, really remarkable,' said Rips. 'Someone intentionally put this information into the Torah.'

That much was clear. But neither of us knew if the danger was real. I told Rips that I could not fully believe it because I still could not accept the open prophecy of the Bible, I still could not accept that there really would be an End of Days.

'If you accept the hidden statement in the Torah,' said Rips, 'then you should also accept the open statement.'

There was a logic to what he said. There was no doubt that the computerized code appeared to support the long-known prophecy of the Bible, and yet for me there was a difference. I had seen one come true, and not the other.

'I believed the Bible code was real the day Rabin was killed,' I explained, recalling the moment.

'I was at a train station, leaning against a wall, talking to a friend on a pay phone. Suddenly he interrupted and said, "Wait a minute, I want to hear the news about Rabin." I had been out all day, I hadn't heard anything, but I instantly knew that the prediction had come true, that Rabin was dead.

'I slid down the wall, all the way to the floor. And I said, to myself but out loud, "Oh my God, it's real."'

Rips said he understood. 'It was my own feeling, exactly, when the Scud missiles were fired at Israel on the second day of the Gulf War, on the date we found three weeks in advance in the Bible code,' he said.

'I was in a sealed room with my whole family. My wife, my five young children, and I were all wearing gas masks. We could hear the air-raid sirens outside. It was 2 AM on the 3rd of Shevat, January 18th 1991. That was the day that had been encoded.

'I knew the missiles were flying at us, we heard that Tel Aviv had already been hit, and all I could think was, "It works! The code works!"'

Rips had been investigating the Bible code for six years by the time the Gulf War started, as predicted, when predicted. But it was not until the night the Scuds hit Israel that he fully believed it was real, just as I had not fully believed it until Rabin was assassinated, as predicted, when predicted.

'I believed it before as a mathematician,' said Rips. 'But this was quite another perspective. It was an odd moment of joy in that sealed room, waiting for the missile to strike.'

Another scientist had once told me of similar mixed feelings, how he had felt when he discovered that all life on Earth might be doomed. I wrote the first cover story about that Apocalyptic warning, Sherry Rowland's discovery that the ozone was being destroyed by man-made chemicals, at a time when he was dismissed as a crackpot, when everyone was calling him 'Chicken Little.' And now I remembered what he told me when he was proven right, and won the Nobel prize.

'There was no moment of Eureka! really,' said Rowland. 'I just came home one night and told my wife, "The work is going very well, but it looks like the end of the world."'

Now, on New Year's Eve in Jerusalem, in the city that the Bible code warned would be the target of an atomic attack that might trigger the real Armageddon, I told Eli Rips that story, and we both laughed.

But I could not forget that, according to the Bible code, within ten years an 'atomic holocaust' in Israel might trigger a third 'World War,' that we might already be in the real 'End of Days.'

There is no way to ignore the clear fact that a computerized code in the Bible, confirmed by some of the most famous mathematicians in the world, a code that accurately predicted the Gulf War, the collision of a comet with Jupiter, and the assassination of Rabin, also seems to state that the Apocalypse starts now, that within a decade we may face the real Armageddon, a nuclear World War.

But the Bible code is more than a warning. It may be the information we need to prevent the predicted disaster.

'Code will save' appears right above 'atomic holocaust,' just below 'the End of Days.'

It is not a promise of divine salvation. It is not a threat of inevitable doom. It is just information. The message of the Bible code is that we can save ourselves.

In the end, what we do determines the outcome. So we are left where we have always been, with one big difference – we now know that we are not alone.

○ ATOMIC HOLOCAUST ☐ IN THE END OF DAYS ◇ CODE WILL SAVE

CODA

Reporters generally tell what has happened, not what will happen.

'Usually, people wait for things to occur before trying to describe them,' wrote Jonathan Schell in his definitive book about the nuclear threat, *The Fate of the Earth*. 'But since we cannot afford under any circumstances to let a holocaust occur, we are forced in this one case to become the historians of the future.'

In the days after Yitzhak Rabin was murdered, I reluctantly came to the same conclusion.

'I know why you're involved in this,' I told Rips late one night a few days after Rabin was killed, and there was no longer any doubt that the Bible code was real. 'You're a mathematician, you're religious, and you read the Bible every day.

'But I don't know why I'm involved. I'm not religious. I don't even believe in God. I'm a total skeptic. There's no one who would be harder to persuade this is real than me.'

'That's why you're involved,' said Rips. 'You can tell the modern world about the Bible code.'

'I'm just the reporter who stumbled onto this,' I replied.

But at exactly the moment the Bible code became life-and-death reality, we discovered that the code also predicted an 'atomic holocaust' in Israel, an attack that might trigger the first nuclear 'World War.'

I felt compelled to warn both Peres and Netanyahu that the code seemed to predict an atomic attack, as I had warned Rabin that the code predicted his assassination.

I never imagined that I would ultimately find myself searching for the details of the real Apocalypse. I never imagined that the 'End of Days' would be encoded in the Bible with the current year. I never imagined that the long-known Biblical prophecies of Armageddon might on some level be real.

I had been a reporter all my life. I started out on the night police beat. I always had a very flat-footed, down-to-earth view of reality. And I was determined to deal with this story the same way I dealt with every other story.

There were two problems. I could not get a face-to-face interview with the encoder. And I could not check out the facts in the future.

Is the Bible code merely giving a scientific gloss to millennium fever, or is it warning us, perhaps just in time, of a very real danger? There is no way to know.

The code may be neither 'right' nor 'wrong.' It probably tells us what might happen, not what will happen.

But since we cannot let our world be destroyed, we cannot simply wait – we must assume that the warning in the Bible code is real.

NOTES

CHAPTER NOTES

Dr Rips has done a formal controlled experiment only in the Book of Genesis, but we consistently find accurate details of modern events also encoded in the rest of the Torah, the first five books of the Bible. The Rabin assassination, for example, was encoded in Numbers and Deuteronomy.

'I would be surprised if the same code we proved existed in Genesis did not exist in the rest of the Torah,' states Rips.

And he agrees that other parts of the Old Testament, like Daniel and Isaiah, might also be encoded. The collision of the comet with Jupiter was encoded in Isaiah, where the date of the impact was also found in advance.

The Bible code itself appears to confirm that the entire Old Testament is encoded. 'He encoded the Torah, and more,' states the code, evidence that not only the first five books, but at least some of the later writings also have hidden information.

○ BIBLE CODE (TORAH)   □ HE ENCODED THE TORAH, AND MORE

Indeed, the clearest encoding of the 'Bible code' uses the Hebrew word 'Tanakh,' the name for the entire Old Testament. 'Tanakh' is actually a Hebrew acrostic of the first letters of the names of all three parts of the Old Testament, the Law, the Prophets, and the Writings.

כשיאמוייהפפמייעושענונחנראשרלאכבכנושעתאכיה*אאה
ורדנתהירתבמתתמרתתעכובלכנתנכיוהראאלהלחנהלהאלהכנ
בכיחבתיובהרויטהמבתתמתשיבויבמכביאלכמכלמחייחנ?וה
שרתדתתרללייוהממשחהאהרשראכבנוכמכעלתלעמכנוובזת חת
יהלאללעתילאייכמאיכביס(נ)לוחללהחלננ(נ)יימ*האמממכבהתדרש
אלכבהכלעשתמתעשילעה?)מ?(שב?כבטשבחדאבהוהרל(נ)י,רחב
והראמשממממ*האכ*שאכ(נ)שעלעכייכותשיכומתשעששלעכבכר
גדרשעמכנ(ס)תאלמכמכבונוכמכפשתשצראהוהומאתמטטמכסכבר
אאה*יינ(ס)לפךאמלדכבדיתרמתובתינד?בנכפלמ?אכ*שתרתרהארשאכב
מושיעברשאיולחנכואמתאיודבעוכתבוכנובתהאתמ

○ BIBLE CODE (TANAKH)   □ SEALED BEFORE GOD

Crossing the words 'Bible code' is a hidden text that states it was 'sealed before God' – an apparent statement that the Bible code is the 'sealed book,' the secret revelation foretold in the plain text of the Bible.

Rips used the standard Hebrew language text of Genesis, known as the *Textus Receptus*, in his experiment. The same full text of the Bible is used in the Bible code computer program.

The best known edition of that text, the *Jerusalem Bible* (Koren Publishing Co., 1992), also contains the most widely accepted English translation of the Old Testament, and it is the primary source of quotes from the plain text in this book. I have also consulted and sometimes used a translation some scholars prefer by Rabbi Aryeh Kaplan, *The Living Torah* (Maznaim, 1981).

Quotes from the New Testament are primarily from the King James Version, although I have also consulted a modern translation known as the New International Version.

The statements by Rips quoted throughout this book come from a series of conversations that took place over the course of five years, primarily at his home in Jerusalem, in his office at Hebrew University, in his office at Columbia University, and in hundreds of telephone interviews.

CHAPTER ONE: THE BIBLE CODE

Chaim Guri called Rabin's office the night I met with him, 1 September 1994, and the next morning the Prime Minister's driver picked up my letter warning of the assassination and delivered it to Rabin. Guri, the winner of Israel's two highest writing awards, the Bialik Prize and the Israel Prize for Literature, had known Rabin since childhood, and remained one of the Prime Minister's closest friends.

Yigal Amir, a 26-year-old Orthodox Jew, fired three shots, hitting Rabin twice, after a political rally in Tel Aviv on the evening of 4 November 1995. He later said that God commanded him to do it, and claimed that the murder was justified by religious law because Rabin was planning to surrender the land that God gave Israel.

'5756,' the Hebrew year encoded with 'Rabin assassination' and 'Tel Aviv,' began in September 1995, and ended in September 1996. The years encoded in the Bible are from the ancient Hebrew calendar, which starts in Biblical time, 3760 years earlier than the modern calendar.

In addition to Guri, two other people knew more than a year before it happened that I had found the Rabin assassination predicted in the Bible code, and that I warned the Prime Minister. When I first found the prediction encoded in 1994, I showed it to Eli Rips, who was then in New York as a visiting professor at Columbia University. And on the same trip I met with Guri, I met with the chief scientist at the Israeli Ministry of Defense, Gen. Isaac Ben-Israel. The memo I gave him, dated 31 August 1994, stated: 'The only time the full name Yitzhak Rabin is encoded in the Bible, the words "assassin that will assassinate" cross his name ... I think Rabin is in real danger, but that the danger can be averted.' Later I met again with Gen. Ben-Israel, along with Rips, who briefed him on the technical details of the Bible code.

A month before the assassination I again tried to reach Rabin directly. He was in the United States to sign an interim peace agreement with Arafat at the White House. I sent a message to his top aide 30 September 1995, stating: 'Last year, I was in contact with Prime Minister Rabin through his close friend, Chaim Guri. He spoke to the Prime Minister after meeting with me, and sent him a letter about a possible threat to Mr Rabin's life. I have uncovered new information that suggests Prime Minister Rabin may be in great danger.' The aide did not get back to me, and I was not able to reach the Prime Minister, who was killed five weeks later.

I spoke again to Guri the day after Rabin was killed, then flew to Israel and met with him in Jerusalem. In the phone call, and at our meeting, he told me his reaction to the prediction of the assassination coming true, and of his immediate call to Gen. Barak. Ehud Barak, the most decorated military hero in Israel, had for many years been the Army's chief of staff, and Guri referred to him that way, but at the time Rabin was killed Barak was actually a cabinet minister.

I first heard about the Bible code by chance, in June 1992, after meeting on an entirely different subject with Gen. Uri Saguy, who was then chief of Israeli military intelligence. The information came from a young officer, but no one at the top level of Israeli intelligence was aware of the Bible code until I brought Rips in to brief some of the technical officers at a later time.

Rips is an associate professor in the department of mathematics at Hebrew University in Jerusalem. The quote that he read to me from the Genius of Vilna came from an English translation of *The Jewish Mind*, by Abraham Rabinowitz (Hillel Press, 1978), pp. 33–4.

Rips' colleague Witztum found in advance the precise date of the first Scud missile attack on Israel, 3 Shevat, 5751 (18 January 1991). Rips confirmed that Witztum told him the date, and that Rips himself saw it encoded in the Bible, three weeks before the Gulf War started. Later, both Rips and his wife told me how they had felt the night that the missile attack did happen on the exact date found in advance.

H.M.D. Weissmandel, the Czech rabbi who found the first evidence of the code, never himself published his discovery. But his students did later publish a limited-edition book that included a brief reference to his code work before World War II, *Torat Hemed* (Yeshiva Mt Kisko, 1958). One of his students, Rabbi Azriel Tauber, said that Weissmandel, in a pre-computer era, wrote out the entire Torah on index cards, with 100 letters on each card, ten rows of ten letters each, and then looked for words spelled out with equidistant skips.

Isaac Newton's search for the Bible code was revealed by the great economist John Maynard Keynes in *Essays and Sketches in Biography* (Meridian Books, 1956), pp. 280–90, 'Newton, the Man.' Richard S. Westfall, in *The Life of Isaac Newton* (Cambridge University Press, 1993), p. 125, also quoted Newton's theological notebooks, and stated that the physicist 'believed that the essence of the Bible was the prophecy of human history.' See also, Westfall's *Never at Rest: A Biography of Isaac Newton* (Cambridge University Press, 1980), pp. 346ff.

I first saw the report of the Rips and Witztum experiment in the original draft they submitted for peer review, and the abstract quoted is from that draft. The paper was ultimately published in an American math journal, Statistical Science, in August 1994 (vol. 9, no. 3), pp. 429–38, 'Equidistant Letter Sequences in the Book of Genesis,' Doron Witztum, Eliyahu Rips, and Yoav Rosenberg. I spoke to the journal editor, Robert Kass, before the article was published. His editorial note is quoted from the pre-print he read to me. It was later published in Statistical Science, p. 306. The full Rips-Witztum paper is reprinted in the Appendix of this book.

The results Rips and Witztum reported in Statistical Science were that the names had matched the dates against odds of four in a million, but in a series of later experiments the actual odds were found to be one in ten million.

The original results were derived by taking the set of 32 names and 64 dates and jumbling them in a million different combinations, so that only one was a completely correct pairing. Rips and Witztum then did a computer run to see which of the million examples got a better result – where the information came together most clearly in the Bible. 'In four cases the random pairing won,' explained Rips. 'The correct pairing won 999,995 times.'

But in a second experiment where all the correct matches of names and dates were eliminated from the jumbled pairings, and the only correct information appeared in the completely accurate list, and 10 million permutations were checked, the results were one in 10 million.

'None of the random pairings came out higher,' said Rips. 'The results were 0 vs. 9,999,999, or one in 10 million.'

Harold Gans told me the results of his independent experiment in a 25 January 1993 telephone interview, and he further detailed it in another telephone interview in December 1996. In his paper submitted to Statistical Science, Gans stated: 'We conclude that these results provide corroboration of the results reported by Witztum, Rips, and Rosenberg.'

Gans stated the odds of finding the cities encoded with the names of the sages were 1 in 200,000.

In the years since the Rips-Witztum paper was published in August 1994, no one has submitted a rebuttal to the math journal, Kass stated in a January 1997 telephone interview.

An Australian scientist, Avraham Hasofer, did publish a brief critique of the Bible code in a small religious journal, B'Or Ha'Torah (no. 8, 1993), pp. 121–31. But that was before Rips and Witztum published their experiment. Hasofer did not address their mathematical evidence that there is a code in Genesis, and Hasofer did not himself run any experiment, or actually investigate the Bible code.

Another Australian mathematician, Brendan McKay, raised questions about the Rips-Witztum experiment on the Internet after this book was written. He suggested that the code found in Genesis may not exist in the rest of the Bible. But McKay was not aware that the Rabin assassination was found in advance, encoded in Numbers and Deuteronomy, and that other major events were found in each of the five books of the Torah.

McKay also questioned the statistical method Rips used. But McKay's paper is only a preliminary draft. It has not passed the peer review process that Rips' work did, and McKay has not submitted it to Statistical Science, or any other referee journal. Rips has responded to McKay, inviting his challenge. 'I think he is not right,' said Rips.

Israel's most famous mathematician, Robert J. Aumann, noted that even if McKay was right, his own preliminary draft stated that the results in the Rips-Witztum experiment would still be 1 in 1000, in ordinary science still very strong results, indeed the most rigorous test ever applied by mathematicians.

Harvard statistician Persi Diaconis, in a letter dated 7 May 1990, in fact set that standard for the Rips-Witztum experiment that proved the existence of the Bible code: 'For publication of such a fantastic claim I think a significance level of 1/1000 or better should be required.'

The experiment carried out by Rips and Witztum in accordance with all Diaconis' demands had a significance level of at least 1/50,000 (and a later experiment showed the odds were really 1/10,000,000). Diaconis recommended that the paper be published in the math journal Statistical Science.

An Israeli mathematician, who asked not to be quoted by name, told me in December 1996 that he has begun a 'preliminary investigation' of the Rips-Witztum experiment. He stated that he has 'no evidence' that their findings are wrong, and in fact stated that 'the math is perfect, and so is the computer science.' However, he questioned the way in which Rips and Witztum chose the names of the sages they matched with the dates of birth and death in the Bible code.

I raised his questions with Rips. Rips told me that he and his colleague Witztum had first compiled a list of 34 sages from a standard reference text, *The Encyclopedia of Prominent Jewish Scholars*, doing it entirely mechanically, using only the names of the men to whom the encyclopedia devoted three or more columns.

Their first experiment, according to Rips, showed 'a very strong correlation between the names and the dates,' apparently proving the existence of a code in Genesis.

Later, the Harvard statistician Persi Diaconis, an independent authority who was supervising their experiment, demanded 'fresh data,' a new list that could not have been selected to succeed.

Diaconis also suggested the experimental method Rips and Witztum used, a million permutations of the names and dates, to test whether the correct pairing of names and dates were really the best match in the Bible code.

Rips and Witztum compiled a second list of 32 names, again mechanically, using in their experiment all the sages to whom the same encyclopedia devoted at least one-and-a-half and less than three columns.

Because many of the sages, especially in pre-modern times, went by several different names, and there were diverse spellings of some of the names, Rips and Witztum then submitted the final list of 32 to the chairman of the Biblical bibliography department at Israel's Bar-Ilan University, Dr Shlomo Z. Havlin.

Havlin, one of the foremost experts on Rabbinical literature in the world, who helped compile Bar-Ilan's famous data bank of ancient Hebrew literature, made the final decision on which spellings of which names Rips and Witztum would use in their experiment. I interviewed Havlin in Jerusalem in December 1996, and he confirmed that he, independently, decided which data would be used by Rips and Witztum in the experiment that proved the existence of the Bible code.

Havlin also made a written statement: 'I have confirmed that each of the two lists of names and denominations were decided by my judgement, and that I scrupulously examined it against the computerized data-bank of the Data Processing Center of Bar-Ilan University.'

These, then, are the facts:

(1) The list of names used in the final experiment was decided by an independent scholar, Havlin at Bar-Ilan;

(2) The names were found encoded with the dates, according to a mathematical test designed by a second independent scholar, Diaconis at Harvard;

(3) The same 32 names, plus the original 34 names, were then found also to match the cities, by a third independent scientist, the Pentagon code-breaker Gans.

The experiment that proved the existence of the Bible code could not have been rigged.

Nonetheless, the Israeli mathematician who declined to be named challenged the results of the Rips-Witztum experiment, claiming that if the columns in the encyclopedia were measured more precisely, three of the 32 names used in the Rips experiment would be deleted, and two other names would be added.

Rips and Witztum accepted his challenge, and ran their entire experiment all over again in December 1996 and January 1997, using the revised list of names demanded by the skeptical mathematician. The results, Rips reported, were 'twenty times better than in our original experiment' – instead of four in a million, two in 10 million. By another way of measuring the odds, the original results were one in 10 million, and the new results five in 100 million.

I performed my own, more limited experiment, checking 20 Bible code findings displayed in this book, to see if any of the same encodings also appeared in a control text of the same size, the first 304,805 letters from the Hebrew translation of *Crime and Punishment.* Half of the names or phrases did not appear at all, and none appeared with coherent, related information.

For example, 'Yitzhak Rabin' did not appear with any skip sequence in *Crime and Punishment,* nor did 'atomic holocaust.' That was expected, because the odds against Rabin's full name appearing in a text of 304,805 letters were 10 to 1, and the odds of 'atomic holocaust' appearing were almost 100 to 1.

Other expressions like 'President Kennedy' and 'Shakespeare' did appear in *Crime and Punishment.* That was also expected, because the odds were that both names would appear with some skip sequence in a text of that size.

However, whereas in the Bible the next words after 'President Kennedy' were 'to die,' and 'Dallas' was encoded in the same place, in *Crime and Punishment* there was no match with the name of the city where he was assassinated, and nothing related to his murder appeared in the same place.

Similarly, 'Shakespeare' appeared once in *Crime and Punishment,* but not with 'Hamlet' or 'Macbeth.'

The pattern was consistent for all twenty names and phrases checked. Sometimes random letter combinations did appear in the novel, but never with coherent information.

'Obviously, if one were to search for enough examples in another book,' said Rips, 'one would finally find some related words that do meet, that appear in the same place. This would be expected by random chance.

'But only in the Bible code is there consistent, coherent information. And no one has found in *War and Peace* or *Crime and Punishment* the accurate prediction of an assassination a year before it happened, or the correct dates of a war three weeks in advance. No one has found anything like that in any other book, in any translation, or in any original Hebrew text, except the Bible.'

The legendary original form of the Bible dictated to Moses by God – 'contiguous, without break of words' – was stated by one of the greatest sages in history, Nachmanides, in his *Commentary on the Torah* (Shilo, 1971), Charles Chavel, ed., vol. I, p. 14. The continuity of the original Bible was also expressed in its original form as a scroll, not as a book with separate pages, but as one continuous parchment that was unrolled.

Einstein's statement that 'the distinction between past, present, and future is only an illusion' comes from a letter he wrote to the family of his lifelong friend Michele Besso on 21 March 1955, Einstein Archive, 7–245, published in *The Quotable Einstein* (Princeton University Press, 1996), p. 61.

Besso was a fellow clerk at the Swiss patent office where the 25-year-old Einstein formulated his Theory of Relativity. The quoted letter was written just after Besso died fifty years later, less than a month before Einstein's own death. The full context of his statement about the true nature of time is therefore poignant: 'Now he has departed from this strange world a little ahead of me. That signifies nothing. For us believing physicists, the distinction between past, present and future is only an illusion, however persistent.'

Stephen Hawking's statement that 'time travel might be within our capabilities' is quoted from his introduction to *The Physics of Star Trek* (Basic Books, 1995), p. xii. Hawking repeats his belief in time travel in the latest edition of his book *A Brief History of Time* (Bantam, 1996) – 'The possibility of time travel remains open' (p. 211). He also notes that any advanced form of space travel would require faster-than-light travel, which automatically means going back in time.

The collision of comet Shoemaker-Levy with Jupiter starting on 16 July 1994, was observed by astronomers around the world, and reported in the international media. The details reported are from a series of stories in the New York Times, and the 23 May 1994, issue of Time magazine.

There is a complete version of the Bible in the original Hebrew almost 1000 years old, the Leningrad Codex, published in 1008 AD. It is the oldest intact copy of the Old Testament. There is an even older copy of the Hebrew Bible at the Shrine of the Book in Jerusalem, called the Aleppo Codex, but part of it was destroyed in a fire. That book, when it was still intact, was used by Maimonides, the great twelfth-century scholar.

Parts of every book of the Bible (except Esther), and a complete copy of Isaiah, were found among the Dead Sea Scrolls, which are more than 2000 years old.

All Bibles in the original Hebrew language that now exist are the same letter for letter. According to Adin Steinsaltz, the foremost translator of ancient Hebrew texts, the Talmud clearly states several times that if a copy of the Torah has even one wrong letter, it cannot be used and must be buried.

The Bible code computer program uses the universally accepted original Hebrew text.

Therefore, there is no question that information about today's world is encoded in a book that existed at least 1000 years ago, and almost certainly 2000 years ago, in exactly the same form it exists today.

My meeting with Kazhdan and Rips at Harvard took place on 22 March 1994, in Kazhdan's office. His quoted comments on the Bible code are from that meeting.

Kazhdan, along with Yale's Piatetski-Shapiro and two other famous mathematicians, also made a written statement that was published in 1988, six years before the Rips-Witztum experiment passed three levels of peer review, noting that although it was premature to say that the code had been established decisively at that point, 'the results obtained are sufficiently striking to deserve a wide audience and to encourage further study.'

When we met at Harvard in 1994, the original Rips experiment had just passed the final peer review. Kazhdan then stated that he believed the Bible code was real, but could not yet explain its existence.

My meeting with Piatetski-Shapiro took place at the Institute for Advanced Study at Princeton, in November 1994, and his quoted statements are from that interview.

Stephen Hawking's statement re: the Uncertainty Principle was published in *A Brief History of Time* (Bantam, 1988), pp. 54–5.

Einstein's statement re: quantum physics and God was made in a 4 December 1926 letter to the physicist Max Born, published in *The Born-Einstein Letters* (Macmillan, 1971), pp. 90–1.

I met with Robert J. Aumann at his office in Hebrew University, Jerusalem, on 25 January 1996, and all his quoted statements were made at that meeting, except for the final statement – 'The Bible code is an established fact' – which he made at a 19 March 1996 meeting of the Israeli Academy of Science, when he introduced Rips, who had been invited to speak to the Academy.

Aumann was the senior mathematician most directly involved in overseeing the original Rips-Witztum experiment that proved the existence of the code, and therefore has the most detailed knowledge of their work. I have met and spoken with Aumann on several occasions since our first meeting. He remains a convinced skeptic: 'Psychologically it is very difficult to accept, but the science is entirely on the level.'

The code's suggestion that there is a 'fifth dimension' led me to meet with the chairman of Harvard's physics department, Sidney Coleman, and one of the leading experts on the origin of the universe, M.I.T. physicist Alan Guth. Both told me, in separate interviews, that most physicists now agree that there is a fifth dimension, but that no one can yet define what it is. Both, however, stated an apparent paradox – that the fifth dimension is smaller than the nucleus of an atom, but that we, our whole universe, are inside it.

The ancient religious text cited by Rips is *The Book of Creation* (*Sefer Yetzirah*), which according to legend was first written by the patriarch Abraham, a thousand years before Moses received the Bible on Mt Sinai. *The Book of Creation* states that we exist in a five-dimensional world, three dimensions of space, a fourth dimension of time, and a fifth spiritual dimension. Modern science confirms the first four, and has no definition of the fifth.

Chapter One, verse five of *The Book of Creation* defines the five dimensions this way: 'A depth of beginning / A depth of end, A depth of good / A depth of evil, A depth of above / A depth of below, A depth of east / A depth of west, A depth of north / A depth of south.' *The Book of Creation*, translated by Aryeh Kaplan (Samuel Weiser, 1990), p. 44.

Rips, in citing this ancient definition of the 'fifth dimension,' noted that every dimension is defined by a system of measurement, and that the fifth dimension may contain all the others because it is defined by the distance between good and evil, and that, said Rips, 'is the greatest distance in the world.'

CHAPTER TWO: ATOMIC HOLOCAUST

There is a consistent prophecy throughout the Old Testament that Israel will be devastated in some terrible war, and it is this prophecy that gave rise to the larger vision of the Apocalypse, best known from the horrifying prediction in the New Testament, the Book of Revelation.

The word 'Apocalypse' comes from Greek, and actually means 'to uncover, to reveal.' But in modern times it has come to mean the final destruction that is revealed in the Bible.

In the Old Testament, the final destruction is very clearly focused on Israel. Its most famous statement is in Daniel 12:1 – 'And there shall be a time of trouble, such as never was since there was a nation.' But the earliest statement of the Apocalypse comes from Isaiah. In Isaiah 9:13 it is stated this way: 'The Lord will cut off Israel, head and tail, in a single day.' In Isaiah 29:1 the threat is very specifically focused on Jerusalem, as it is in Daniel 9:12, which states: 'Under the whole Heaven there has not been done the like of what has been done against Jerusalem.'

Both Daniel and Isaiah 29 make it clear that the ultimate danger is in a time yet to come, that the destruction of Jerusalem is not only in the past, but also in the future.

The best known prophecy of the 'Final Battle' is in Revelation 20:7–9, which predicts that Satan will lead a great army in an attack on Jerusalem. The names of the nations in the invading Satanic horde, 'Gog and Magog' (20:8), actually come from the Book of Ezekiel in the Old Testament, where they are described simply as enemies who will invade Israel from the North at some unstated time in the future (Ezekiel 38–9). The very word 'Armageddon,' which also comes from Revelation (16:16), is actually a Greek transliteration of the name of a city in northern Israel, Megiddo.

In the current tense Middle East environment, it is already hard to remember that at the time Rabin was killed Israel was almost uniquely at peace. That was accomplished largely by the Rabin-Arafat handshake on the White House lawn on 13 September 1993. And it did not break down until the wave of terrorism began, as predicted in the code, on 25 February 1996.

The letters that spell out the Hebrew year 5756 also spell out a question that I have translated, 'Will you change it?' In fact, the 'it' is implied in the Hebrew, but not stated. The literal Hebrew translation is a question in plural form: 'Will you change?' The question is not whether we will be changed, but whether we will change something else.

So the best English translation of the question formed by the letters that spell out the year 5756, the English words that give the clearest sense of the Hebrew, are as stated, 'Will you change it?'

My original letter to Shimon Peres was dated 9 November 1995, and was delivered to him that day by Elhanan Yishai, who had known the Prime Minister since Peres was thirteen, and remained a close friend and ally in the Labor party. Peres' reaction was told to me by Yishai after their meeting less than a week after Rabin was killed.

I met with Peres' press secretary Eliza Goren at the Prime Minister's office a few days later, and her quoted comment is from that meeting. I again saw Goren in New York on 10 December 1995, and at that time gave her another version of the same letter I had earlier sent the Prime Minister.

The quote from the US Senate report on the danger of nuclear terrorism is from the opening statement of Senator Sam Nunn, vice chairman of the Senate Permanent Subcommittee on Investigations, as transcribed in the original report of the 31 October 1995 session. It appears in slightly altered words in the final committee report, 'Global Proliferation of Weapons of Mass Destruction' (Sen. Hrg. 104–422), p. 4.

The statement that 'even potatoes are much better guarded' than nuclear weapons in the collapsed Soviet Union was made by Mikhail Kulik, the official who investigated the theft of 13.5 kilograms of enriched uranium from a nuclear-submarine shipyard near Murmansk. It is quoted in Scientific American (January 1996), p. 42, 'The Real Threat of Nuclear Smuggling,' Phil Williams and Paul Woessner.

The danger was further confirmed by several nuclear terrorism experts in and out of the US government, including Pentagon and CIA officials who spoke to me on a background basis.

The offer by a top Russian scientist to sell a Soviet missile system he had helped develop was made to me at a meeting in Moscow in September 1991. The obviously impoverished condition of top nuclear scientists that so shocked me in the days right after the Soviet Union first started to collapse apparently still exists to this day.

In October 1996 the chief of the most important nuclear weapons design facility in Russia, Vladimir Nechai, committed suicide because of the shame he felt in not being able to pay his scientists for months at a time. In a New York Times column 15 November 1996, another Russian official who attended his funeral noted the condition of the nuclear scientists who were there: 'Here was the pride of Russian science; here were the physicists of world stature, dressed in their threadbare jackets and faded shirts with frayed cuffs.' The official, Grigory Yavlinsky, concluded, 'In Russia, no one can guarantee the security of thermonuclear programs.'

My telephone conversation with Gen. Jacob Amidror took place in November 1995. Amidror was then deputy chief of Aman, Israeli military intelligence. He is now the top aide to the Defense Minister.

Gen. Danny Yatom first contacted me by letter dated 18 December 1995, but we did not talk until the first week of January, 1996. Yatom's letter stated, 'Following your letter dated December 10, 1995, to the Prime Minister, Mr Shimon Peres, he has asked me to meet with you for discussions.'

In our later telephone conversations Yatom, who was then Peres' top military advisor, arranged for me to meet directly with the Prime Minister. Yatom's quoted statement is from a telephone conversation.

My 26 January 1996 meeting with Shimon Peres at the Prime Minister's office in Jerusalem was arranged through Yatom, and attended by Goren. Peres' quoted questions are from that meeting.

Kaddafi's statement was released through the Libyan news agency on 27 January 1996, and reported in Israeli newspapers the next day. The quote is translated from the daily Ha'aretz.

My meeting with Gen. Yatom was on 28 January 1996, at the Prime Minister's office in Jerusalem. Yatom told me he had already talked to Peres about our meeting, and also said he had read Kaddafi's statement. His quoted statements are from that meeting.

Peres' speech, stating the danger of nuclear terrorism, took place in Jerusalem 30 January 1996. It is quoted from a 31 January report in the Jerusalem Post. Peres later made a similar statement on ABC's 'Nightline' (29 April 1996): 'It is the first time in history that an evil and malicious movement, covered by a religious lining, may acquire these terrible weapons. Imagine what would have happened if Hitler had a nuclear bomb.'

CHAPTER THREE: ALL HIS PEOPLE TO WAR

The 25 February 1996, terrorist bombing in Jerusalem and the series of bombings over the next nine days were reported throughout the world. The account here is taken from the New York Times and the Jerusalem Post.

Although that date, 5th Adar in the Hebrew calendar, had been found the day Rabin died nearly four months earlier, because the prediction 'all his people to war' seemed so unlikely to come true so soon, I did not tell Prime Minister Peres when I met with him in January. At the last minute, the night before the Sunday morning attack I did try to reach Gen. Yatom, but there was no answer at his office.

I met with Yatom 30 April 1996, outside the Israeli Embassy in Washington, as we had arranged in a phone conversation earlier that day.

I called Eli Rips 28 May 1996, the day before the Israeli election, and told him that I found 'Prime Minister Netanyahu' encoded in the Bible. It was Rips who discovered, during that phone conversation, that the word 'elected' crossed Netanyahu's name. I told Rips I did not believe it would happen and asked him what he thought about the apparent false prediction in the Bible code. He suggested we wait to see the outcome.

Rips agreed that it was clearly against the odds that two statements of death would cross 'Prime Minister Netanyahu,' but said he was not sure if those words, which appear in the plain text of the Bible, had meaning in relation to the modern event, the living man, encoded in the same place.

'But I had the same reservations about the prediction of Rabin's assassination,' said Rips, 'so this time I don't know what to say.'

The words with the name 'Amir' on the table where 'Netanyahu' appears with 'Yitzhak Rabin' – 'He changed the nation, he will make them evil' – appear in reverse in the plain text of the Bible overlapping 'Amir,' whose name also appears in reverse. Both are in the same verse of the Bible where the words 'name of the assassin' appear in the plain text, Numbers 35:11.

I first spoke to Ben-Zion Netanyahu 3 June 1996, by telephone and sent him the quoted letter to the Prime Minister dated 29 May. I spoke to him again on 9 June, and he confirmed that he had received my letter and given it to the Prime Minister Friday, 7 June.

Professor Netanyahu's book, *The Origins of the Inquisition*, was published in 1995 by Random House. It is dedicated to his other son, Jonathan, who died 4 July 1976, leading the famous rescue at Entebbe.

Rips returned the elder Netanyahu's phone call in my presence on 31 July 1996. Rips confirmed to him that the Bible code was a scientifically proven fact, and that both 'atomic holocaust' and 'holocaust of Israel' were encoded in the Bible. I met with Ben-Zion Netanyahu at his home in Jerusalem the same day, 31 July. His quoted statements are from that meeting.

The next day, 1 August, I saw the elder Netanyahu again at his home in Jerusalem in the late evening. His quoted statements are from that meeting.

My last conversation with Ben-Zion Netanyahu on that trip to Israel took place on 3 August, by telephone, and the quotes are from that phone conversation.

The last letter I sent Prime Minister Netanyahu was dated 20 August 1996, and was again sent to him through his father.

CHAPTER FOUR: THE SEALED BOOK

The 'sealed book' is described in Revelation 5:1–5, and the story of the Messiah opening the 'seven seals' is told in Revelation 6–8.

The original version of the same story appears in Daniel 12:1–4.

It is striking that in the New Testament the sealed book is opened to unleash the four horsemen of the Apocalypse, to cause the dead to cry for vengeance on the living, to trigger a great earthquake and cause the Sun, Moon, and stars to go black, and finally to cause 'silence in Heaven.'

However, in the original story told in the Old Testament, the sealed book is opened to save the world from disaster. 'And at that time thy people shall be rescued, everyone that shall be found written in the book' (Daniel 12:1).

Isaac Newton's focus on Daniel and Revelation is revealed by several biographers, including Keynes. In describing Newton's hidden papers, Keynes wrote (p. 286): 'Another large section is concerned with all branches of Apocalyptic writings from which he sought to deduce the secret truths of the Universe – the Book of Daniel, the Book of Revelations.'

The 'End of Days' appears four times in the original words of the Bible – Genesis 49:1–2, Numbers 24:14, Deuteronomy 4:30, and Deuteronomy 31:29. A second Biblical expression of the 'End of Days' appears in the last words of Daniel 12:13.

There are three ways to write any Hebrew year with letters, and I checked all three for each of the next 120 years, to see which best matched both Biblical expressions of the 'End of Days.' Out of 360 possible matches for each of the two ways the Bible originally stated the 'End,' only one year matched both – 5756, in the modern calendar the year that began in September 1995 and ended in September 1996.

The 'time of trouble' is foretold in Daniel 12:1. The promise of salvation, 'thy people shall be rescued,' is also in Daniel 12:1.

One of the first Dead Sea Scrolls found was a non-Biblical prophecy of 'The War Between the Sons of Light and the Sons of Darkness,' in which the Final Battle is described in detailed military terms. For a more detailed discussion of Apocalyptic prophecies through the ages, see *When Time Shall Be No More*, Paul Boyer (Harvard University Press, 1992).

The Bible itself describes God giving Moses the Torah in Exodus 24:12. And Moses is clearly identified as the man who wrote down 'the words of this Torah in a book' in Deuteronomy 31:24.

The description of God coming down on Mt Sinai is vividly told in Exodus 19:16–20, the source of the description in this book.

Paul Davies is quoted from *The Mind of God* (Touchstone, 1993), p. 96.

The New York Times reported 18 February 1997, that 'quantum computers' may be within our reach, that mankind may be ready to harness the world inside atoms and create 'an information-processing method so powerful that it would be to ordinary computing what nuclear energy is to fire.'

The astronomer Carl Sagan suggested that an advanced alien technology 'might seem to us like magic' in *Pale Blue Dot* (Random House, 1994), p. 352.

The author of *2001*, Arthur C. Clarke, made a similar observation: 'Any sufficiently advanced technology is indistinguishable from magic' (*Profiles of the Future*, Holt, Rinehart, and Winston, 1984).

Paul Davies' imagined 'alien artifact' is described in his book *Are We Alone?* (Basic Books, 1995), p. 42. Stanley Kubrick, in his famous movie version of Clarke's *2001*, showed a mysterious black monolith that seemed to reappear at successive stages of human evolution, each time we were ready to be taken to a higher level. When I told him about the Bible code, Kubrick's immediate reaction was, 'It's like the monolith in *2001*.'

The beginning of the Bible as a stone carving is told in Deuteronomy 27:2–8, in which Moses instructs the people to 'write very plainly upon stones all the words of this Torah.'

The quote from Jack Miles appears in *God: A Biography* (Knopf, 1995), p. 365.

Joseph's nickname, 'Zaphenath-Paneah,' appears in Genesis 41:45. There is a discussion of all the scholarly speculation of its possible meanings in Kaplan, *The Living Torah*, p. 207, including an Egyptian hieroglyphic representation of the name. The 'revealer of secrets' passage is from Daniel 2:47. Miles' statement that the God assisting Joseph was apparently able to reveal the future, but not change it, is quoted from *God*, p. 365, and his comparison of the future to a 'vast reel of film' that can be previewed is quoted from p. 365.

The quote Rips read to me from Isaiah 45:7, in which God Himself clearly states He is both good and evil, caused a nation-wide furor when it was quoted by a rabbi in Bill Moyers' 1996 PBS series, 'Genesis.' It was striking that the statement was such a surprise, and so controversial, because it was not hidden, but openly stated in a 2500-year-old book of the Bible, both in the original Hebrew, and in all standard English translations including the King James Version. If after several millennia most people still did not know, and could not accept, what was plainly stated in the Bible as the words of God, how could they accept a hidden code in the Bible?

The alternate translation of the final words of the Book of Daniel is not hidden in a code; it is simply another way of reading the plain words of the text.

CHAPTER FIVE: THE RECENT PAST

Isaiah's statement that 'to see the future, you must look backwards' comes from verse 41:23, and is more fully discussed in Chapter Eight.

It has a special meaning in the Bible, but it is also a statement that anyone who knows the history of the world would make. It is what Churchill said, 'The farther backward you can look, the farther forward you are likely to see.' And the philosopher George Santayana said, 'Those who cannot remember the past are condemned to repeat it.'

Doron Witztum, Rips' colleague, discussed his code research with me when we met in June 1992 at his home in Jerusalem. Witztum also self-published a limited edition of his code findings, *The Additional Dimension* (Israel, 1989). The Holocaust material cited in Chapter One was included in that publication.

One significant fact I noticed from the first week I spent with Eli Rips searching the Bible code is that we were able to find in the code names and places determined by known events in world history, or by what was on the front page of a newspaper that day, things I asked him to find on the spot. Similarly, when people later asked me to find names or events I had not thought to look for, they too were often encoded with relevant information.

A publisher I met with while researching this book, Sonny Mehta at Knopf, asked me to look for Mahatma Gandhi. 'M. Gandhi' was encoded in a single skip sequence with the words 'He will be killed,' just as 'President Kennedy' was immediately followed in a single skip sequence by the words 'to die.'

The Sadat assassination was found in the Bible code by Rips' colleague Witztum.

The purchase of what is now known as the Tomb of the Patriarchs in Hebron 4000 years ago by Abraham is told in Genesis 23, where the entire transaction is described in detail, including the bargaining between Abraham and Ephron, a Hittite, before they settled on the price, '400 shekels of silver.'

The Aum Shinrikyo cult's plans were documented in a US Senate committee report on the threat of terrorists using unconventional weapons, 'Global Proliferation of Weapons of Mass Destruction,' Permanent Subcommittee on Investigations (Sen. Hrg. 104–422). 'The world was forced to pay attention on the morning of March 20, 1995,' said the committee vice chairman Senator Nunn, citing the day that poison gas was spread through the Tokyo subway system. 'The cult, known as Aum Shinrikyo, thus gained the distinction of becoming the first group, other than a nation during wartime, to use chemical weapons on a major scale. I believe this attack signals the world has entered into a new era' (p. 5).

The Senate report cited a book published by the cult leader, *Second Set of Predictions*, Shoko Asahara, in which he stated: 'I am certain that in 1997, Armageddon will break out.' According to an independent American expert on terrorism, documents seized at the time of Asahara's arrest revealed that he had set a new and earlier date for Armageddon, 1996.

The details of the Oklahoma City bombing come from reports in the New York Times, Time, and Newsweek.

A nuclear terrorism expert at the Pentagon later told me that if the Oklahoma bombers had the amount of plutonium that could fit in a Coca-Cola can, and had included that in their crude truck bomb made of fertilizer and fuel oil, that they could have made Oklahoma City uninhabitable for at least a century.

CHAPTER SIX: ARMAGEDDON

The story of the discovery of the Dead Sea Scrolls is recounted in Millar Burrows' authoritative book, *The Dead Sea Scrolls* (Viking, 1956), pp. 4–5. There have been several versions told, but all involve a Bedouin stumbling onto the 2000-year-old Dead Sea Scrolls by accident. Some believe he was not a shepherd boy, but a smuggler.

Norman Golb in his book *Who Wrote the Dead Sea Scrolls?* (Touchstone, 1995) states that the Dead Sea Scrolls were saved to preserve the Bible and other Temple writings from the Romans, before they destroyed Jerusalem in 70 AD.

The caves where the scrolls were found are located at Qumran in the cliffs above the Dead Sea.

The Isaiah scroll was the one complete book of the Bible found among the Dead Sea Scrolls. The original was on display, wrapped around the drum that stands in the center of the Shrine of the Book, until the curators realized that the ancient parchment was cracking. A facsimile is now wrapped around the drum, and the original is being restored.

The architect of the Shrine, Armand Bartos, in a telephone interview on 21 October 1996, revealed that the drum was designed to retract and be covered over by steel plates to protect the Isaiah scroll in case of nuclear war. It appears that the device he designed is no longer functional.

The Apocalypse is described in Isaiah 29, and the first Biblical reference to a 'sealed book' is in Isaiah 29:11.

The alternate translation of Isaiah 29:17-8, which states that the sealed book will be opened, and its secrets revealed, is not hidden in a skip code, but simply in a slightly different set of word breaks in the original text.

I checked 'World War' and 'atomic holocaust' against all three ways to write each Hebrew year for the next 120 years. Out of 360 possible matches for each of the two expressions, only two years matched both – 5760 and 5766, in the modern calendar the years 2000 and 2006. Rips later checked the statistics for the matches of 'World War' and 'atomic holocaust' with those two years and agreed that the results were 'exceptional.'

The estimate that there are 50,000 nuclear weapons now in the world comes from nuclear proliferation experts at the Pentagon. The same experts state that both American and Russian land-based ballistic missiles can reach any target on Earth within half an hour, and that submarine-launched nuclear missiles can reach most major cities within fifteen minutes. A nuclear World War could cause far more destruction within hours than World War II caused in six years. See also Jonathan Schell, *The Fate of the Earth* (Knopf, 1982).

The Mezuzah contains fifteen verses from the last book of the original Bible, Deuteronomy 6:4-9 and 11:13-21, a total of 170 words, always written in 22 lines. The small scroll is rolled up and inserted in a wooden or metal case, affixed to the upper part of the right doorpost, following the commandment in the Bible: 'And thou shalt write them on the doorposts of thy house.' In Hebrew the word for 'doorpost' is 'Mezuzah.'

Senator Nunn's statement is quoted from 'Global Proliferation of Weapons of Mass Destruction' (Sen. Hrg. 104–422), p. 4. Senator Richard Lugar's statement is quoted from the same Senate report, pp. 10–11.

Peres' statement is quoted from his 30 January 1996 speech in Jerusalem.

Jerusalem is the only city among the nine most likely targets of a nuclear attack that is a clear statistical match in the Bible code with either 'atomic holocaust' or 'World War,' and it matches both against high odds. The other cities checked are Washington, New York, London, Paris, Tokyo, Beijing, Moscow, and Tel Aviv. Paris is the only other possible match with 'World War,' but the full hidden text seems to link that encoding to a former Israeli Prime Minister: 'from Paris, Peres.'

The encoding of 'Jerusalem' that matches both 'atomic holocaust' and 'World War' is the best encoding of the name of that city in the Bible, the one with the shortest skip sequence. It appears in a single verse, Deuteronomy 5:9.

Moreover, the ancient Biblical name for Jerusalem, 'Ariel,' also appears with both 'World War' and 'atomic holocaust.' That is the name of the city used in the first vision of the Apocalypse, in Isaiah 29:1–2.

'Ariel' has a second literal meaning in Hebrew, 'altar hearth,' the place where a burnt offering was made. And in Isaiah 29:2 the shocking connection is openly stated: 'It shall be to me as an altar hearth.' There follows Isaiah's vision of a future destruction of Jerusalem, words that appear to describe an atomic holocaust.

Schell's description of the atomic bombing of Hiroshima on 6 August 1945, is quoted from *The Fate of the Earth*, p. 37. Only a few sentences of his detailed description are quoted, and they are quoted without ellipses.

Schell's description of a ground explosion of a nuclear bomb, that also seems to echo the ancient words of Isaiah, is quoted from *The Fate of the Earth*, pp. 50–1, 53. Again, excerpts from a long detailed description are quoted here without ellipses.

Schell also notes that the 12.5-kiloton atomic bomb dropped on Hiroshima was 'by present-day standards a small one, and in today's arsenals it would be classed among the merely tactical weapons' (p. 36).

For an extensive discussion of the long, bloody history of religious conflict in Jerusalem see Karen Armstrong, *Jerusalem* (Knopf, 1996). In his review of the book, the New York Times Jerusalem bureau chief Serge Schmemann noted: 'Three great monotheistic religions deem it sacred, yet no city has a comparable history of carnage, destruction, and strife' (New York Times Book Review, 8 December 1996, p. 13).

The 'Armageddon' verse is quoted from the King James Version of the New Testament, Revelation 16:14 and 16:16.

The etymology of the word 'Armageddon' is confirmed in *The Oxford Companion to the Bible* (Oxford University Press, 1993), p. 56. It is noted there that the word 'Armageddon' is found only in Revelation 16:16, where it is specifically identified as the 'Hebrew' name for the location of the Final Battle. The Oxford commentary then states: 'Scholars generally explain Armageddon (NRSV: "Harmagedon") as a Greek transliteration of the Hebrew phrase *har megiddo* ("the mountain of Megiddo").'

The 'Gog and Magog' verse is quoted from the King James Version, Revelation 20:7–8.

The Oxford commentary (p. 256) notes that Revelation apparently misquotes Ezekiel 38–39 where 'Gog' is identified as the ruler of the land of 'Magog.' The Oxford commentary also states, 'The specific location of Magog is unknown.'

The original version in Ezekiel 38:15 clearly predicts that Israel will be invaded from the north. 'Syria' is encoded with that verse, and the ancient names for Iran and Libya appear in Ezekiel 38:5. The slaughter that ensues is stated in Ezekiel 39:17–18.

Einstein's vision of World War III and World War IV was quoted in a display of his original handwritten manuscript of the Theory of Relativity at the Israel Museum in Jerusalem, which also houses the Shrine of the Book, where the Dead Sea Scrolls are displayed. It is also published in *The Quotable Einstein*, p. 223.

CHAPTER SEVEN: APOCALYPSE

'The great terror' is foretold in Deuteronomy 34:12, the last verse of the original Bible, the last words the Bible says God dictated to Moses on Mt Sinai.

Kaplan's translation of the last three verses of the Torah states: 'No other prophet like Moses has arisen in Israel, whom God knew face to face. No one else could reproduce the signs and miracles that God let him display in the land of Egypt, or any of the mighty acts or great sights that Moses displayed before the eyes of all Israel.'

The hidden text of the last verse is not really in a code, but revealed by slightly different word breaks in the original text. The warning is very clear – 'for everyone, the great terror: fire, earthquake' – and it cannot be by chance that this is the last secret revealed in the Bible.

Three years are a very good mathematical match with 'the great terror,' the years 2000, 2014, and 2113. It is striking that all of the Apocalyptic dangers, whether man-made or natural disasters, appear in the Bible code to be grouped at least roughly within those same time frames.

The 'great earthquake' is foretold in Revelation 16:18 and 16:20. An earlier vision of the 'great earthquake' was in Ezekiel 38:19–20, where the location is clearly stated to be 'the land of Israel.' And an even earlier version was in Isaiah 13:13, where the threatened earthquake seems global, or even cosmic.

The full spelling of 'Los Angeles' in Hebrew does not appear in the Bible code, but the abbreviated form 'L.A. Calif.' is more clearly encoded with 'great earthquake' than any other major city in the world, and it appears also with 'fire, earthquake.' Both encodings appear with the same year, '5770,' in the modern calendar 2010.

The US Geological Survey report predicting a major southern California earthquake before 2024 was published in the Bulletin of the Seismological Society of America (vol. 5, no. 2), pp. 379–439, in April 1995.

I also interviewed the Survey's California coordinator David Schwartz on 23 October 1996, and he confirmed that a massive earthquake is expected in southern California within the next 30 years, and added that northern California is the second most likely area in the United States to be hit in the near future. 'No one yet knows how good we are at this,' said Schwartz, 'but those are the two biggest bullseyes on the map.'

The official Chinese government estimate of the number killed in the great 1976 earthquake in Tangshan was 242,000, but according to the New York Times the number killed was 800,000.

I told my then publisher, Dick Snyder, in April 1993 that the Bible code indicated Japan would be hit by a series of major earthquakes. The Okushiri quake happened 12 July 1993, and was encoded with the name of the epicenter and the month. My meeting with the Japanese cabinet minister Wakako Hirōnaka took place at her office in Tokyo in September 1993. The great Kobe earthquake struck on 16 January 1995, killing more than 5000.

Virtually all scientists now believe that the dinosaurs were wiped out by an asteroid that slammed into what is now the Gulf of Mexico approximately 65 million years ago. The latest findings suggest that it caused a firestorm across all of North America, immediately killing everything on this continent, and that the fallout from the explosion blotted out the Sun around the world, eventually killing all the dinosaurs. The original asteroid extinction theory was proposed in 1980 by Walter Alvarez, a geologist at Berkeley. The latest findings were published in the November issue of Geology Magazine by Peter Schultz and Stephen D'Hondt.

The creation of 'the great Tanin' is told in Genesis 1:21. The name of the dragon the Bible says God fought, 'Rahab,' comes from Isaiah 51:9. It is a plea to God: 'Awake, as in the ancient days, in the generations of old. Art thou not who cut Rahab in pieces, and pierced through the dragon?' The Hebrew word here is again 'Tanin.'

The oldest known Creation myth was written thousands of years before the Bible, in Sumer, the area near the Persian Gulf now called Iraq. The Sumerian myth begins with the slaying of a 'dragon' by a 'god.' And nearly every ancient civilization around the world had a similar primal myth.

Brian Marsden's warning that the comet Swift-Tuttle might strike the Earth on 14 August 2126, was made on 15 October 1992. The quoted New York Times report was published 27 October 1992. The quoted Newsweek report was published 23 November 1992.

The 1994 collision of Shoemaker-Levy with Jupiter was reported around the world. The account here is from the New York Times and Time magazine.

Eleanor Helin, the NASA scientist in charge of tracking asteroids and comets was quoted in the New York Times 14 May 1996, and the plans for preventing a collision with the Earth were reported in both the Times and Newsweek.

The ancient tale about the king who broke the big rock into pebbles before hurling it at his son is told in two ancient commentaries, Midrash Psalms 6:3 and Midrash Yalkut Shimoni 2:635. Later, an 18th-century sage, the Genius of Vilna, related this tale to the ultimate fate of one of two foreseen Messiahs, the one who according to legend will come first, in an effort to prevent the horror of the End of Days. Like the king's son, said the Genius of Vilna, he 'will not suffer the death penalty. He must, however, still suffer the pain of the smaller rocks.' Kol HaTor, chapter 1, paragraph 6.

The comet that hit Jupiter crumbled into twenty pieces before it bombarded the planet. It is striking that the Hebrew name for the planet Jupiter, 'Zedek,' which means 'justice,' is the root of a name used for the Messiah who comes first, 'Zadik,' which means 'the just one.'

The theory that an ancient collision by a comet may have inspired later Apocalyptic scenarios in the Bible is quoted from Timothy Ferris, 'Is This the End?,' New Yorker magazine, 27 January 1997, p. 55. The odds of a comet or asteroid striking the Earth are stated on p. 49.

CHAPTER EIGHT: THE FINAL DAYS

The Jerusalem Post report that Netanyahu was scheduled to meet with King Hussein in Amman 25 July 1996, appeared in the weekly edition published 21 July. The date of the scheduled trip was also published in several other Israeli newspapers that week. The reason the trip was delayed, King Hussein's sudden illness, was confirmed by the Prime Minister's press office. Netanyahu's 5 August meeting with Hussein was reported in the Jerusalem Post 6 August.

'Both trips were decided on the day I was elected,' Netanyahu stated at a news conference, referring to his already completed visit to Cairo and his then upcoming July visit to Amman. Both trips were found encoded in the Bible a week before Netanyahu was elected, where his election was itself forecast in advance.

A more formal statement of the Uncertainty Principle is made by Stephen Hawking: 'The more accurately you try to measure the position of a particle, the less accurately you can measure its speed, and vice versa.' The upshot, according to Hawking, is that quantum physics can only 'predict a number of different possible outcomes' and 'not a single definite result.' *A Brief History of Time*, p. 55.

My meeting with Dore Gold took place just before midnight on 10 September 1996, at the Essex House Hotel in New York. My fax to Gen. Yatom was dated 11 September and sent that day. I spoke with our go-between Gen. Ben-Israel 10 September and again on 12 September, and he told me that he had met with Yatom, and that Yatom confirmed he had received the message and Israeli intelligence was checking out the potential danger of an atomic attack.

My final fax to Yatom was sent 16 September.

The assassination of Austrian Archduke Ferdinand on 28 June 1914, is accepted by all historians as the immediate cause of World War I. A 1996 PBS documentary, 'The Great War,' reconfirmed that fact, and an Oxford historian on the show said that the assassination not only triggered the war, but also led inexorably to the Russian Revolution. Indeed, PBS raised the question of what might have happened if the Archduke's carriage had turned right instead of left, if it had not crossed the path of the Serbian nationalist who shot him: 'A wrong turn by the Archduke's driver brought the heir to the Austrian throne face to face with Gavrilo Princip,' the Serbian assassin.

The assassination set off a chain reaction. Again, from PBS: 'On July 28, 1914, Austria declared war against Serbia. But war between Austria and Serbia meant war between Austria and Russia. That meant war between Russia and Germany. And that meant war between Germany and France. And that meant war between Germany and Britain. In a flash, the whole continent was going to be at war.'

The 'Butterfly Effect' is cited by James Gleick in *Chaos* (Penguin, 1987), p. 8. He also quotes a much older version of the same concept, from a nursery rhyme (p. 23):

'For want of a nail, the shoe was lost;
For want of a shoe, the horse was lost;
For want of a horse, the rider was lost;
For want of a rider, the battle was lost;
For want of a battle, the kingdom was lost!'

The 9th of Av is not only by tradition the date that the First Temple was destroyed in 586 BC and the Second Temple in 70 AD, but also the date that England expelled the Jews in 1290, Spain expelled the Jews in 1492, and the day that the gas chambers of Treblinka began to operate in 1942, beginning the Holocaust. See Aryeh Kaplan, *Handbook of Jewish Thought* (Maznaim, 1979), vol. II, pp. 339–40.

Some historians suggest that the Nazis chose the day deliberately: 'The mass expulsions from Warsaw began on July 22, 1942, the day before the 9th of Av. On the following day, the 9th of Av, the gas chambers of Treblinka began to operate. The organization of these actions on a somber Jewish holiday was no coincidence. The Nazis studied the Jewish calendar and frequently scheduled the most destructive actions [on such dates]. Within two months, 300,000 Jews were sent to their death.' Nora Levin, *The Holocaust* (Schocken Books, 1973), p. 318.

According to the Talmud God cursed that day because it was the date in Biblical times that the first scouts Moses sent ahead into the Promised Land came back with an 'evil report,' telling the ancient Israelites that they could not conquer it.

'Ariel' is the ancient name of Jerusalem used in the first warning of the Apocalypse in Isaiah 29:1–2.

The paradoxical quote from the Talmud on the coexistence of free will and foreknowledge comes from Mishnah Avot 3:15, and is attributed to Rabbi Akiva.

In Hebrew the name 'Jacob,' which means both 'he will prevent' and 'he will delay,' also means 'he will follow,' specifically track, or even shadow like a detective. So the name of the Biblical Patriarch may suggest that he is in some way still watching over his people. The name Jacob was given after a mysterious wrestling match with an unidentified night visitor (Genesis 32:25–29) became the name of the country, 'Israel.' In Hebrew, 'Israel' means 'he will fight God.'

The Bible itself explains Jacob's new name that way: 'Thy name shall be called no more Jacob, but Israel; for thou hast fought with God and with men, and hast prevailed' (Genesis 32:29).

The three days of warfare starting on 25 September 1996, was reported throughout the world. The account here is taken from the New York Times and the Jerusalem Post. The archaeological tunnel under the Temple Mount in Jerusalem connects the holy places of three religions: the Wailing Wall, the Dome of the Rock and the Via Dolorosa, the route Jesus is said to have walked to his crucifixion.

The word 'annexed' that appears twice with 'Holocaust of Israel' is used by Israeli authorities to describe the only two territories captured in the 1967 war that were formally made part of Israel, the Golan Heights and East Jerusalem. The Golan formerly belonged to Syria, which still claims it, and which recently moved elite troops into position around it. East Jerusalem was part of Jordan, and is claimed by the Palestinians as the capital of their homeland.

The name 'Arafat' appears only twice with no skips in the original text of the Bible, and one of those times appears with the only meeting of the two Biblical expressions of the 'End of Days.' In fact, it appears directly below that phrase, against very high odds. Moreover, the next words in the hidden text following his name state, 'Remember! Don't forget the confirmation of the End Time.'

The 'exile under Ishmael' is foretold primarily in the Zohar, an ancient commentary, part of the so-called 'hidden Midrash' which reveals the secrets not stated openly in the Torah. There are several references in the Zohar to a future time of warfare in Israel in the 'End of Days,' before the coming of the Messiah. In Zohar Genesis 1:19A it is stated that 'the children of Ishmael will prepare to arouse all the nations of the world to come against Jerusalem.' It is also stated, however, that Israel might be saved from the attack.

The story of Isaac and Ishmael, Abraham's two sons, is told in Genesis 21. Ishmael's mother was a servant, Hagar the Egyptian, and when Isaac was born his mother Sarah told her husband Abraham, 'Get rid of that slave woman and her son, for that slave woman's son will never share in the inheritance with my son Isaac' (21:10). When Ishmael was born, the plain words of the Bible seem to foretell the battle to come: 'He will be a wild donkey of a man;

his hand will be against everyone and everyone's hand will be against him' (Genesis 16:12).

The middle-of-the-night handshake between Netanyahu and Arafat 15 January 1997, was reported that day in the New York Times. Two days earlier, when first reports of the deal emerged, the Times reported: 'American officials had no illusion that the Hebron agreement would preclude further crises and confrontations, given the fundamental mutual mistrust and antipathy between the conservative Israel Government and Mr Arafat. The scope of the further withdrawals, and the issues still to be negotiated – Jerusalem, borders, Jewish settlements – are expected to raise at least as many passions and crises as Hebron. Militant Jewish settlers are bound to view the Hebron withdrawal as a betrayal. Rejectionist Islamic groups among the Palestinians may try to use terror again to derail the agreements.'

The series of events in March 1997 is recounted from reports in the New York Times and the Jerusalem Post. The quote from King Hussein's letter to Netanyahu is taken from a New York Times report on 12 March 1997. The 21 March suicide bombing was reported in the Times the next day.

Richard P. Feynman is quoted from his book, *Six Easy Pieces* (Helix, 1995), p. 135. Feynman also states that he believes the Uncertainty Principle relates to all things and that therefore 'at the present time we must limit ourselves to computing probabilities' (p. 136).

Feynman further states that he does not believe we will ever 'beat that puzzle': 'No one has ever found (or even thought of) a way around the Uncertainty Principle. So we must assume that it describes a basic characteristic of nature' (pp. 136, 132).

I was, by chance, reading Feynman's book as I was flying to Israel, and learned that Netanyahu was scheduled to go to Jordan on the day the Bible code had predicted in advance. When that trip was suddenly delayed, I realized that the great physicist must be right, we cannot be sure what will happen, we can only state probabilities.

The science writer Timothy Ferris, in the New York Times Magazine, 29 September 1996, stated that quantum physics 'remains a highly successful branch of science.' His article was entitled, 'Weirdness Makes Sense' (pp. 143ff).

The Nobel laureate Gabriel García Márquez, in his novel *One*

Hundred Years of Solitude, tells of the discovery of a manuscript which reveals a family's history 'one hundred years ahead of time.' As García Márquez describes it, he seems to have imagined the true nature of the Bible and its code on a smaller scale. The writer 'had not put events in the order of man's conventional time, but had concentrated a century of daily episodes in such a way that they coexisted in one instant' (Harper, 1991), p. 421. I thought of it when Rips told me that the whole Bible code had to be written at once, in a single flash.

My original meeting with Rabbi Adin Steinsaltz took place at his office in Jerusalem on 30 June 1992, two days after I first met with Eli Rips, and I have met with him on several of my return visits to Israel. We discussed the true nature of time, and the way it might be revealed by the reversal of tenses in the Torah at that first meeting and on other occasions. Steinsaltz told me that although the statement of the future as the past and the past as the future is unique to the Bible, there is no extensive commentary on the reversal of tenses.

Steinsaltz first pointed me to Isaiah 41:23, the verse in the Bible that specifically related seeing the future to 'saying things backwards.' It was not until years later that I independently discovered that the verse, read backwards, stated the year of the threatened holocaust, '5756.'

Rips calculated the odds that all the Apocalyptic dangers stated in the code would match a single expression of the year 2006, 'in 5766,' at about one thousand to one. He agreed it was 'remarkable' that this one year among 120 uniquely matched all the dangers checked – 'the End of Days,' 'World War,' 'Atomic Holocaust,' 'Holocaust of Israel,' and 'Great Earthquake.' Rips also agreed it was 'striking' that several expressions of the same years 2000 and 2006 likewise matched the same dangers, but said there was no clear way to measure that mathematically.

'We can be certain it is non-random, that it was intentionally encoded,' said Rips. 'We cannot be certain whether that means the danger is real.'

The date of the first Scud missile attack, 18 January 1991, was reported in the New York Times, and confirmed in *Facts on File Yearbook 1991,* p. 28. Eight Scuds were fired at Israel at about 2 AM

18 January (Israel time). Two hit Tel Aviv. Three landed near Haifa. Three fell in open fields. Jerusalem was not hit. The US had launched Desert Storm, starting the Gulf War, the day before, 17 January 1991.

'Code will save,' the words that appear above 'atomic holocaust' and below 'the End of Days,' also has a second translation in Hebrew, 'codes of Moses.'

Exodus 2:10 tells how Moses was given his name. According to the Bible, he was born in Egypt at a time when the Pharaoh decreed that all male Hebrew infants be killed. His mother, to save him, built a small Ark, and set it afloat in the Nile. The Pharaoh's daughter found the child when she came to the river to bathe, and adopted him as her own:

'And she called his name Moses; and she said, Because I drew him out of the water.'

In Hebrew, it is a play on words. According to the authoritative Alcalay dictionary (Massada, 1990), p. 1517, 'Moses' actually means, 'to pull out, extricate, rescue.'

CODA

Jonathan Schell's statement 'We are forced in this one case to be historians of the future' appears in *The Fate of the Earth*, p. 21.

NOTES ON ILLUSTRATIONS

The names and events encoded in the Bible use the same Hebrew that appears in the plain text of the Bible and the same Hebrew used by Israelis today.

The years encoded in the Bible are from the ancient Hebrew calendar, which starts in Biblical time, 3760 years earlier than the modern calendar. The equivalent years in the modern calendar are also noted with all the Bible code print-outs.

The names of people and places are taken from standard reference sources, like the Hebrew Encyclopedia. The Hebrew spellings for more current events are those used by Israeli newspapers.

The translations of all encodings have been confirmed by the authoritative R. Alcalay Hebrew-English dictionary (Massada, 1990) and the standard unabridged Hebrew dictionary, A. Even-Shoshan (Kiryat Sefer, 1985). And all the Bible code material quoted in this book has been checked by Israeli translators, who worked with me during the entire five-year investigation.

Many of the most important Bible code print-outs reproduced in this book were seen and confirmed by Dr Rips. The translations of the Rabin assassination material were also confirmed by Rabbi Adin Steinsaltz, the leading translator of ancient Hebrew texts.

All of the Bible code print-outs displayed in this book have been confirmed by statistics to be encoded beyond chance. The word combinations are mathematically proven to be non-random.

The statistics are calculated automatically by computer, according to the mathematical model designed by Rips and Witztum, and validated by independent peer review.

The computer scores the matches between words, using two tests – how closely they appear together, and whether the skips that spell out the search words are the shortest in the Bible. (For a more detailed explanation see Appendix.)

Hebrew reads right to left, but words are encoded in both directions, and, as in a crossword puzzle, also up and down.

Sometimes the original text of the Bible, with only slightly different word breaks between the existing letters, reveals precise information about events in the modern world. In this book, it is called the 'hidden text.' We can use the hidden words encoded with 'Watergate' to show how it works.

The plain text of the fourth book of the Bible, Numbers 3:24, refers to a clan of one of the Twelve Tribes of Israel, 'the chief of the house of the father of the Gershonites.' The original Hebrew text of that verse is reproduced below:

ן ש י א ב י ת ב א ל ג ר ש נ י

CHIEF OF THE HOUSE OF THE FATHER OF THE GERSHONITES

However, the same word that in Biblical Hebrew meant 'chief' or 'ruler,' in modern Hebrew is the word for 'President,' the word used by Israelis today for 'President Clinton' or their own 'President Weizmann.'

And, with a slight change in word breaks, the same letters in Numbers 3:24 spell out an entirely new sentence: 'President, but he was kicked out.' Again, the original Hebrew is reproduced below:

ן ש י א ב י ת א ב ל ג ר ש

PRESIDENT, BUT HE WAS KICKED OUT

So, the only time 'Watergate' is encoded anywhere in the Bible, it appears in the same place that the hidden text describes Nixon's forced resignation. The words in the Bible are exact. 'Watergate,' 'President,' and 'kicked out' were the words used by Israeli newspapers in reporting Nixon's downfall.

In some cases, the Bible code uses a condensed form of Hebrew, as one would expect in a code. And the Bible code, like the Bible itself, sometimes drops letters that are generally used in modern Hebrew, primarily the vuv and the yud.

All the Bible code print-outs displayed in this book are cited below, with chapter and verse numbers from the Bible, showing where they are encoded. All the code print-outs that differ even slightly from common Hebrew, or that require further explanation for people who don't read Hebrew, are detailed.

CHAPTER ONE: THE BIBLE CODE

• 'Yitzhak Rabin' is encoded starting in Deuteronomy 2:33 and ending in Deuteronomy 24:16. It is the only time his full name is encoded anywhere in the Bible. 'Assassin that will assassinate' appears in Deuteronomy 4:42, and 'assassinate' crosses Rabin's name. It is the only time those words appear in the Bible. (p. 4).

• 'Yitzhak Rabin,' as noted, appears in Deuteronomy 2:33–Deuteronomy 24:16. 'Name of assassin who will assassinate' appears in Deuteronomy 4:42. The name of Rabin's assassin, 'Amir,' appears in Numbers 35:11, and the plain text of the same verse again includes the words 'name of assassin.' (p. 6)

• 'Rabin assassination' is encoded from Exodus 36:37 to Leviticus 22:5. The year he was killed appears in Exodus 39:3–4, and crosses both 'Rabin assassination' and the place he was killed, 'Tel Aviv.' The name of the city is encoded from Exodus 33:5 to Leviticus 4:9. (p. 6)

• 'Fire on 3rd Shevat,' the Hebrew date equivalent to 18 January 1991, the day of the first Scud missile attack in the Gulf War, is encoded in Genesis 14:2–12. The name of Iraq's leader, 'Hussein,' is encoded in Genesis 14:9–14. Both the words 'war' and 'missile,' although only marked once on the table, appear twice, and the second 'missile' crosses 'enemy.' (p. 8)

The full code sequence actually states 'Hussein picked a day.' It is encoded in Genesis 14:6–17, the same chapter of the Bible where 'fire on 3rd Shevat' is encoded. But the two phrases are too long to fit together on a single print-out. The literal translation of the encoded words would be 'Hussein marked a day,' as if he circled it on a calendar.

The modern Hebrew spelling of the name 'Hussein' would generally have one more letter, a vuv, but the spelling encoded in the Bible is an accepted alternative form, and consistent with Biblical Hebrew. The encoding of his name with the date was clearly intentional; the attack did happen as predicted 'on 3rd Shevat.'

• 'Yitzhak Rabin,' as noted above, appears in Deuteronomy 2:33–Deuteronomy 24:16. (p. 15)

• 'Assassin who will assassinate,' as noted above, appears in Deuteronomy 4:42. (p. 15)

• 'Amir' appears in Numbers 33:14–15. It is the third way in which the name of the assassin is encoded with the murder. (p. 16)

• 'Clinton' is encoded starting in Genesis 24:8 and ending in Numbers 26:24. His name is spelled in the Bible code exactly as it is spelled in the Israeli press. 'President' appears connected to 'Clinton' in Numbers 7:2. It is, again, exactly the word used for 'President' in modern Israel. (p. 19)

• 'Watergate' is encoded from Genesis 28:21 to Numbers 19:18. 'Who is he? President, but he was kicked out,' as explained in detail above, appears in Numbers 3:23–24. (p. 19)

• 'Economic collapse' is encoded from Exodus 20:9 to Deuteronomy 11:6. It appears only once in the entire Bible, and the year it began, 1929, appears in the same place. The equivalent Hebrew year, '5690,' is encoded in Numbers 10:8. (p. 20)

• 'Man on Moon' is encoded from Numbers 19:20–Numbers 27:1. 'Spaceship' crosses it, encoded in Numbers 22:25. (p. 21)

• 'Shoemaker-Levy,' the name of the comet that struck Jupiter, is encoded starting at Genesis 19:38 and ending at Genesis 38:19. 'Jupiter' is encoded in Genesis 30:41 to Genesis 31:1. (p. 22)

• 'Shoemaker-Levy' is again encoded in Isaiah 25:11 to Isaiah 27:4. 'Jupiter' is encoded in Isaiah 26:16. And the date the comet struck the planet, '8th Av,' appears in Isaiah 26:20. (p. 23)

There are two ways to spell 'Jupiter' in Hebrew, and both are encoded with the name of the comet that struck the planet. The first spelling is a transliteration of 'Jupiter,' and is encoded in Genesis; only part of the name is displayed in the print-out because the table is too wide to be reproduced in full. The second is the Hebrew name for the•planet, 'Zedek,' which is encoded in Isaiah with the date the comet hit Jupiter.

• 'Hitler' is encoded in Genesis 8:19–21. He is identified as 'Nazi and enemy' in Genesis 8:17–18. He is called an 'evil man' in Genesis 8:21. 'Slaughter' is encoded in Genesis 8:20. (p. 25)

• 'Shakespeare' is encoded from Leviticus 23:24 to Numbers 1:34. 'Hamlet' is encoded in Leviticus 3:13–14:27. 'Macbeth' is also encoded starting in the same verse of the Bible, Leviticus 3:13, and ending in Leviticus 7:29. (p. 31)

• 'Wright Brothers' is encoded from Genesis 30:30 to Genesis 43:14. 'Airplane' appears in Genesis 33:7–8. (p. 32)

• 'Edison' is encoded from Numbers 14:19–17:19. 'Lightbulb' appears in Numbers 11:26–27. 'Electricity' appears in Numbers 13:1–2. (p. 32)

• 'Newton' is encoded from Numbers 18:30 to Numbers 21:5. 'Gravity' crosses his name encoded in Numbers 19:20. In Hebrew, the word that means 'gravity' is usually prefaced by the words 'force of,' and without that would mean 'attraction' or 'pull.' But since it is encoded with 'Newton,' the scientist who discovered 'gravity,' the meaning seems clear, and the encoding intentional. (p. 33)

• 'Einstein' appears once in the Bible encoded from Exodus 21:29 to Numbers 31:39. The word 'science,' and the overlapping statement 'a new and excellent understanding,' both appear in Numbers 3:34 and cross the name 'Einstein.' 'They prophesied a brainy person' appears in Numbers 11:26. (p. 33)

CHAPTER TWO: ATOMIC HOLOCAUST

• 'All his people to war' appears in Deuteronomy 2:32, just above 'assassin who will assassinate,' which crosses 'Yitzhak Rabin' as noted above. (p. 36)

• 'Holocaust of Israel' is encoded once in the Bible, from Genesis 49:17 to Deuteronomy 28:64. '5756' appears in Exodus 17:2, the only time the year appears anywhere in the plain text of the Bible without any skips. (p. 36)

• 'Atomic holocaust' is encoded from Numbers 29:9 to Deuteronomy 8:19. It appears only once in the Bible, and the odds against it appearing at all are at least 100 to 1. 'In 5756' is encoded in Deuteronomy 12:15. (p. 37)

• 'The next war' is encoded from Genesis 36:15 to Numbers 12:8. 'It will be after the death of the Prime Minister' appears in the verse right above, Genesis 25:11. (p. 39)

On the same table that 'the next war' is encoded, in the same verse that states 'It will be after the death of the Prime Minister,' both the names 'Yitzhak' and 'Rabin' are encoded, but the full code print-out is too big to be reproduced here, so we see only the Prime Minister's first name.

• 'Libyan artillery' is encoded from Exodus 21:22 to Numbers 1:38. The same unique appearance of '5756' in Exodus 17:2 that appears with 'holocaust of Israel' also appears here. (p. 43)

• The name 'Libya' appears three times with 'atomic holocaust,' once crossing those words, and twice more on the same line, appearing all three times in Exodus 34:6–7. The Hebrew word that means 'total destruction' appears twice in that same verse of the Bible. Right before the first encoding of 'Libya' are the words 'It was exploded.' Right after the third encoding of 'Libya' are the words 'They were revealed.' (p. 44)

• 'Atomic artilleryman' is encoded from Deuteronomy 4:40 to Deuteronomy 6:24. The opening of the first verse, Deuteronomy 4:40, states, 'In order that you prolong thy days.' In Hebrew the same letters also spell out 'address, date.' The apparent location, 'the Pisgah,' crosses the second letter of 'atomic artilleryman' in Deuteronomy 4:49. (p. 45)

CHAPTER THREE: ALL HIS PEOPLE TO WAR

• 'Autobus' is encoded from Numbers 9:2 to Numbers 14:35. 'Bombing' or 'explosion' appears in the same place, encoded in

Numbers 10:23–4. 'Jerusalem' crosses 'autobus,' encoded in Numbers 11:1–4. The full name of the city is encoded in the Bible, but the print-out is too wide to be reproduced in full here. (p. 50)

• 'Autobus' is encoded again in Genesis 34:7–35:5. 'They will ride, and there will be terror' appears in the last verse, Genesis 35:5, crossing 'autobus.' 'Fire, great noise' appears in the previous verse, Genesis 34:4. (p. 51)

• 'Prime Minister Netanyahu' is encoded one time in the Bible, from Exodus 19:12 to Deuteronomy 4:47. Crossing his name is the word 'elected,' encoded in Numbers 7:83. His nickname, 'Bibi,' is encoded in the same verse. (p. 53)

• 'Netanyahu' appears without skips in the hidden text of Deuteronomy 1:21, on the same table where 'Yitzhak Rabin,' 'Amir,' 'name of assassin,' and 'all his people to war' also appear together (see Chapter One). Right before 'Netanyahu' in the hidden text are the words, 'for the great horror.' (p. 55)

• 'The next war' is encoded from Genesis 36:15 to Numbers 12:8. 'It will be after the death of the Prime Minister' appears in the verse right above, Genesis 25:11. Overlapping those words, encoded in the same verse, is the statement 'another will die.' (p. 58)

• 'Prime Minister Netanyahu' is cited above. The words 'surely he will be killed' that cross his name appear in Exodus 19:2. The words 'his soul was cut off' appear in Exodus 31:14. The word 'murdered' appears twice in Numbers 31:17. (p. 59)

CHAPTER FOUR: THE SEALED BOOK

• 'In the End of Days' appears in the plain text of Genesis 49:1, which states: 'And Jacob called to his sons, and said, Gather yourselves together, that I may tell you that which shall befall you in the End of Days.' The year, 'in 5756,' is encoded from Genesis 48:17 to Genesis 49:6. (p. 62)

The 'End of Days' appears four times in the original five books of the Bible. In the Jerusalem Bible it is translated as 'the last days' and 'the latter days.' But Kaplan notes that the literal meaning is 'the End of Days' (*The Living Torah*, p. 245).

• 'World War' is encoded once in the Bible, from Deuteronomy 4:28 to Deuteronomy 17:4. 'In the End of Days' appears in the plain text of the Bible just above, in Numbers 24:14. (p. 63)

• 'Atomic holocaust,' as already noted, also appears once (Numbers 29:9 to Deuteronomy 8:19). Again, 'in the End of Days' appears just above, in the same verse that appears with 'World War,' Numbers 24:14. (p. 63)

• The second Biblical expression of the 'End of Days,' which appears only in the plain text of Daniel, is encoded from Deuteronomy 4:34 to Deuteronomy 32:28. 'In 5756' is encoded just above, in Deuteronomy 1:25. (p. 64)
In its original Biblical context it is always taken to foretell a future time of trouble, the Apocalypse. But the last words of Daniel are also seen as foretelling 'the days of the Messiah.'

• 'Amir,' Rabin's assassin, is encoded in the same skip sequence as 'End of Days,' from Numbers 16:3 to Numbers 29:8. 'War' appears in the plain text of Deuteronomy 4:34, the verse where 'End of Days' begins. (p. 66)

• The two Biblical expressions of the 'End of Days' appear together one time, in the plain text of Deuteronomy 4:30, and encoded from Numbers 28:9 to Deuteronomy 19:10. Both 'plague' and the plea 'Save!' appear in the same place in Numbers 14:37–38. (p. 67)

• 'It was made by computer' is encoded in Exodus 32:16–17, where the plain text states, 'And the tablets were the work of God, and the writing was the writing of God, engraved on the tablets.' (p. 69)

• 'Bible code' is encoded from Deuteronomy 12:11 to Deuteronomy 12:17. The Hebrew word used for 'Bible' is 'Tanakh,' which means the entire Old Testament. 'Sealed before God' appears in Deuteronomy 12:12. (p. 72)

• 'Computer' is encoded in Daniel 12:4–6. The plain text of Daniel 12:4 states, 'But thou, O Daniel, shut up the words, and seal the book, until the time of the End.' (p. 72)

• '5757,' the Hebrew year equivalent to 1997, is encoded from Daniel 10:8 to Daniel 11:22. The current year also appears with the famous words from Daniel 12:4, 'Shut up the words, and seal the book, until the time of the End.' In the same place, at Daniel 11:13 and Daniel 11:40, there twice appear the same words which have two possible translations: 'for you, the encoded' and 'for you, the hidden secrets.' (p. 76)

CHAPTER FIVE: THE RECENT PAST

• 'World War' is encoded from Deuteronomy 4:28 to Deuteronomy 17:4. 'It will strike them, to destroy, annihilate' appears in Deuteronomy 9:19, crossing 'World War.' (p. 78)

The word 'second' is encoded right above 'World War,' but is not included in the code print-out because in Hebrew the word 'war' is female in gender, and the word 'second' appears here in the male form. However, it seems clearly intended, because the full hidden text states 'second and third,' and that phrase crosses 'this world devastated, World War,' which is spelled out in a single skip sequence.

• 'Roosevelt' is encoded once in the Bible, from Genesis 40:11 to Deuteronomy 9:1. He is identified as 'President' in Numbers 25:18, and the hidden text of that same verse states, 'He gave the order to strike on the day of the great defeat.' The last letter of the Hebrew word for 'great defeat' does not appear in the print-out, because it is one column too wide. (p. 78)

• 'Atomic holocaust,' as noted above, is encoded from Numbers 29:9 to Deuteronomy 8:19. The year of Hiroshima, 1945, in the Hebrew calendar '5705,' appears in Deuteronomy 8:19, crossing the last letter of 'atomic holocaust.' 'Japan' is encoded in Numbers 29:9. (p. 78)

• 'President Kennedy' is encoded once in the Bible, from Genesis 34:19 to Genesis 50:4. The next words in the same skip sequence, 'to die,' are encoded from Genesis 27:46 to Genesis 31:51. 'Dallas' appears in the same place, starting at Genesis 10:7 to Genesis 39:4. (p. 79)

• 'Oswald' is encoded from Numbers 34:6 to Deuteronomy 7:11. 'Name of the assassin who will assassinate' appears in Deuteronomy

4:42, the same verse that is encoded with the Rabin assassination, and the name of his assassin, Amir. (p. 80)

• 'Ruby' is encoded in Deuteronomy 2:8 with 'Oswald,' and the words 'he will kill the assassin,' which appear in Numbers 35:19. (p. 80)

• 'R.F. Kennedy' is encoded in Exodus 26:21–2. In the hidden text of those verses, intertwined with his name, twice appear the words 'second ruler will be killed.' The name of his assassin, 'S. Sirhan,' is encoded from Exodus 19:18 to Exodus 29:13, crossing the name 'Kennedy' in the code. (p. 81)

• 'Toledano' is encoded from Genesis 31:39 to Genesis 42:34. The only time his name appears, the entire code sequence spells out 'captivity of Toledano' (Genesis 24:6 to Genesis 30:20). The name of the city, 'Lod,' appears in Genesis 39:14. The words 'Don't shed blood' appear in the plain text of Genesis 37:22, and the statement 'he will die' appears in the hidden text of Genesis 30:20. (p. 83)

• 'Goldstein' is encoded from Genesis 31:10 to Leviticus 25:16. 'Man from the house of Israel who will slaughter' appears across his name in Leviticus 17:3. The name of the city where he committed the massacre, 'Hebron,' appears in Numbers 3:19. (p. 84)

'Goldstein' is generally spelled with one more letter, a vuv, but this is an accepted alternate spelling, and it is consistent with Biblical Hebrew.

• 'Oklahoma' is encoded from Genesis 29:25 to Genesis 35:5. 'Death' crosses the name of the city that was bombed in Genesis 30:20. 'There will be terror' appears in the plain text of Genesis 35:5, the last verse in which 'Oklahoma' is encoded. (p. 87)

• 'Murrah Building' is encoded from Genesis 35:3 to Genesis 46:6. The words 'desolated, slaughtered' appear in Genesis 35:3, crossing the 'M.' 'Killed, torn to pieces' appears in Genesis 37:33, again crossing the name of the building. (p. 88)

• 'His name is Timothy' is encoded in Genesis 37:12–19, and 'McVeigh' is encoded in Genesis 37:8–9. (p. 88)

His name is encoded with the day and the hour that he allegedly blew up the Federal office building in Oklahoma City, killing 168 people. It was exactly 'two years from the death of Koresh,' the leader of a lunatic religious cult. Those words are also encoded with 'McVeigh,' but are not shown on the smaller scale table reproduced in the book.

CHAPTER SIX: ARMAGEDDON

• Both 'in 5760' and 'in 5766,' the years 2000 and 2006 in the modern calendar, are encoded with 'World War' in Deuteronomy 11:14–15. The two years are encoded in the same verses of the Bible. They overlap each other. 'In 5766' is simply 'in 5760' with one more letter, spelling out the later year. There is no way to know whether one or both of the years is intended. Both match 'World War' against very high odds, and both are better matches than any other year. No other year appears on the original 'World War' table in the Bible code. Mathematically, 'in 5766' is a slightly better match, but '5760' appears a second time on the same table, encoded in Numbers 28:5–6. (pp. 93, 94)

• 'Atomic holocaust,' like 'World War,' is encoded with both the years 2000 and 2006. Both years again appear in Deuteronomy 11:14–15. Again there is no way to know which of the two years is intended. Both are a very good match mathematically. Although '5766' is again a slightly better match, these two years are the only years in the next 120 that match both 'atomic holocaust' and 'World War.' (p. 94)

• 'Terrorism' is encoded with 'World War' in Deuteronomy 3:13, and the words 'war to the knife' appear just above in Deuteronomy 1:44. (p. 96)

• 'Communism' is encoded once in the Bible, from Genesis 41:34 to Numbers 26:12. The connecting words 'fall of' are encoded in Numbers 22:27–8. 'Russian' is encoded in the same place, between Numbers 26:12 and Numbers 34:2. 'In China' is encoded just below in Deuteronomy 22:21, and the word 'next' appears in the same verse. (p. 98)

• 'Atomic weapon' is encoded once in the Book of Isaiah, from 32:1 to 65:18. 'Jerusalem' and 'scroll' and 'He opened it' all appear in the hidden text of the last verse, Isaiah 65:18. In fact, they overlap each other. The 'M' in 'atomic' is also the 'M' in 'Jerusalem,' and the same 'M' is the 'M' in 'Megillah,' the Hebrew word for 'scroll,' and overlapping 'scroll' are the words 'He opened it,' which in Hebrew begins with the same 'M.' Since the plain words of Isaiah state that a 'sealed book' will be opened, revealing the details of an Apocalypse that it almost openly describes as an atomic attack on Jerusalem, the encoding of 'atomic weapon' is clearly intentional. But in modern Hebrew it would usually be spelled with one more letter. (p. 100)

• 'Ariel,' the ancient name for Jerusalem, appears in the hidden text of Deuteronomy 4:28, where the encoding of 'World War' begins. (p. 101)

• 'Armageddon' is encoded from Genesis 44:4 to Exodus 10:16, and 'Asad holocaust' follows in the same skip sequence from Genesis 30:6 to Genesis 41:57. The 'Armageddon' code print-out uses the Hebrew words 'Har Megiddo,' which means 'Mt Megiddo.' Bible scholars agree that this Hebrew name is the origin of the word 'Armageddon,' which is really a Greek transliteration of the name of that location in northern Israel. The word 'Armageddon' does not appear in the plain text of the Old Testament, only in the New Testament. (p. 102)

• 'Syria' is encoded in Ezekiel 38:10–15, starting at the verse that states, 'And thou shalt come from thy place in the far North, thou and many peoples with thee, a great horde, and a mighty army.' 'Gog, land of Magog' appears in the plain text of Ezekiel 38:2. (p. 103)

CHAPTER SEVEN: APOCALYPSE

• The year 2113 is encoded from Deuteronomy 29:24 to Deuteronomy 33:14. 'Empty, depopulated, desolated' appears in Deuteronomy 33:14. 'For everyone, the great terror: fire earthquake' appears in the hidden text of the last verse of the original Bible, Deuteronomy 34:12 (p. 106)

• 'Great earthquake' is encoded from Exodus 39:21 to Deuteronomy 18:17. It also appears with both the years 2000 and 2006. Again, they overlap each other, encoded in Leviticus 27:23. 'In 5760,' the year

2000 in the Hebrew calendar, however appears twice, encoded again in Exodus 39:21. (p. 106)

• 'Los Angeles' is not encoded in the Bible, but its abbreviated form 'L.A. Calif.' is encoded twice, in Leviticus 23:10–12, and in Genesis 27:9–30. Against high odds, 'L.A. Calif.' appears with 'great earthquake' (Exodus 9:24 to Numbers 23:11), and again with 'fire, earthquake' (Genesis 27:17). And both encodings appear with the same year, 2010. That year, '5770' in the Hebrew calendar, is encoded with 'great earthquake' in Numbers 4:23. And '5770' actually overlaps 'fire, earthquake' in Genesis 27:17. (p. 108)

• 'China' appears in Numbers 33:12 with 'great earthquake' and 'in 5760' (cited above). The year of the last 'great earthquake' in China, 1976, is encoded in Leviticus 27:24. (p. 109)

• 'Kobe, Japan' is encoded from Numbers 5:14 to Deuteronomy 1:7. Both 'fire, earthquake' and 'the big one' appear in the hidden text of Deuteronomy 10:21. (p. 111)

• 'Year of the plague' is encoded once in the Bible, from Exodus 16:10 to Deuteronomy 2:34. 'Israel and Japan' appears in the hidden text of Exodus 16:10, crossing 'year of the plague.' (p. 111)

• 'Japan' appears in Leviticus 14:18, with 'great earthquake.' The years 2000 and 2006 appear just below in Leviticus 27:23. (p. 112)

• 'Economic collapse' is encoded once in the Bible, from Exodus 20:9 to Deuteronomy 11:6. 'Earthquake struck Japan' appears just below in the hidden text of Deuteronomy 31:18. (p. 112)

• 'Dinosaur' is encoded once in the Bible, from Genesis 36:14 to Deuteronomy 30:14. 'Dragon' crosses 'dinosaur,' encoded in Deuteronomy 4:25. The name of the dragon the Bible says God battled, appears in the hidden text of Deuteronomy 10:10, which states, 'It will strike Rahab.' 'Asteroid' crosses 'dinosaur,' encoded in Deuteronomy 24:19–21; one letter does not fit on the Bible code print-out reproduced here. (p. 114)

• 'Swift' is encoded from Leviticus 15:19 to Leviticus 23:29. The year the comet is predicted to return, 2126, is encoded in Leviticus 24:5. 'In the seventh month, it came' appears in Leviticus 23:39. 'The seventh month' would ordinarily mean the seventh month in the Hebrew calendar, but in this context instead seems to be a statement that the comet will come in July, and therefore safely pass by the Earth. (p. 116)

• 'Comet' is encoded from Leviticus 18:20 to Deuteronomy 27:1. The year 2006 is encoded in Leviticus 27:23. 'Year predicted for world' appears right above, in Leviticus 25:46. (p. 118)

   The year 2012 also appears with 'comet,' in Deuteronomy 1:4. 'Earth annihilated' appears just above in Exodus 34:10. But, with 2012, also in the hidden text of Deuteronomy 1:4 are the words 'It will be crumbled, I will tear it to pieces.' (p. 119)

CHAPTER EIGHT: THE FINAL DAYS

• 'Prime Minister Netanyahu' is encoded once, from Exodus 19:12 to Deuteronomy 4:47. 'July to Amman' appears with no skips in the hidden text of Leviticus 26:12–13. It also appears only once in the Bible. (p. 121)

• 'Delayed' appears in Leviticus 14:39, just above 'July to Amman.' (p. 122)

• 'Delayed' appears three times on the same table with 'Prime Minister Netanyahu,' right above 'July to Amman,' overlapping 'his soul was cut off' in Exodus 31:14, and crossing 'murdered,' encoded from Numbers 19:10 to Deuteronomy 17:11. (p. 124)

• 'The next war' is encoded once in the Bible, from Genesis 36:15 to Numbers 12:8. 'Another will die, Av, Prime Minister' appears in the hidden text of Genesis 25:11, one line above. (p. 124)

• '9th of Av is the day of the Third' appears in the hidden text of Numbers 19:12, with 'World War' and the ancient name for Jerusalem, 'Ariel.' 'Third' does not agree in gender with 'war,' which is in Hebrew a female word. But, the '9th of Av' was the date of the first and second destructions of Jerusalem, and since the Bible code warns that a third World War may begin with the third destruction of Jerusalem on the same date, the encoding is clearly intentional. And the Hebrew is perfect if it describes the 'third' destruction of Jerusalem. (p. 126)

• '9th Av, 5756,' the date in the Hebrew calendar equivalent to 25 July 1996, is encoded from Genesis 45:27 to Leviticus 13:55. 'Bibi' and 'delayed' are intertwined with a hidden text that states 'five futures, five roads' in Numbers 7:35. (p. 127)

• 'Holocaust of Israel' is encoded once from Genesis 49:17 to Deuteronomy 28:64. The year 2000, '5760' in the ancient calendar, crosses it encoded in Exodus 12:4. 'You delayed' overlaps the year in the hidden text of Exodus 12:4–5. (p. 129)

• 'They delayed the year of the plague' is encoded as a single skip sequence from Genesis 1:3 to Deuteronomy 2:34. 'Israel and Japan' crosses it in Exodus 16:10. (p. 129)

• 'Friend delayed' appears in the hidden text of Numbers 14:14, where the plain words foretell 'the End of Days.' Both appear just above 'World War.' (p. 130)

• 'Tunnel' is encoded with the same skip sequence as 'Holocaust of Israel,' running parallel to it from Exodus 17:2 to Numbers 14:36. (p. 131)

• 'Ramallah' appears in Numbers 32:25, crossing 'atomic holocaust' (Numbers 29:9 to Deuteronomy 8:19). The full hidden text states, 'Ramallah fulfilled a prophecy.' (p. 132)

• 'Annexed' appears twice with 'holocaust of Israel,' in Leviticus 13:2 and Leviticus 27:15. (p. 132)

• 'Arafat' appears in Deuteronomy 9:6, right below 'in the End of Days' (Deuteronomy 4:30), the only time those words in the plain text of the Bible appear with the second Biblical expression of the 'End of Days,' encoded from Numbers 28:9 to Deuteronomy 19:10. (p. 133)

• 'They told the future backwards' appears in Isaiah 41:23, which can also be translated 'They told the things that are to come here-after,' or 'They told the letters in reverse.' '5756,' in the modern calendar 1996, appears backwards in the same verse of Isaiah. (p. 137) 'They changed the time' overlaps the year, also spelled out backwards in Isaiah 41:23. (p. 137)

• 'Code will save' appears in Numbers 26:64, right above 'atomic holocaust,' and right below 'in the End of Days' (Numbers 24:14). In Hebrew, the same letters that spell 'code will save' also spell 'codes of Moses.' (p. 140)

CHAPTER NOTES

• 'Bible code' is encoded from Genesis 41:46 to Numbers 7:38. The Hebrew word used here for 'Bible' is 'Torah,' the name for the first five books of the Old Testament, which the Bible says God dictated to Moses. The same word that means 'code' also is a verb, so the full phrase can also be read, 'He encoded the Torah, and more.' The additional words 'and more' appear in Numbers 20:20 to Deuteronomy 28:8. (p. 145)

• 'Bible code' is encoded again from Deuteronomy 12:11 to Deuteronomy 12:17. The Hebrew word used here for 'Bible' is 'Tanakh,' which means the entire Old Testament. 'Sealed before God' appears in Deuteronomy 12:12. (p. 146)

APPENDIX

APPENDIX

The original experiment that proved the existence of the Bible code was published in a U.S. scholarly journal, Statistical Science, a review journal of the Institute of Mathematical Statistics (vol. 9, no. 3), in August 1994, pp. 429–438.

The journal editor, Robert E. Kass of Carnegie-Mellon University, stated in a prefatory note: 'Our referees were baffled: their prior beliefs made them think the Book of Genesis could not possibly contain meaningful references to modern-day individuals, yet when the authors carried out additional analyses and checks the effect persisted.'

In the nearly three years since the Rips-Witztum-Rosenberg paper was published, no one has submitted a rebuttal to the math journal.

Statistical Science 1994, Vol. 9, No. 3, 429–438

Equidistant Letter Sequences
in the Book of Genesis

Doron Witztum, Eliyahu Rips and Yoav Rosenberg*

Abstract: It has been noted that when the Book of Genesis is written as two-dimensional arrays, equidistant letter sequences spelling words with related meanings often appear in close proximity. Quantitative tools for measuring this phenomenon are developed. Randomization analysis shows that the effect is significant at the level of 0.00002.

Key words and phrases: Genesis, equidistant letter sequences, cylindrical representations, statistical analysis.

1. INTRODUCTION

The phenomenon discussed in this paper was first discovered several decades ago by Rabbi Weissmandel [7]. He found some interesting patterns in the Hebrew Pentateuch (the Five Books of Moses), consisting of words or phrases expressed in the form of equidistant letter sequences (ELS's) – that is, by selecting sequences of equally spaced letters in the text.

As impressive as these seemed, there was no rigorous way of determining if these occurrences were not merely due to the enormous quantity of combinations of words and expressions that can be constructed by searching out arithmetic progressions in the text. The purpose of the research reported here is to study the phenomenon systematically. The goal is to clarify whether the phenomenon in question is a real one, that is, whether it can or cannot be explained purely on the basis of fortuitous combinations.

The approach we have taken in this research can be illustrated by the following example. Suppose we have a text written in a

* Eliyahu Rips is Associate Professor of Mathematics, Hebrew University of Jerusalem, Givat Ram, Jerusalem 91904, Israel. Doron Witztum and Yoav Rosenberg did this research at Jerusalem College of Technology, 21 Havaad Haleumi St, P.O.B. 16031, Jerusalem 91160, Israel.

foreign language that we do not understand. We are asked whether the text is meaningful (in that foreign language) or meaningless. Of course, it is very difficult to decide between these possibilities, since we do not understand the language. Suppose now that we are equipped with a very partial dictionary, which enables us to recognise a small portion of the words in the text: 'hammer' here and 'chair' there, and maybe even 'umbrella' elsewhere. Can we now decide between the two possibilities?

Not yet. But suppose now that, aided with the partial dictionary, we can recognise in the text a pair of conceptually related words, like 'hammer' and 'anvil.' We check if there is a tendency of their appearances in the text to be in 'close proximity.' If the text is meaningless, we do not expect to see such a tendency, since there is no reason for it to occur. Next, we widen our check; we may identify some other pairs of conceptually related words: like 'chair' and 'table,' or 'rain' and 'umbrella.' Thus we have a sample of such pairs, and we check the tendency of each pair to appear in close proximity in the text. If the text is meaningless, there is no reason to expect such a tendency. However, a strong tendency of such pairs to appear in close proximity indicates that the text might be meaningful.

Note that even in an absolutely meaningful text we do not expect that, deterministically, every such pair will show such tendency. Note also, that we did not decode the foreign language of the text yet: we do not recognise its syntax and we cannot read the text.

This is our approach in the research described in the paper. To test whether the ELS's in a given text may contain 'hidden information,' we write the text in the form of two-dimensional arrays, and define the distance between ELS's according to the ordinary two-dimensional Euclidean metric. Then we check whether ELS's representing conceptually related words tend to appear in 'close proximity.'

Suppose we are given a text, such as Genesis (G). Define an equidistant letter sequence (ELS) as a sequence of letters in the text whose positions, not counting spaces, form an arithmetic progression; that is, the letters are found at the positions

$$n, n + d, n + 2d, \ldots, n + (k-1)d.$$

```
צ ו מ פ פ ס ק ר ו י ב א ת י ב ו ו י ח א ו פ ס ו י
ע ל ע י ו נ שׁ ג צ ר א ב ו ב ז ע מ ר ק ב ו מ נ א
כ ה נ ח מ ה יׁ ה ו י מ י ש ר פ מ ג ב כ ר מ ג ו מ
ע ב ר ש א ד סׁא ה נ ר ג ד ע ו א ב י ו ד א מ ד ב
ו ל ו ד ג דׁמ מ שׁ ו פ ס י וׁ ד ר י י ה ר ב
מ י ת ע ב ש ל ב א ו י ב א ל ש ע י ו ד א מ ד ב כ
```

FIG. 1.

We call *d* the *skip*, *n* the *start* and *k* the *length* of the ELS. These three parameters uniquely identify the ELS, which is denoted (n, d, k).

Let us write the text as a two-dimensional array – that is, on a single large page – with rows of equal length, except perhaps for the last row. Usually, then, an ELS appears as a set of points on a straight line. The exceptional cases are those where the ELS 'crosses' one of the vertical edges of the array and reappears on the opposite edge. To include these cases in our framework, we may think of the two vertical edges of the array as pasted together, with the end of the first line pasted to the beginning of the second, the end of the second to the beginning of the third and so on. We thus get a cylinder on which the text spirals down in one long line.

It has been noted that when Genesis is written in this way, ELS's spelling out words with related meanings often appear in close proximity. In Figure 1 we see the example of פטיש (hammer) and סדן (anvil); in Figure 2, צדקיהו (Zedekia) and מתניה (Matanya), which was the original name of King Zedekia (Kings II, 24:17). In Figure 3 we see yet another example of החנוכה (the Chanuka) and חשמונאי (Hasmonean), recalling that the Hasmoneans were the priestly family that led the revolt against the Syrians whose successful conclusion the Chanuka feast celebrates.

Indeed, ELS's for short words, like those for פטיש (hammer) and סדן (anvil), may be expected on general probability grounds to appear close to each other quite often, in any text. In Genesis, though, the phenomenon persists when one confines attention to the more 'noteworthy' ELS's, that is, those in which the skip $|d|$ is *minimal* over the whole text or over large parts of it. Thus for פטיש (hammer), there is no ELS with a smaller skip than that of Figure 1 in all of Genesis; for סדן (anvil), there is none in a section of text comprising 71% of G; the other four words are minimal over the whole text of G. On the face of it, it is not clear whether or not this can be attributed to chance. Here we develop a method for testing the significance of the phenomenon according to accepted statistical principles. After making certain choices of words to compare and ways to measure proximity, we perform a randomization test and obtain a very small p-value, that is, we find the results highly statistically significant.

FIG. 2.

FIG. 3.

2. OUTLINE OF THE PROCEDURE

In this section we describe the test in outline. In the Appendix, sufficient details are provided to enable the reader to repeat the computations precisely, and so to verify their correctness. The authors will provide, upon request, at cost, diskettes containing the program used and the texts G, I, R, T, U, V and W (see Section 3).

We test the significance of the phenomenon on samples of pairs of related words (such as hammer–anvil and Zedekia–Matanya). To do this we must do the following:

(i) define the notion of 'distance' between any two words, so as to lend meaning to the idea of words in 'close proximity';

(ii) define statistics that express how close, 'on the whole,' the words making up the sample pairs are to each other (some kind of average over the whole sample);

(iii) choose a sample of pairs of related words on which to run the test;

(iv) determine whether the statistics defined in (ii) are 'unusually small' for the chosen sample.

Task (i) has several components. First, we must define the notion of 'distance' between two given ELS's in a given array; for this we use a convenient variant of the ordinary Euclidean distance. Second, there are many ways of writing a text as a two-dimensional array, depending on the row length; we must select one or more of these arrays and somehow amalgamate the results (of course, the selection and/or amalgamation must be carried out according to clearly stated, systematic rules). Third, a given word may occur many times as an ELS in a text; here again, a selection and amalgamation process is called for. Fourth, we must correct for factors such as word length and composition. All this is done in detail in Sections A.1 and A.2 of the Appendix.

We stress that our definition of distance is not unique. Although there are certain general principles (like minimizing the skip d) some of the details can be carried out in other ways. We feel that varying these details is unlikely to affect the results substantially. Be that as it may, we chose one particular definition, and have, throughout, used *only* it, that is, the function $c(w, w')$ described in Section A.2 of the Appendix had been defined before any sample was chosen, and it underwent no changes. [Similar remarks apply to choices made in carrying out task (ii).]

Next, we have task (ii), measuring the overall proximity of

pairs of words in the sample as a whole. For this, we used two different statistics P_1 and P_2, which are defined and motivated in the Appendix (Section A.5). Intuitively, each measures overall proximity in a different way. In each case, a small value of P_i indicates that the words in the sample pairs are, on the whole, close to each other. No other statistics were *ever* calculated for the first, second or indeed any sample.

In task (iii), identifying an appropriate sample of word pairs, we strove for uniformity and objectivity with regard to the choice of the pairs and to the relation between their elements. Accordingly, our sample was built from a list of personalities (p) and the dates (Hebrew day and month) (p') of their death or birth. The personalities were taken from the *Encyclopedia of Great Men in Israel* [5].

At first, the criterion for inclusion of a personality in the sample was simply that his entry contain at least three columns of text and that a date of birth or death be specified. This yielded 34 personalities (the *first list* – Table 1). In order to avoid any conceivable appearance of having fitted the tests to the data, it was later decided to use a fresh sample, without changing anything else. This was done by considering all personalities whose entries contain between 1.5 and 3 columns of text in the *Encyclopedia*; it yielded 32 personalities (the *second list* – Table 2). The significance test was carried out on the second sample only.

Note that personality–date pairs (p, p') are not word pairs. The personalities each have several appellations, there are variations in spelling and there are different ways of designating dates. Thus each personality–date pair (p, p') corresponds to several word pairs (w, w'). The precise method used to generate a sample of word pairs from a list of personalities is explained in the Appendix (Section A.3).

The measures of proximity of word pairs (w, w') result in statistics P_1 and P_2. As explained in the Appendix (Section A.5), we also used a variant of this method, which generates a smaller sample of word pairs from the same list of personalities. We denote the statistics P_1 and P_2, when applied to this smaller sample, by P_3 and P_4.

EQUIDISTANT LETTER SEQUENCES IN THE BOOK OF GENESIS

TABLE 1
The first list of personalities

Personality	Name	Date
1. The Ra'avad of Posquieres	רבי אברהם, הראב"ד	כ"ז כסלו, בכ"ז כסלו, כ"ז בכסלו
2. Rabbi Avraham, son of the Rambam	רבי אברהם	י"ח כסלו, בי"ח כסלו, י"ח בכסלו
3. Rabbi Avraham Ibn-Ezra	רבי אברהם, אבן עזרא, בן עזרא, הראב"ע	א' אדר א', בא' אדר א', א' באדר א'
4. Rabbi Eliyahu Bahur	רבי אליהו, הבחור, בעל הבחור	בו' בשבט, ו' בשבט
5. Rabbi Eliyahu of Vilna	רבי אליהו, הגאון	ט"ו ניסן, בט"ו ניסן, ט"ו בניסן י"ח ניסן, בי"ח ניסן, י"ח בניסן י"ט תשרי, בי"ט תשרי, י"ט בתשרי
6. Rabbi Gershon Ashkenazi	רבי גרשון, הגרשני	י' אדר ב', בי' אדר ב', י' באדר ב'
7. Rabbi David Gans	רבי דוד, דוד גנז, דוד גאנז, צמח דוד	ה' אלול, בה' אלול, ה' באלול
8. The Taz	רבי דוד, דוד הלוי, בעל הט"ז	כ"ז שבט, בכ"ז שבט, כ"ז בשבט
9. Rabbi Haim Ibn-Attar	רבי חיים, בן עטר, אבן עטר, אור החיים	ט"ו תמוז, בט"ו תמוז, ט"ו בתמוז י"ה תמוז, בי"ה תמוז, י"ה בתמוז
10. Rabbi Yehudah, son of the Rosh	רבי יהודה	י"ז תמוז, בי"ז תמוז, י"ז בתמוז
11. Rabbi Yehudah He-Hasid	רבי יהודה	י"ג אדר, בי"ג אדר, י"ג באדר
12. Maharal of Prague	רבי יהודה, רבי ליוא, המהר"ל, מהר"ל מפרג	י"ח אלול, בי"ח אלול, י"ח באלול
13. Rabbi Yehonathan Eybeschuets	רבי יונתן, איבשיץ, בעל התמום	כ"א אלול, בכ"א אלול, כ"א באלול
14. Rabbi Heshil of Cracow	רבי יהושע, רבי העשיל	כ' תשרי, בכ' תשרי, כ' בתשרי
15. The Sema	רבי יהושע, בעל הסמ"ע	י"ט ניסן, בי"ט ניסן, י"ט בניסן
16. The Bach	רבי יואל, סירקש, בעל הב"ח	בכ' אדר, כ' באדר
17. Rabbi Yom-Tov Lipman Heller		ר' אלול, בו' אלול, ו' באלול
18. Rabbenu Yonah	רבי יונה, רבנו יונה	ח' חשון, בח' חשון, ח' בחשון
19. Rabbi Yosef Caro	רבי יוסף, יוסף קרו, יוסף קארו, מהר"י קרו, מהר"י קארו, בית יוסף, המחבר	י"ג ניסן, בי"ג ניסן, י"ג בניסן
20. Rabbi Yehezkel Landa	בעל הצל"ח	י"ח חשון, בי"ח חשון, י"ח בחשון י"ז אייר, בי"ז אייר, י"ז באייר
21. The Pnei–Yehoshua	פני יהושע	כ"ח כסלו, בכ"ח כסלו, כ"ח בכסלו י"ד שבט, בי"ד שבט, י"ד בשבט
22. Rabbenu Tam	רבי יעקב, רבנו תם	ד' תמוז, בד' תמוז, ד' בתמוז
23. The Rif	רבי יצחק, אלפסי, רב אלפס	
24. The Besht	רבי ישראל, בעל שם טוב, הבעש"ט	י"ח אלול, בי"ח אלול, י"ח באלול
25. The Maharam of Rothenburg	רבי מאיר, המהר"ם	י"ט אייר, בי"ט אייר, י"ט באייר
26. The Levush	רבי מרדכי, מרדכי יפה, הלבוש, בעל הלבוש	ג' אדר ב', בג' אדר ב', ג' באדר ב'
27. The Rema	רבי משה, איסרלש	י"ח אייר, בי"ח אייר, י"ח באייר
28. The Ramhal	לוצטו, לוצאטו, הרמח"ל	כ"ו אייר, בכ"ו אייר, כ"ו באייר
29. The Rambam	רבי משה, הרמב"ם	בכ' טבת, כ' בטבת י"ד ניסן, בי"ד ניסן, י"ד בניסן
30. Hacham-Zvi	רבי צבי, חכם צבי	בא' אייר, א' באייר
31. The Shach	רבי שבתי, שבתי כהן, שבתי הכהן, בעל הש"ך	א' אדר א', בא' אדר א', א' באדר א'
32. Rashi	רבי שלמה	כ"ט תמוז, בכ"ט תמוז, כ"ט בתמוז
33. The Maharshal	רבי שלמה, לוריא, מהרש"ל, המהרש"ל	י"ב כסלו, בי"ב כסלו, י"ב בכסלו
34. The Maharsha	אידלש, מהרש"א, המהרש"א	ה' כסלו, בה' כסלו, ה' בכסלו

TABLE 2
The second list of personalities

Personality	Name	Date
1. Rabbi Avraham Av-Beit-Din of Narbonne	רבי אברהם, הראב"ד, הרב אב"ד, הראב"ד, האשכול	כ' חשון, בכ' חשון, כ' בחשון
2. Rabbi Avraham Yizhaki	רבי אברהם, יצחקי, זרע אברהם	י"ג סיון, בי"ג סיון, י"ג בסיון
3. Rabbi Avraham Ha-Malakh	רבי אברהם, המלאך	י"ב תשרי, בי"ב תשרי, י"ב בתשרי
4. Rabbi Avraham Saba	רבי אברהם, אברהם סבע, צרור המר	
5. Rabbi Aaron of Karlin	רבי אהרן	י"ט ניסן, בי"ט ניסן, י"ט בניסן
6. Rabbi Eliezer Ashkenazi	מעשי השם, מעשי י/ה/ו/ה	כ"ב כסלו, בכ"ב כסלו, כ"ב בכסלו
7. Rabbi David Oppenheim	רבי דוד, אופנהים	ז' תשרי, בז' תשרי, ז' בתשרי
8. Rabbi David Ha-Nagid	רבי דוד, דוד הנגיד	
9. Rabbi David Nieto	רבי דוד, דוד ניטו	כ"ח טבת, בכ"ח טבת, כ"ח בטבת
10. Rabbi Haim Abulafia	רבי חיים	ו' ניסן, בו' ניסן, ו' בניסן
11. Rabbi Haim Benbenest	רבי חיים, בנבנשת	י"ט אלול, בי"ט אלול, י"ט באלול
12. Rabbi Haim Capusi	רבי חיים, כפוסי, בעל נס, בעל הנס	י"ב שבט, בי"ב שבט, י"ב בשבט
13. Rabbi Haim Shabetai	רבי חיים, חיים שבתי, מהרח"ש, המהרח"ש	י"ג ניסן, בי"ג ניסן, י"ג בניסן
14. Rabbi Yair Haim Bacharach	חות יאיר	בא' טבת, א' בטבת
15. Rabbi Yehudah Hasid	רבי יהודה	ה' חשון, בה' חשון, ה' בחשון
16. Rabbi Yehudah Ayash	רבי יהודה, מהר"י עיאש	א' תשרי, בא' תשרי, א' בתשרי
17. Rabbi Yehosef Ha-Nagid	רבי יהוסף	בט' טבת, ט' בטבת
18. Rabbi Yehoshua of Cracow	רבי יהושע, מגני שלמה	בכ"ז אב, כ"ז באב
19. The Maharit	רבי יוסף, מטרני, יוסף טרני, טראני, מטראני, מהריט"מ, המהריט"ם, מהרי"ט, המהרי"ט	י"ד תמוז, בי"ד תמוז, י"ד בתמוז
20. Rabbi Yosef Teomim	רבי יוסף, תאומים, פרי מגדים	בד' איר, ד' באיר
21. Rabbi Yakov Beirav	רבי יעקב, יעקב בירב, מהר"י בירב, הריב"ד	ל' ניסן, בל' ניסן, ל' בניסן
22. Rabbi Israel Yaakov Hagiz	חאגיז, בעל הלק"ט	כ"ו שבט, בכ"ו שבט, כ"ו בשבט
23. The Maharil	רבי יעקב, מולין, יעקב סג"ל הלוי, מהר"י סג"ל, מהרי"ל הלוי, המהרי"ל, המהרי"ל	כ"ב אלול, בכ"ב אלול, כ"ב באלול
24. The Yaabez	היעב"ץ, הריעב"ץ, עמדין, הרי עמדן, הר"י עמדין	ל' ניסן, בל' ניסן, ל' בניסן
25. Rabbi Yizhak Ha-Levi Horowitz	רבי יצחק, הורוויץ, יצחק הלוי	בו' איר, ו' באיר
26. Rabbi Menahem Mendel Krochmal	רבי מנחם, קרוכמל, רבי מענדל, צמח צדק	בב' שבט
27. Rabbi Moshe Zacuto	רבי משה, זכותא, זכותו, משה זכות, משה זכות, משה זכות, מהרם זכות, מהרמ"ז, המהרמ"ז, המזל"ן, קול הרמ"ז	ט"ז תשרי, בט"ז תשרי, ט"ז בתשרי, י"ו תשרי, בי"ו תשרי, י"ו בתשרי
28. Rabbi Moshe Margalith	רבי משה, מרגלית, פני משה	י"ב טבת, בי"ב טבת, י"ב בטבת
29. Rabbi Azariah Figo	רבי עזריה	א' אדר א', בא' אדר א', א' באדר א'
30. Rabbi Immanuel Hai Ricchi	א"ח הע"ר, ישר לבב	בא' אדר, א' באדר
31. Rabbi Shalom Sharabi	רבי שלום, מזרחי, שרעבי, שר שלום, מהרש"ש, המהרש"ש	בי' שבט, י' בשבט
32. Rabbi Shelomo of Chelm	רבי שלמה	כ"א תמוז, בכ"א תמוז, כ"א בתמוז

Finally, we come to task (iv), the significance test itself. It is so simple and straightforward that we describe it in full immediately.

The second list consists of 32 personalities. For each of the 32! permutations π of these personalities, we define the statistic P_1^π obtained by permuting the personalities in accordance with π, so that Personality i is matched with the dates of Personality $\pi(i)$.

The 32! numbers P_1^π are ordered, with possible ties, according to the usual order of the real numbers. If the phenomenon under study were due to chance, it would be just as likely that P_1 occupies any one of the 32! places in this order as any other. Similarly for P_2, P_3 and P_4. This is our null hypothesis.

To calculate significance levels, we chose 999,999 random permutations π of the 32 personalities; the precise way in which this was done is explained in the Appendix (Section A.6). Each of these permutations π determines a statistic P_1^π; together with P_1, we have thus 1,000,000 numbers. Define the *rank order* of P_1 among these 1,000,000 numbers as the number of P_1^π not exceeding P_1; if P_1 is tied with other P_1^π, half of these others are considered to 'exceed' P_1. Let ρ_1 be the rank order of P_1, divided by 1,000,000; under the null hypothesis, ρ_1 is the probability that P_1 would rank as low as it does. Define ρ_2, ρ_3 and ρ_4 similarly (using the same 999,999 permutations in each case).

After calculating the probabilities ρ_1 through ρ_4, we must make an overall decision to accept or reject the research hypothesis. In doing this, we should avoid selecting favorable evidence only. For example, suppose that $\rho_3 = 0.01$, the other ρ_i being higher. There is then a temptation to consider ρ_3 only, and so to reject the null hypothesis at the level of 0.01. But this would be a mistake; with enough sufficiently diverse statistics, it is quite likely that just by chance, some one of them will be low. The correct question is, 'Under the null hypothesis, what is the probability that at least one of the four ρ_i would be less than or equal to 0.01?' Thus denoting the event '$\rho_i \leq 0.01$' by E_i, we must find the probability not of E_3, but of 'E_1 or E_2 or E_3 or E_4.' If the E_i were mutually exclusive, this probability would be 0.04; overlaps only decrease the total probability, so that it is in any case less than or equal to 0.04. Thus we can reject the null hypothesis at the level of 0.04, but not 0.01.

More generally, for any given δ, the probability that at least one of the four numbers ρ_i is less than or equal to δ is at most 4δ. This is known as the Bonferroni inequality. Thus the overall significance level (or p-value), using all four statistics, is $\rho_0 := 4 \min \rho_i$.

3. RESULTS AND CONCLUSIONS

In Table 3, we list the rank order of each of the four P_i among the 1,000,000 corresponding P_i^π. Thus the entry 4 for P_4 means that for precisely 3 out of the 999,999 random permutations π, the statistic P_4^π was smaller than P_4 (none was equal). It follows that min $\rho_i = 0.000004$, so $\rho_0 = 4$ min $\rho_i = 0.000016$. The same calculations, using the same 999,999 random permutations, were performed for control texts. Our first control text, R, was obtained by permuting the letters of G randomly (for details, see Section A.6 of the Appendix). After an earlier version of this paper was distributed, one of the readers, a prominent scientist, suggested to use as a control text Tolstoy's *War and Peace*. So we used text T consisting of the initial segment of the Hebrew translation of Tolstoy's *War and Peace* [6] – of the same length as G. Then we were asked by a referee to perform a control experiment on some early Hebrew text. He also suggested to use randomization on words in two forms: on the whole text and within each verse. In accordance, we checked texts I, U and W: text I is the Book of Isaiah [2]; W was obtained by permuting the words of G randomly; U was obtained from G by permuting randomly words within each verse. In addition, we produced also text V by permuting the verses of G randomly. (For details, see Section A.6 of the Appendix.) Table 3 gives the results of these calculations, too. In the case of I, min ρ_i is approximately 0.900; in the case of R it is 0.365; in the case of T it is 0.277; in the case of U it is 0.276; in the case of V it is 0.212; and in the case of W it is 0.516. So in five cases $\rho_0 = 4$ min ρ_i exceeds 1, and in the remaining case $\rho_0 = 0.847$;

TABLE 3
Rank order of P_i among one million P_i^π

	P_1	P_2	P_3	P_4
G	453	5	570	4
R	619,140	681,451	364,859	573,861
T	748,183	363,481	580,307	277,103
I	899,830	932,868	929,840	946,261
W	883,770	516,098	900,642	630,269
U	321,071	275,741	488,949	491,116
V	211,777	519,115	410,746	591,503

that is, the result is totally nonsignificant, as one would expect for control texts.

We conclude that the proximity of ELS's with related meanings in the Book of Genesis is not due to chance.

APPENDIX: DETAILS OF THE PROCEDURE

In this Appendix we describe the procedure in sufficient detail to enable the reader to repeat the computations precisely. Some motivation for the various definitions is also provided.

In Section A.1, a 'raw' measure of distance between words is defined. Section A.2 explains how we normalize this raw measure to correct for factors like the length of a word and its composition (the relative frequency of the letters occurring in it). Section A.3 provides the list of personalities p with their dates p' and explains how the sample of word pairs (w, w') is constructed from this list. Section A.4 identifies the precise text of Genesis that we used. In Section A.5, we define and motivate the four summary statistics P_1, P_2, P_3 and P_4. Finally, Section A.6 provides the details of the randomization.

Sections A.1 and A.3 are relatively technical; to gain an understanding of the process, it is perhaps best to read the other parts first.

A.1 The Distance between Words

To define the 'distance' between words, we must first define the distance between ELS's representing those words; before we can do that, we must define the distance between ELS's in a given array; and before we can do that, we must define the distance between individual letters in the array.

As indicated in Section 1, we think of an array as one long line that spirals down on a cylinder; its *row length h* is the number of vertical columns. To define the distance between two letters x and x', cut the cylinder along a vertical line between two columns. In the resulting plane each of x and x' has two integer coordinates, and we compute the distance between them as usual, using these coordinates. In general, there are two possible values for this distance, depending on the vertical line that was chosen for cutting the cylinder; if the two values are different, we use the smaller one.

Next, we define the distance between fixed ELS's e and e' in a fixed cylindrical array. Set

$f :=$ the distance between consecutive letters of e,

$f' :=$ the distance between consecutive letters of e',

$\ell :=$ the minimal distance between a letter of e and one of e',

and define $\delta(e, e') := f^2 + f'^2 + \ell^2$. We call $\delta(e, e')$ the *distance* between the ELS's e and e' in the given array; it is small if both fit into a relatively compact area. For example, in Figure 3 we have $f = 1, f' = \sqrt{5}, \ell = \sqrt{34}$ and $\delta = 40$.

Now there are many ways of writing Genesis as a cylindrical array, depending on the row length h. Denote by $\delta_h(e, e')$ the distance $\delta(e, e')$ in the array determined by h, and set $\mu_h(e, e') := 1/\delta_h(e, e')$; the larger $\mu_h(e, e')$ is, the more compact is the configuration consisting of e and e' in the array with row length h. Set $e = (n, d, k)$ (recall that d is the skip) and $e' = (n', d', k')$. Of particular interest are the row lengths $h = h_1, h_2, \ldots$, where h_i is the integer nearest to $|d|/i$ ($\frac{1}{2}$ is rounded up). Thus when $h = h_1 = |d|$, then e appears as a column of adjacent letters (as in Figure 1); and when $h = h_2$, then e appears either as a column that skips alternate rows (as in Figure 2) or as a straight line of knight's moves (as in Figure 3). In general, the arrays in which e appears relatively compactly are those with row length h_i with i 'not too large.'

Define h_i' analogously to h_i. The above discussion indicates that if there is an array in which the configuration (e, e') is unusually compact, it is likely to be among those whose row length is one of the first 10 h_i or one of the first 10 h_i'. (Here and in the sequel 10 is an arbitrarily selected 'moderate' number.) So setting

$$\sigma(e, e') := \sum_{i=1}^{10} \mu_{h_i}(e, e') + \sum_{i=1}^{10} \mu_{h_i'}(e, e'),$$

we conclude that $\sigma(e, e')$ is a reasonable measure of the maximal 'compactness' of the configuration (e, e') in any array. Equivalently, it is an inverse measure of the minimum distance between e and e'.

Next, given a word w, we look for the most 'noteworthy' occurrence or occurrences of w as an ELS in G. For this, we chose those ELS's $e = (n, d, k)$ with $|d| \geq 2$ that spell out w for which $|d|$ is minimal over all of G, or at least over large portions of it. Specifically, define the *domain of minimality* of e as the maximal segment T_e of G that includes e and does not include any other ELS $\hat{e} = (\hat{n}, \hat{d}, \hat{k})$ for w with $|\hat{d}| < |d|$. If e' is an ELS for another word w', then $T_e \cap T_{e'}$ is called the *domain of simultaneous minimality* of e and e'; the length of this domain, relative to the whole of G, is the 'weight' we assign to the pair (e, e'). Thus we define $\omega(e, e') := \lambda(e, e')/\lambda(G)$, where $\lambda(e, e')$ is the length of $T_e \cap T_{e'}$, and $\lambda(G)$ is the length of G. For any two words w and w', we set

$$\Omega(w, w') := \sum \omega(e, e')\sigma(e, e'),$$

where the sum is over all ELS's e and e' spelling out w and w', respectively. Very roughly, $\Omega(w, w')$ measures the maximum closeness of the more noteworthy appearances of w and w' as ELS's in Genesis – the closer they are, the larger is $\Omega(w, w')$.

When actually computing $\Omega(w, w')$, the sizes of the lists of ELS's for w and w' may be impractically large (especially for short words). It is clear from the definition of the domain of minimality that ELS's for w and w' with relatively large skips will contribute very little to the value of $\Omega(w, w')$ due to their small weight. Hence, in order to cut the amount of computation we restrict beforehand the range of the skip $|d| \leq D(w)$ for w so that the expected number of ELS's for w will be 10. This expected number equals the product of the relative frequencies (within Genesis) of the letters constituting w multiplied by the total number of all equidistant letter sequences with $2 \leq |d| \leq D$. [The latter is given by the formula $(D - 1)(2L - (k - 1)(D + 2))$, where L is the length of the text and k is the number of letters in w.] The same restriction applies also to w' with a corresponding bound $D(w')$. Abusing our notation somewhat, we continue to denote this modified function by $\Omega(w, w')$.

A.2 The Corrected Distance

In the previous section we defined a measure $\Omega(w, w')$ of proximity between two words w and w' — an inverse measure of the distance between them. We are, however, interested less in the absolute distance between two words than in whether this distance is larger or smaller than 'expected.' In this section, we define a 'relative distance' $c(w, w')$, which is small when w is 'unusually close' to w', and is 1, or almost 1, when w is 'unusually far' from w'.

The idea is to use perturbations of the arithmetic progressions that define the notion of an ELS. Specifically, start by fixing a triple (x, y, z) of integers in the range $\{-2, -1, 0, 1, 2\}$; there are 125 such triples. Next, rather than looking for ordinary ELS's (n, d, k), look for '(x, y, z)-perturbed ELS's' $(n, d, k)^{(x, y, z)}$, obtained by taking the positions

$$n, n + d, \ldots, n + (k - 4)d, n + (k - 3)d + x,$$
$$n + (k - 2)d + x + y, n + (k - 1)d + x + y + z,$$

instead of the positions $n, n + d, n + 2d, \ldots, n + (k - 1)d$. Note that in a word of length k, $k - 2$ intervals could be perturbed. However, we preferred to perturb only the three last ones, for technical programming reasons.

The *distance* between two (x, y, z)-perturbed ELS's $(n, d, k)^{(x, y, z)}$ and $(n', d', k')^{(x, y, z)}$ is defined as the distance between the ordinary (unperturbed) ELS's (n, d, k) and (n', d', k').

We may now calculate the '(x, y, z)-proximity' of two words w and w' in a manner exactly analogous to that used for calculating the 'ordinary' proximity $\Omega(w, w')$. This yields 125 numbers $\Omega^{(x, y, z)}(w, w')$, of which $\Omega(w, w') = \Omega^{(0, 0, 0)}(w, w')$ is one. We are interested in only some of these 125 numbers; namely, those corresponding to triples (x, y, z) for which there actually exist some (x, y, z)-perturbed ELS's in Genesis for w, and some for w' [the other $\Omega^{(x, y, z)}(w, w')$ vanish]. Denote by $M(w, w')$ the set of all such triples, and by $m(w, w')$ the number of its elements.

Suppose $(0, 0, 0)$ is in $M(w, w')$, that is, both w and w' actually appear as ordinary ELS's (i.e., with $x = y = z = 0$) in the text. Denote by $v(w, w')$ the number of triples (x, y, z) in $M(w, w')$ for which $\Omega^{(x, y, z)}(w, w') \geq \Omega(w, w')$. If $m(w, w') \geq 10$ (again, 10 is an arbitrarily selected 'moderate' number),

$$c(w, w') := v(w, w')/m(w, w').$$

If $(0, 0, 0)$ is not in $M(w, w')$, or if $m(w, w') < 10$ (in which case we consider the accuracy of the method as insufficient), we do not define $c(w, w')$.

In words, the corrected distance $c(w, w')$ is simply the rank order of the proximity $\Omega(w, w')$ among all the 'perturbed proximities' $\Omega^{(x, y, z)}(w, w')$; we normalize it so that the maximum distance is 1. A large corrected distance means that ELS's representing w are far away from those representing w', on a scale determined by how far the *perturbed* ELS's for w are from those for w'.

A.3 The Sample of Word Pairs

The reader is referred to Section 2, task (iii), for a general description of the two samples. As mentioned there, the significance test was carried out only for the second list, set forth in Table 2. Note that the personalities each may have several appellations (names), and there are different ways of designating dates. The sample of word pairs (w, w') was constructed by taking each name of each personality and pairing it with each designation of that personality's date. Thus when the dates are permuted, the total number of word pairs in the sample may (and usually will) vary.

We have used the following rules with regard to Hebrew spelling:

1. For words in Hebrew, we always chose what is called the *grammatical orthography* – 'ktiv dikduki.' See the entry 'ktiv' in Even-Shoshan's dictionary [1].

2. Names and designations taken from the Pentateuch are spelled as in the original.
3. Yiddish is written using Hebrew letters; thus, there was no need to transliterate Yiddish names.
4. In transliterating foreign names into Hebrew, the letter 'א' is often used as a *mater lectionis*; for example, 'Luzzatto' may be written 'לוצטו' or 'לוצאטו.' In such cases we used both forms.

In designating dates, we used three fixed variations of the format of the Hebrew date. For example, for the 19th of Tishri, we used חשרי יט, חשרי ביט and יטנחשרי. The 15th and 16th of any Hebrew month can be denoted as יה or טו and יו or טז, respectively. We used both alternatives.

The list of appellations for each personality was provided by Professor S. Z. Havlin, of the Department of Bibliography and Librarianship at Bar-Ilan University, on the basis of a computer search of the 'Responsa' database at that university.

Our method of rank ordering of ELS's based on (x, y, z)-perturbations requires that words have at least five letters to apply the perturbations. In addition, we found that for words with more than eight letters, the number of (x, y, z)-perturbed ELS's which actually exist for such words was too small to satisfy our criteria for applying the corrected distance. Thus the words in our list are restricted in length to the range 5–8. The resulting sample consists of 298 word pairs (see Table 2).

A.4 The Text

We used the standard, generally accepted text of Genesis known as the *Textus Receptus*. One widely available edition is that of the Koren Publishing Company in Jerusalem. The Koren text is precisely the same as that used by us.

A.5 The Overall Proximity Measures P_1, P_2, P_3 and P_4

Let N be the number of word pairs (w, w') in the sample for which the corrected distance $c(w, w')$ is defined (see Sections A.2 and A.3). Let k be the number of such word pairs (w, w') for which $c(w, w') \leq \frac{1}{5}$. Define

$$P_1 := \sum_{j=k}^{N} \binom{N}{j} \left(\frac{1}{5}\right)^j \left(\frac{4}{5}\right)^{N-j}$$

To understand this definition, note that *if* the $c(w, w')$ were independent random variables that are uniformly distributed over $[0, 1]$, *then* P_1 would be the probability that at least k out of N of them are less than or equal to 0.2. However, we do *not* make or use any such assumptions about uniformity and independence. Thus P_1, though calibrated in probability terms, is simply an ordinal index that measures the number of word pairs in a given sample whose words are 'pretty close' to each other [i.e., $c(w, w') \leq \frac{1}{5}$], taking into account the size of the whole sample. It enables us to compare the overall proximity of the word pairs in different samples; specifically, in the samples arising from the different permutations of the 32 personalities.

The statistic P_1 ignores all distances $c(w, w')$ greater than 0.2, and gives equal weight to all distances less than 0.2. For a measure that is sensitive to the actual size of the distances, we calculate the product $\Pi c(w, w')$ over all word pairs (w, w') in the sample. We then define

$$P_2 := F^N \left(\prod c(w, w') \right),$$

with N as above, and

$$F^N(X) := X \left(1 - \ln X + \frac{(-\ln X)^2}{2!} + \ldots + \frac{(-\ln X)^{N-1}}{(N-1)!} \right).$$

To understand this definition, note first that if $x_1, x_2, \ldots, x_N$ are independent random variables that are uniformly distributed over $[0, 1]$, then the distribution of their product $X := x_1 x_2 \ldots x_N$ is given by $\mathrm{Prob}(X \leq X_0) = F^N(X_0)$; this follows from (3.5) in [3], since the $-\ln x_i$ are distributed exponentially, and $-\ln X = \Sigma_i(-\ln x_i)$. The intuition for P_2 is then analogous to that for P_1: *If* the $c(w, w')$ were independent random variables that are uniformly distributed over $[0, 1]$, *then* P_2 would be the probability that the product $\Pi c(w, w')$ is as small as it is, or smaller. But as before, we do not use any such uniformity or independence assumptions. Like P_1, the statistic P_2 is calibrated in probability terms; but rather than thinking of it as a probability, one should think of it simply as an ordinal index that enables us to compare the proximity of the words in word pairs arising from different permutations of the personalities.

We also used two other statistics, P_3 and P_4. They are defined like P_1 and P_2, except that for each personality, all appellations starting with the title 'Rabbi' are omitted. The reason for considering P_3 and P_4 is that appellations starting with 'Rabbi' often use only the given names of the personality in question. Certain given names are popular and often used (like 'John' in English or 'Avraham' in Hebrew); thus several different personalities were called Rabbi Avraham. If the phenomenon we are investigating is real, then allowing such appellations might have led to misleadingly low values for $c(w, w')$ when π matches one 'Rabbi Avraham' to the dates of another 'Rabbi Avraham.' This might have resulted in misleadingly low values P_1^π and P_2^π for the permuted samples, so in misleadingly low significance levels for P_1 and P_2 and so, conceivably, to an unjustified rejection of the research hypothesis. Note that this effect is 'one-way'; it could not have led to unjustified acceptance of the research hypothesis, since under the null hypothesis the number of P_i^π exceeding P_i is in any case uniformly distributed. In fact, omitting appellations starting with 'Rabbi' did not affect the results substantially (see Table 3); but we could not know this before performing the calculations.

An intuitive feel for the corrected distances (in the original, unpermuted samples) may be gained from Figure 4. Note that in both the first and second samples, the distribution for R looks quite random, whereas for G it is heavily concentrated near 0. It is this concentration that we quantify with the statistics P_i.

A.6 The Randomizations

The 999,999 random permutations of the 32 personalities were chosen in accordance with Algorithm P of Knuth [4], page 125. The pseudorandom generator required as input to this algorithm was that provided by Turbo-Pascal 5.0 of Borland Inter Inc. This,

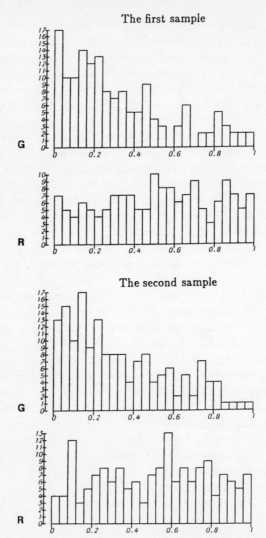

FIG. 4. *The distribution of value of $c(w, w')$ in the interval* [0, 1].

in turn, requires a seed consisting of 32 binary bits; that is, an integer with 32 digits when written to the base 2. To generate this seed, each of three prominent scientists was asked to provide such an integer, just before the calculation was carried out. The first of the three tossed a coin 32 times; the other two used the parities of the digits in widely separated blocks in the decimal expansion of π. The three resulting integers were added modulo 2^{32}. The resulting seed was 01001 10000 10011 11100 00101 00111 11.

The control text R was constructed by permuting the 78,064 letters of G with a single random permutation, generated as in the previous paragraph. In this case, the seed was picked arbitrarily to be the decimal integer 10 (i.e., the binary integer 1010). The control text W was constructed by permuting the words of G in exactly the same way and with the same seed, while leaving the letters within each word unpermuted. The control text V was constructed by permuting the verses of G in the same way and with the same seed, while leaving the letters within each verse unpermuted.

The control text U was constructed by permuting the words within each verse of G in the same way and with the same seed, while leaving unpermuted the letters within each word, as well as the verses. More precisely, the Algorithm P of Knuth [4] that we used requires $n - 1$ random numbers to produce a random permutation of n items. The pseudorandom generator of Borland that we used produces, for each seed, a long string of random numbers. Using the binary seed 1010, we produced such a long string. The first six numbers in this string were used to produce a random permutation of the seven words constituting the first verse of Genesis. The *next* 13 numbers (i.e., the 7th through the 19th random numbers in the string produced by Borland) were used to produce a random permutation of the 14 words constituting the second verse of Genesis, and so on.

ACKNOWLEDGEMENTS

We express our gratitude to Yaakov Rosenberg who prepared the software for the permutation test. Our thanks are due to the Jerusalem College of Technology for the use of its facilities, which made this study possible. We would like to express special gratitude to Dr R. Yehezkel, D. Pisanti, A. Sherman and M. Rosen. We thank the Michlalah, Jerusalem College for Women, for the permission to use their computer. We thank personally Dr I. Isaak and H. Rosenfeld for their help.

We thank the Venice Jewish community in Los Angeles and Mr Bernard Goldstein of London for their help with computer facilities.

The text of the Book of Genesis on a disc was obtained through the kindness of the late Rabbi S. D. Sassoon; another text was given to us by Dr M. Katz, to whom we express our sincere gratitude.

We wish to express our thanks to Dr S. Srebrenik and to Professor D. Michelson for helpful discussions and valuable suggestions. We thank Professor S. Z. Havlin and Dr I. Gottlieb for valuable advice. We thank Y. Orbach for help on linguistic matters. We thank M. Goldberg and G. Freundlich for assistance.

REFERENCES

[1] Even-Shoshan, A. (1989). *A New Dictionary of the Hebrew Language*, Kiriath Sefer, Jerusalem.

[2] FCAT (1986). The Book of Isaiah, file ISAIAH.MT. Facility for Computer Analysis of Texts (FCAT) and Tools for Septuagint Studies (CATSS), Univ. Pennsylvania, Philadelphia. (April 1986.)

[3] Feller, W. (1966). *An Introduction to Probability Theory and Its Applications* 2. Wiley, New York.

[4] Knuth, D. E. (1969). *The Art of Computer Programming* 2. Addison-Wesley, Reading, MA.

[5] Margalioth, M., ed. (1961). *Encyclopedia of Great Men in Israel; a Bibliographical Dictionary of Jewish Sages and Scholars from the 9th to the End of the 18th Century* 1–4. Joshua Chachik, Tel Aviv.

[6] Tolstoy, L. N. (1953). *War and Peace*. Hebrew translation by L. Goldberg, Sifriat Poalim, Merhavia.

[7] Weissmandel, H. M. D. (1958). *Torath Hemed*. Yeshivath Mt Kisco, Mt Kisco.

ACKNOWLEDGEMENTS

This adventure began by chance five years ago when I learned that a highly respected Israeli mathematician had discovered a hidden code in the Bible that revealed modern events. I went to see Eli Rips one evening in June of 1992, thinking I would know within an hour that there was nothing to his claim.

In the five years since then, we have spoken at least weekly, and met many times. The overwhelming evidence that the Bible code is real came from many sources, but this book could not have been written without Eli's constant help. It was written independently of him, however, and the views expressed in it are not his, except for his quoted remarks.

Many Israeli scholars assisted my research. Rabbi Adin Steinsaltz gave me much of his valuable time. Yakir Aharonov, a leading physicist, helped me understand some of the difficult scientific concepts that may be involved. Robert Aumann, who investigated Rips' work more thoroughly than any mathematician, met with me repeatedly and patiently explained the proofs of the code.

A number of Israeli government officials have also helped in important ways. I won't thank them by name, because in the current environment that might make their jobs more difficult.

Several friends took time to read, criticize, and encourage. One, Jon Larsen, did far more. Jon was the first friend I told about the Bible code, and he was the first person to read this book in manuscript. His advice has been incredibly good at every step, and to the extent this book works it owes much to him.

Jane Amsterdam joined in at a critical later stage, full of enthusiasm. Both she and Jon took chances for me, and did naturally, without hesitation, things that took courage.

My friend and attorney, Michael Kennedy, was involved from the beginning, and, as he has all through my life, helped in every way. His associate, Ken Burrows, a true author's lawyer, kept the project on course.

Finally, I want to thank my translator, Gilad, a brilliant young Israeli whose grandfather helped make Hebrew a living language again after World War II, and my research assistants Hilary and Elizabeth.

And especially Vendela, who worked with me every day and helped me write this book. I would not have made it without her.

INDEX

INDEX

Boldface page numbers refer to illustrated Bible code print-outs.

Abraham, 8, 20, 71, 133, 134, 156, 174
    tomb of, 85, 164
Additional Dimension, The (Witztum), 164
airplane, 32, **32**
Aleppo Codex, 154
alien civilizations, 70, 163
Alvarez, Walter, 170
American Revolution, 31
Amidror, Jacob, 41–2, 159
Amir, Yigal, 5, **6**, 14, 15–16, **15**, **16**, 26,
    54, **55**, 80, 89, 147, 160–61
    'End of Days' and, 66–7, **66**
Apocalypse, 61–2, 66, 76, 77, 119–20,
    137–40, 161, 171
    derivation of term, 157
    'great terror' in, 105, 106, **106**, 169
    natural disasters in, *see* asteroids;
        comets; earthquakes
    predicted in Isaiah, 92, 99–101, 126,
        135–7, 157, 166, 167, 173
    see also Armageddon; 'End of Days'
Apollo, 11, 14, 19–20
Arabs, 38, 56, 62, 103, 130–34
    in Kiryat-Arba, 85
    massacred at Hebron mosque, 83–5,
        84
Arab terrorists, 40–47, 49–51, 134
Arafat, Yasir, 39, 51, 56, 60, 130, 133,
    134, 147, 157
    'End of Days' and, 132, **133**, 174, 175
Ark of the Covenant, 69
Armageddon, 64, 76, 77, 86, 92–6, 101–
    4, 120, 122, 125, 130, 132, 134, 137,
    165

earthquakes linked to, 105
Gog and Magog in, 35, 103, **103**, 105,
    157, 168
in Hebrew language, 102
Syria and, 102–4, **102**, **103**, 168
as transliteration of Megiddo, 102,
    157, 168
Armstrong, Karen, 168
Armstrong, Neil, 19–20
Asad, Hafez, 102, **102**
Asahara, Shoko, 86, 165
assassinations, 79–82
    of John F. Kennedy, 3, 4, 14, 26, 79–
        81, **79**
    pattern of, 81
    of Robert F. Kennedy, 3, 4, 79, 81,
        81
    of Sadat, 3, 4, 79, 82, 164
    World War I triggered by, 125, 172
    see also Rabin, Yitzhak, assassination
        of
asteroids, 113, **114**, 116–18, 170
    defense against, 117
    'Earth crossers', 116–17
atomic holocaust, 35–60, 91–104, 120,
    134, 136–40, 157–60
    author's warnings of, 40, 41, 43–5, 46,
        52, 56, 56–7, 122–3
    delayed, 121–30, **129**, 136–7
    'End of Days' and, 62, **63**, 64, 65, 74,
        139, **140**
    in Hebrew calendar, 35–7, **36**, **37**, 40,
        42, **43**, 44, **44**, 52–3, 56, 60, 92–6,
        94, 122, 128, **129**, 137, **137**, 166

atomic holocaust – *contd*
 of Hiroshima, *see* Hiroshima, atomic
  bombing of
 Jerusalem in, 35, 99–101, **100**, 103,
  135, 157, 167, 173
 Libya in, 42, **43**, 44–5, **44**, 46–7, 159
 Netanyahu and, 54–60
 nuclear terrorism in, 40–47, 96–7, 99,
  101, 123, 159, 165
 possible prevention of, **45**, 46, 137–
  40, **140**
 Ramallah and, 131, **132**
 staging areas for, 42, 45–6, 52
 World War III and, *see* World War
  III
Aumann, Robert J., 28, 150, 155–6
Aum Shinrikyo, 85–6, 89, 165
Auschwitz, 26

Bach, Johann Sebastian, 31
Balaam, 'End of Days' foretold by, 62,
 129
Barak, Ehud, 5, 148
Bar-Ilan University, 151–2
Bartos, Armand, 91–2, 166
Beethoven, Ludwig van, 31
Ben-Israel, Isaac, 5, 147, 172
Bers, Lipman, 24
Besso, Michele, 154
Bible, 154–5
 as alien artifact, 71, 164
 origins of, 13, 22, 68–71
 prophecy in, 72–4
 reversal of time in, 136–7, **137**
 see also Torah
Bible code, 1–2, 3–34, 141–2, **185**, 147–
 56
 as computer program, 8, 10, 13–18,
  30, 71–2, 91–2, 139
 computer programs for, 1, 8, 10–12,
  21, 71–2, 146
 in continuous letter strand, 13–14,
  14–15
 control texts for, 11, 14, 18, 153
 crossword-puzzle structure of, 8, 13,
  14, 15, 29, 30
 delay in, 121–30, **122**, **124**, **127**, **129**,
  130, 136–7, **137**

 early references to, 8–9, 29
 explanations for, 24–6
 good vs. evil in, 75, 163
 holographic structure of, 30, 135
 inclusiveness of, 14, 28–34
 independent evaluations of, 11–12,
  17–18, 24–6, 28–9, 149–51
 interlocking words in, 14
 Newton's search for, 9–10, 18, 33, 61,
  65, 149, 162
 non-human intelligence and, 23, 27,
  34, 57–8, 65, 70–71, 135
 peer review process applied to, 12–
  13, 155
 prevention made possible by, 5, 7, 26–
  7, 38, 40, **45**, 46, 74, 75–6, **76**, 86,
  119, 121–30, **129**, 137–40, **140**, 158
 probabilities in, 7, 27, 28–9, 43, 46,
  75, 86, 93, 123
 proof of God in, 26, 34, 41, 57, 75
 publication on, 11–12, 17
 as 'sealed book,' 64–76, 92, 95, 100,
  139, 146, **146**
 searches of, 13–16
 skip sequences in, 9, 13–14, 66, 79,
  164
 source of, 68–76
 statistical significance of, 10, 11, 16,
  17, 28, 38, 44, 53, 149, 151, 152, 166
 time-locked nature of, 10, 30, 37, 65,
  71, 72
biological weapons, 86, 97
Book of Creation, The (Sefer Yetzirah)
 (Kaplan, trans.), 156
Booth, John Wilkes, 81
B'Or Ha'Torah, 150
Born, Max, 155
Boyer, Paul, 162
Brief History of Time, A (Hawking), 154,
 155, 172
Burrows, Millar, 165
'Butterfly Effect,' 125, 172

California, earthquakes in, 107–9, **108**,
 169
Chaos (Gleick), 125, 172
chemical weapons, 86, 97, 165
China, 102

earthquakes in, 107, 109, **109**, 170
fall of communism in, 97, **98**
Christians, early, 67
Churchill, Winston, 31, 77, 164
Clarke, Arthur C., 70, 163
Clinton, Bill, 14, 19, **19**, 52
CNN, 16
Coleman, Sidney, 156
Columbia University, 24, 146, 147
comets, 113–20, 169–70
  crumbled, 119, **119**, 171
  defense against, 117, 171
  'Earth crossers,' 116–17
  in Hebrew calendar, **114**, 115–16,
    117–19, **118**, **119**
  Shoemaker-Levy, 4, 22–4, **22**, **23**, 68,
    116–17, 119, 145, 154, 170–71
  Swift-Tuttle, 113–16, **116**, 117, 170
Commentary on the Torah (Nachmanides),
  153
communism, 31, 97, **98**
  Chinese, fall of, 97, **98**
  see also Soviet Union
computer programs, 1, 8, 10–12, 21, 71–
  2, 146
  Bible code as, 8, 10, 13–18, 30, 71–2,
    91–2, 139
computers, 10, 13, 68–72, **69**, **72**, 73,
  91–2
  quantum, 69
creation myths, 113, 170
Czechoslovakia, 9, 24, 148

Dallas, 14, 79, **79**, 81
Daniel, Book of, 74, 145, 157, 162, 163,
  164
  'End of Days' in, 61, 62, 64, 67, 72, 76,
    146, 161
  'sealed book' in, 61, 62, 64–5, 67, 72,
    76, 146, 161–3
Davies, Paul, 70, 71, 162
Dead Sea, 46, 67, 91, 166
Dead Sea Scrolls, 67, 91–2, 99, 104, 135,
  154–5, 162, 165–6, 168
Dead Sea Scrolls, The (Burrows), 165
Defense Department, U.S., 3
depression, economic, 112
  Great, 19, **20**

Deuteronomy, Book of, 9, 23, 81, 129,
  145, 162, 163, 166, 167, 169
D'Hondt, Stephen, 170
Diaconis, Persi, 150–51, 152
dinosaurs, 113, **114**, 117, 170
Dome of the Rock, 131, 174
Doomsday cult, 85–6
dragon, 113, **114**, 170

'Earth crossers,' 116–17
earthquakes, 105–12, 169–70
  in California, 107–9, **108**, 169
  in China, 107, 109, **109**, 170
  in Ezekiel, 105, 109, 169
  in Hebrew calendar, 105–12, **106**,
    108, **109**, **111**, **112**, 137
  in Isaiah, 105, **106**, 169
  in Israel, 107, 109
  in Japan, 107, 109–12, **111**, **112**, 170
  linked to Armageddon, 105, 167
  in Revelation, 105, 169
Ebola virus, 86
economic collapse, 19, **20**
  in Japan, 112, **112**
Edison, Thomas A., 32, **32**
Egypt, 39
  Joseph in, 73–4, 163
  Ten Plagues of, 86
Eichmann, Adolf, 26
Einstein, Albert, 32–3, **33**, 104, 123,
  168
  chance as viewed by, 27, 155
  time as viewed by, 18, 154
Elba, 31
electricity, 32, **32**
Eliot, T.S., 18
*Encyclopedia of Prominent Jewish Scholars,
  The*, 151
'End of Days,' 61–76, 77, 89, 171,
  Arafat and, 132, **133**, 174
  atomic holocaust and, 62, **63**, 64, 65,
    74, 139, **140**
  in Daniel, 61, 62, 65, 67, 72, 76, 162
  delayed, 128–30, **130**
  as foretold by Balaam, 62, 129
  as foretold by Jacob, 36, 61, 72, 128
  as foretold by Moses, 61–2, 72, 128–
    9

'End of Days' – *contd*
  in Hebrew calendar, 60, 61–2, **62**, 64,
    64, 65–7, **66**, **76**, 137, 162
  natural disasters in, *see* asteroids;
    comets; earthquakes
  New Testament and, 67
  plague and, 66, **67**
  possible prevention of, 75, 75–6, **76**
  Rabin assassination and, 61–2, 66, **66**
  recurring expectations of, 67–8
  in Revelation, 61, 67, 75–6
  World War III and, 62, **63**, 64, 74
  see also Apocalypse; Armageddon
Entebbe, commando raid on, 59, 161
'Equidistant Letter Sequences in the
    Book of Genesis' (Witztum, Rips
    and Rosenberg), 10–12, 17, 149,
    198–220
Exodus, Book of, 9, 20, 69, 82, 97, 162,
    177
extinctions, 113, 117, 120, 170
Ezekiel, Book of, 103, 157, 168
  earthquakes in, 105, 109, 169

Fate of the Earth, The (Schell), 99–100,
    141, 166, 167–8, 177
Ferdinand, Archduke of Austria, 125,
    172
Ferris, Timothy, 120, 171, 175
Feynman, Richard P., 134, 175
fifth dimension, 34, 156
Final Battle, 35, 67, 75, 103, 111, 125,
    157, 162, 168
  see also Armageddon; atomic
    holocaust; World War III
'final solution,' 26, 77
fire, 105, **106**, 107, **108**, 110, **111**, **112**
free will, 29, 75, 127–8, 173

Gandhi, Mohandas K. 'Mahatma,' 79,
    82, 164
Gans, Harold, 11–12, 149–50, 152
García Márquez, Gabriel, 175–6
Genesis, Book of, 8, 9, 17, 18, 20, 21, 23,
    36, 73, 79, 81, 83, 85, 113, 128, 145,
    145, 146, 150, 151, 162, 163, 164–
    5, 170, 173–4, 175
Genius of Vilna, 7–8, 29, 148, 171

Geological Survey, U.S., 107, 169
germ warfare, 86
Gleick, James, 125, 172
God: A Biography (Miles), 72–3, 163
Gog and Magog, 35, 103, **103**, 105, 157,
    168
Golan Heights, 132, 174
Golb, Norman, 165
Gold, Dore, 123, 172
Goldstein, Baruch, 83, **84**
Gorbachev, Mikhail, 41
Goren, Eliza, 40, 158, 159
gravity, 33, **33**
Great Depression, 19, **20**
'Great War, The,' 172
group theory, 3
Gulf War, 4, 14, 74, 123, 177
  in Hebrew calendar, 7, 8–9, **8**, 138,
    148
Guri, Chaim, 3, 5–6, 147–8
Guth, Alan, 156

Hamas terrorists, 51
Hamlet (Shakespeare), 31, **31**
Har Homa housing project, 134
Harvard University, 3, 4, 25, 150–51,
    152, 155, 156
Hasofer, Avraham, 17, 150
Havlin, Schlomo Z., 151–2
Hawking, Stephen, 18, 27, 123, 154, 155,
    172
Hebrew calendar:
  American Revolution in, 31
  atomic holocaust in, 35–7, **36**, **37**, 40,
    42, **43**, 44, **44**, 52, 56, 60, 92–6, **94**,
    122–3, 128, **129**, 166
  comets in, 115–16, **116**, 117–19, **118**,
    119
  earthquakes in, 105–12, **106**, **108**,
    109, **111**, **112**, 137
  'End of Days' in, 60, 61–2, **62**, 64, **64**,
    65–7, **66**, **76**, 137, 162
  Great Depression in, 19, **20**
  Gulf War in, 7, 8–9, **8**, 138, 148
  Hiroshima in, 37, **78**, 79
  Holocaust in, 77, 96
  Jupiter comet collision in, 23, **23**, 116
  1929 Hebron riot in, 85

9th of Av in, 125–7, **126**, **127**, 173
opening of 'sealed book' in, 76, **76**
Rabin assassination in, 4, 5–7, **6**, 39, 82, 147
Russian communist revolution in, 31
Sadat assassination in, 82
Swift-Tuttle comet in, 115, **116**
terrorist attacks in, 49, 50, 51
Tokyo nerve gas attack in, 86
World War III in, 92–6, **93**, **94**, 124–6, **126**, 128, 166
World War II in, 77, **78**, 96
Hebrew language, 9, 55, 146, 155, 167
    Armageddon in, 102
    'Israel' in, 173
    Jacob's name in, 128, 173–4
    Joseph's name in, 73
    letters equated with numbers in, 39–40, 128, 162
    Moses's name in, 177
    planet Jupiter in, 171
    'thought' in, 69, 70
    'Zaphenath-Paneah' in, 73–4, 163
Hebrew University, 3, 4, 24, 146, 148, 155
Hebron, 133
    1929 riot in, 85
    terrorist attacks in, 83–5, **84**, 134
    Tomb of the Patriarchs in, 85, 164
Heisenberg, Werner, 27
Helin, Eleanor, 116–17, 171
Hirōnaka, Wakako, 110, 170
Hiroshima, atomic bombing of, 4, 93, 167–8
    description of, 99–100
    in Hebrew calendar, 37, **78**, 79
Hitler, Adolf, 14, 25–6, **25**, 31, 55, 77
Holocaust, 4, 25–6, 55, 77, 96, 164, 173
Homer, 31
Hussein, King of Jordan, 121–2, 133–4, 171
Hussein, Saddam, 8, **8**, 14

intelligence, non-human, 23, 27, 34, 57–8, 65, 70–71, 135
International Astronomical Union, 113
Intifada, 39
Iran, 103, 168

Isaac, 85, 133, 174
Isaiah, Book of, 23, 75, 91–2, 145, 163, 164
    Apocalypse predicted in, 92, 99–101, 126, 135–7, 157, 166, 167, 173
    in Dead Sea Scrolls, 91–2, 99, 104, 135, 155, 166
    earthquakes in, 105, 169
    Rahab in, 113, 170
    'sealed book' in, 92, 100, 166
    in Shrine of the Book, 91–2, 104, 166
    time and, 77, 136–7, 164, 176
Ishmael, 133, 174
Islambuli, Chaled, 82
Israel, 3–19, 28, 35–60, 77, 96, 102, 121–40, 157–61
    Academy of Science of, 28, 156
    annexed territories in, 132, **132**, 174
    earthquakes in, 107, 109
    'holocaust of,' 35–7, **36**, 42–3, 52, 56, 110, 120, 121, 122, 123, 128, **129**, 131, **131**, 132, **132**, 141, 174; *see also* Armageddon; atomic holocaust
    Japan and, 111–12, 128, **129**
    Ministry of Defense of, 5
    Mossad (intelligence agency) of, 46, 52, 123, 148, 172
    National Library of, 9
    in 1967 Six Day War, 99, 131, 132
    1996 election in, 52–3
    nuclear arsenal of, 45
    plague in, 111, **111**, 128, **129**
    Ramat David Air Force Base of, 102
    terrorism in, 39, 40–47, 49–51, **50**, **51**, 53, 82–5, **83**, **84**, 134, 157, 160
    see also Jerusalem
'Is This the End?' (Ferris), 171

Jacob, 85, 173–4
    'End of Days' foretold by, 36, 61, 72, 128
Japan, 77, **78**, 79, 109–12
    earthquakes in, 107, 109–12, **111**, **112**, 170
    economic collapse in, 112, **112**
    Israel and, 111–12, 128, **129**
    plague in, 111, **111**, 128, **129**
    Tokyo nerve gas attack in, 85–6, 164

Japan – *contd*
  see also Hiroshima, atomic bombing of
Jerusalem, 7, 133, 166, 167, 168
  ancient name for, 99, 101, **101**, 125–
    6, **126**, 167, 173
  in atomic holocaust, 35, 99–101, **100**,
    103, 135, 157, 167, 173
  in Isaiah, 99–101, 167, 173
  Shrine of the Book in, 91–2, 104, 154,
    166, 168
  terrorism in, 49–51, **50**, **51**, 134, 160
  tunnel under Temple Mount in, 131,
    131, 174
  in World War III, 101, **101**, 103, 125–
    6, **126**
Jerusalem (Armstrong), 168
Jerusalem Bible, 146
Jerusalem Post, 18, 82, 121, 160, 171,
  174, 175
Jesus Christ, 67
Jewish Mind, The (Rabinowitz), 148
Jordan:
  Netanyahu's delayed trip to, 59, 121–
    8, **121**, **122**, **124**, 171, 175
  Pisgah mountains of, 42, 45–6, **45**, 52
Joseph, 73–4, 163
Jupiter, comet collision with, 4, 21–3,
  22, **23**, 68, 116–17, 119, 145, 154,
  170–71

Kaddafi, Muammar, 42, 44, 45–6, 47, 159
Kaplan, Aryeh, 146, 156, 163, 169, 173
Kass Robert, 12–13, 149, 150
Kazhdan, David, 25, 155
Kennedy, John F., 3, 4, 14, 26, 79–81, **79**,
  153, 164
Kennedy, Robert F., 3, 4, 79, 81, **81**
Keynes, John Maynard, 9–10, 149, 162
Kiryat-Arba, 85
Kobe, Japan, earthquake in, 110–11,
  111, 170
Koresh, David, cult of, 87–8
Kubrick, Stanley, 163
Kulik, Mikhail, 158

Leningrad Codex, 154
Libya, 42, **43**, 44–5, **44**, 46–7, 103, 159,
  168

Life of Isaac Newton, The (Westfall), 149
lightbulb, 32, **32**
Lincoln, Abraham, 79, 81
Living Torah, The (Kaplan), 146, 163, 169
Los Angeles, earthquakes in, 107–9,
  108, 169
Lugar, Richard, 97, 167

Macbeth (Shakespeare), 31, **31**
McKay, Brendan, 150
McVeigh, Timothy, 87–9, **88**
Maimonides, 154
Marconi, Guglielmo, 32
Marsden, Brian, 113–15, 117, 170
Megiddo, 102, **102**, 157, 168
Mehta, Sonny, 164
Messiah, 61, 66, 161, 171, 174
Mezuzah, 95–6, 134, 166–7
Midrash, 75, 133, 171, 174
Miles, Jack, 72–3, **74**, 163
Mind of God, The (Davies), 70, 162
Moon landing, 4, 14, 19–20, **21**
Moses, 13, 23, 72, 153, 162, 169, 173
  burning bush and, 71
  'End of Days' foretold by, 61–2, 72,
    128
  meaning of name, 177
  on Mount Sinai, 7, 68–71, 73, 162
  Promised Land viewed by, 42, 45, 52
Moyers, Bill, 163
Mozart, Wolfgang Amadeus, 31
Murrah Federal Building, 87–9, **88**

Nachmanides, 153
Napoleon I, Emperor of France, 31
NASA, 116, 171
National Security Agency, U.S., 11
natural disasters, 105–20, 169–71
  see also asteroids; comets; earthquakes
Nazis, 14, **25**, 26, 77, 85, 173
Near-Earth Asteroid Tracking, 116
Nebo, Mount, 45
Nechai, Vladimir, 159
nerve gas, 85
Netanyahu, Benjamin 'Bibi,' 52–60, **55**,
  160, 175
  author's warning letters to, 56, 60, 141
  election of, 52–4, **53**, 59, 160, 171–2

Jordan trip delayed by, 59, 121–8, **121**, **122**, **124**, 171, 175
  possible death of, 53, 58–60, **58**, **59**, 124–5, **124**, 160
Netanyahu, Ben-Zion, 55–6, 56–8, 59–60, 161
Netanyahu, Jonathan, 59, 161
Newsweek, 115, 165, 170, 171
New Testament, 61, 67, 101, 103
Newton, Sir Isaac, 32–3, **33**
  Bible code sought by, 9–10, 18, 33, 61, 65, 149, 162
  time as viewed by, 10
Newtonian physics, 25, 26
New York Times, 18, 69, 113–15, 154, 159, 162–3, 165, 168, 170, 171, 174, 175, 176
9th of Av, 125–7, **126**, **127**, 173
Nixon, Richard, 19, **19**
Northridge earthquake, 107
nuclear arsenals, 41, 44–5, 46, 96–7, 97, 158, 166
nuclear terrorism, 40–47, 96–7, 99, 101, 123, 158–9, 165
nuclear war; *see* atomic holocaust
Numbers, Book of, 9, 129, 145, 161, 162
Nunn, Sam, 86, 97, 158, 165, 167

Oklahoma City bombing, 85, 87–9, **87**, **88**, 165
Okushiri, Japan, earthquake in, 110, 170
Origins of the Inquisition, The (Netanyahu), 161
Oswald, Lee Harvey, 26, 80–81, **80**
ozone layer, 139

Pearl Harbor, 77–9
Pentagon, 12, 116, 152, 158, 165, 166
Peres, Shimon, 38, 49, 52, 167
  author's warnings to, 40, 42, 43–5, 46–7, 49, 123, 127, 141, 158, 159, 160
  in 1996 election, 53–4
  nuclear terrorism danger foreseen by, 46–7, 97, 123, 159–60
physics, 136
  Newtonian, 25, 26

quantum, 3, 26, 27, 34, 122, 134, 172, 175
Physics of Star Trek, The (Krauss), 154
Piatetski-Shapiro, I., 25–6, 155
Picasso, Pablo, 31
Pisgah mountains, 42, 45–6, **45**, 52
plague, 66, **67**, 85–6, 111, **111**, 128, **129**
Princip, Gavrilo, 125, 172

quantum computers, 69, 162–3
quantum physics, 3, 26, 27, 34, 122, 134, 172, 175

Rabin, Yitzhak, assassination of, 3–7, **4**, **6**, 14, 26, 35–40, 51, 53, 60, 66, 68, 74, 89, 123, 138, 145
  'all his people to war' and, 35, **36**, 37–8, 49–51, 55, **55**, 134
  assassin in, 3, **4**, **6**, 4–7, 14, **15**, 15–16, **16**, 35, **36**, 49, 54–5, **55**, 79, 80, 160; *see also* Amir, Yigal
  author's letters warning of, 3, 5, 6–7, 40, 42, 44, 82, 141, 147–8
  'End of Days' and, 61–2, 66, **66**
  in Hebrew calendar, 4, 5–7, **6**, 39, 82, 147
  'next war' and, 39, **39**, 58, **58**, 79, 82
  search for, 14–16, **15**, **16**
Rabinowitz, Abraham, 148
radio, 32
Rahab, 113, **114**, 170
Ramallah, 131, 132
Ramat David Air Force Base, 102
Red Sea fault line, 109
Rembrandt, 31
Revelation, Book of, 35, 67, 75–6, 101, 105–6, 157, 168
  earthquakes in, 105, 169
  'sealed book in,' 61, 161
Rips, Eliyahu, 3–18, 24–5, 28–34, 35–8, 42–3, 53, 56–7, 65–7, 75, 122, 127–8, 131, 133, 134–5, 137–9, 141, 145–6, 147, 148, 149–52, 153, 155, 156, 160–61, 163, 164, 167, 176
Romans, ancient, 91, 99, 125, 165–6
Roosevelt, Franklin D., 31, 77, **78**
Rowland, Sherry, 139
Ruby, Jack, **80**, 81

Russia, 31, 77, 97, **98**, 102, 172
  see also Soviet Union
Russian missiles, 8, 14

Sadat, Anwar, 3, 4, 5, 79, 82, 164
Sagan, Carl, 70, 163
Saguy, Uri, 148
San Francisco, earthquakes in, 107
Santayana, George, 164
Sarah, 85, 174
Sarin (nerve gas), 85–6
Schell, Jonathan, 99–100, 141, 166, 167–8, 177
Schmemann, Serge, 168
Schultz, Peter, 170
Schwartz, David, 169–70
Scud missiles, 8, 14, 138, 148, 176–7
'sealed book,' 61–76, 161–4
  Bible code as, 64–76, 92, 95, 100, 139, 146, **146**
  in Daniel, 61, 62, 64, 67, 72, 76, 145, 161
  in Isaiah, 92, 100, 166
  opening of, 76, **76**, 92, 100, **100**
  in Revelation, 61, 161
Second Set of Predictions (Asahara), 165
Senate, U.S., 41, 85–6, 97, 158, 165, 167
'seven seals,' 61, 161
Shakespeare, William, 31, **31**, 153
Shoemaker-Levy comet, 4, 21–3, **22**, **23**, 68, 116–17, 119, 145, 154, 170–71
Shrine of the Book, 91–2, 104, 154, 166, 168
Sinai, Mount, 7, 68–71, 73, 162
Sirhan Sirhan, 81, **81**
Snyder, Dick, 170
Soviet Union, 24, 31
  collapse of, 41, 96–7, **98**, 158–9
  nuclear arsenal of, 41, 44, 96–8, 158
spaceship, 14, 19, **21**
Stalin, Joseph, 31, 77
Statistical Science, 12, 149, 150, 151
Steinsaltz, Adin, 135, 155, 176
Sumer, 170
Swift-Tuttle comet, 113–16, **116**, 117, 170

Syria, 39, 46, 132, 174
  Armageddon and, 102–4, **102**, **103**, 168
  World War III and, 102–3, **103**

Talmud, 119, 127, 155, 173
Tanakh, 146, **146**
Tanin, 113, 170
Tauber, Azriel, 148
Tel Aviv, 5, **6**, 14, 82, 147, 177
  terrorism in, 49, 50, 51, 134
Teller, Edward, 117
Temple Mount, tunnel under, 131, **131**, 174
Ten Commandments, 69
terrorism, 82–9
  Hamas, 51
  in Hebrew calendar, 49, 50, 51
  in Israel, 39, 40–47, 49–51, **50**, **51**, 53, 82–5, **83**, **84**, 134, 157, 159
  in Japan, 85–6, 165
  nuclear, 40–47, 96–7, 99, 101, 123, 159, 165
  in Oklahoma City, 85, 87–9, **87**, **88**, 165
  reverse, against Hebron mosque, 83–5, **84**
Textus Receptus, 146
Theory of Relativity, 34, 154
  original manuscript of, 104, 168
time, 18, 154
  biblical reversal of, 136–7, **137**, 176
  Isaiah and, 77, 136–7, 164, 176
Time, 136, 154, 165, 171
Tokyo, Japan, 110
  nerve gas attack in, 85–6, 164
Toledano, captivity of, 82–3, **83**
Tomb of the Patriarchs, 85, 164
Torah, 7–8, 9, 68, 145–6, **145**, 155, 162, 169, 174
  original form of, 15, 153
Torat Hemed, 148
tunnel under Temple Mount, 131, **131**, 174
2001, 70, 163

Uncertainty Principle, 27, 122, 134, 155, 172, 175

Unified Field Theory, 17, 34
United States, 31, 77, 102
    earthquakes in, 107–9, 108

Wailing Wall, 131, 174
Wall Street Journal, 2, 38
'War of the Sons of Light with the Sons
    of Darkness,' 91, 162
Washington Post, 2, 38
Watergate crisis, 4, 19, **19**
Waterloo, 31
Weissmandel, H.M.D., 9, 148
Westfall, Richard S., 149
When Time Shall Be No More (Boyer), 162
Who Wrote the Dead Sea Scrolls? (Golb),
    165–6
Williams, Gareth, 117
Witztum, Doron, 10–12, 17, 26, 148,
    149–51, 164
World War I, 125, 172
World War II, 4, 26, 31, 77–9, **78**, 93,
    166

    in Hebrew calendar, 77, **78**, 96
World War III, 38, 51, 91–104, 120, 139,
    141, 168
    delayed, 122–30, **130**
    'End of Days' and, 62, **63**, 64, 74
    in Hebrew calendar, 92–6, **93**, **94**,
        124–6, **126**, 128, 166
    Jerusalem in, 101, **101**, 103, 124–6,
        126
    Syria and, 102–3, **103**
    see also atomic holocaust
Wright Brothers, 32, **32**

Yale University, 3, 4, 25–6, 155
Yatom, Danny, 42, 46–7, 52, 123, 159,
    160, 172
Yavlinsky, Grigory, 159
Yishai, Elhanan, 40, 158

'Zaphenath-Paneah,' 73, 163
Zohar, 174
Zyklon B, 26